EARLY CONNECTICUT HOUSES

An Historical and Architectural Study

By
Norman M. Isham
and
Albert F. Brown

Dover Publications, Inc., New York

This Dover edition, first published in 1965, is an
unabridged and unaltered republication of the
work first published by The Preston and Rounds
Company in 1900.

The publisher is grateful to The Pequot Library
of Southport, Connecticut for making a copy of the
book available for reproduction purposes.

Standard Book Number: 486-21476-1
Library of Congress Catalog Card Number: 65-26654

Manufactured in the United States of America

Dover Publications, Inc.
180 Varick Street
New York, N. Y. 10014

TO

FRANCIS STILES, WILLIAM ANDREWS, JOHN ELDERKIN

WILLIAM HAYDEN, JARVIS BOYKIN

AND THE OTHERS

THE EARLY CRAFTSMEN OF CONNECTICUT

PREFACE.

———

THIS book is based upon the examination and measurement of a considerable number of the older houses of Connecticut. We have not attempted to record every example. From the wealth of old work now standing in the State circumstances of time and expense, as well as the limits of our book, have caused us to select typical dwellings and to leave unmeasured much that is of great interest and value. Our aim has been not to make a mere list of old houses with a description of each one, but rather to trace the development of planning and the survivals and the changes of building methods in the architectural history of the colony. We can only hope that our work may be the means of enlivening and assisting the already awakened interest in these monuments of our colonial history, so that we may have uniform and accurate records of all of them, for we are sadly aware that many must have escaped our notice.

We owe many thanks for assistance cheerfully and generously given, in all the towns where we have carried on our investigations. Especially are our thanks due to the owners and the occupants of the old houses, who have constantly put their dwellings at our disposal, often at some inconvenience, no doubt, to themselves, and have allowed us to measure and sketch at our leisure.

The architectural illustrations will explain themselves. We have personally examined every building now standing of which we give a drawing.   The reader may rest assured that the figures given on the plans and sections are reproductions of actual measurements. The external views are in all cases from photographs.

A word may be necessary about the map.   This we have brought in, not to enter the lists in behalf of any ideas of historical geography we may have, but to give a clearer notion of the original arrangement and extent of the territories of the different settlements wherein are the houses of which the text treats. We think it accurate enough for this purpose, even if in it two or possibly three periods may overlap.

The word Connecticut, as used in our text, has two meanings. One is that of the present State, the other that of the settlements on the Connecticut river in distinction from New Haven.   This latter meaning we have tried to convey, where we could, by adding the word "jurisdiction," or some similar term, to the common name.   In the same way the expression " New Haven jurisdiction " is used to distinguish between New Haven itself and the league of which it was the head.   In other cases the context will make clear the meaning.

CONTENTS.

CHAPTER I.

INTRODUCTION - - - - - - - - - - - - 1

CHAPTER II.

THE EARLIEST PERIOD IN THE CONNECTICUT COLONY, 1635–1675 - - 12

    1. The John Clark House, Farmington.

    2. The Gleason House, Farmington.

    3. The Lewis House, Farmington.

    4. The Cowles House, Farmington.

    5. The Whitman House, Farmington.

    6. The Moore House, Windsor.

    7. The Joseph Whiting House, Hartford.

    8. The Dorus Barnard House, Hartford.

CHAPTER III.

THE SECOND PERIOD IN THE CONNECTICUT COLONY, 1675–1700 - - 49

    1. The Hollister House, South Glastonbury.

    2. The Patterson House, Berlin.

    3. The John Barnard House, Hartford.

CHAPTER IV.

The Third Period in the Connecticut Colony, 1700–1750.   -   -   67

  1. The Barrett House, Wethersfield.

  2. The Meggatt House, Wethersfield.

  3. The Sheldon Woodbridge House, Hartford.

  4. The Webb House, Wethersfield.

  5. The Ebenezer Grant House, South Windsor.

CHAPTER V.

The Earliest Period in the New Haven Colony, 1638–1675   -   -   93

  1. The Theophilus Eaton House, New Haven.

  2. The Henry Whitfield House, Guilford.

  3. The Baldwin House, Branford.

CHAPTER VI.

The Second Period in the New Haven Colony, 1675–1700   -   -   130

  1. The Thomas Painter House, West Haven.

  2. The Stowe House, Milford.

  3. The Harrison House, Branford.

  4. The Goldsmith - Cleveland House, Southold.

CHAPTER VII.

The Third Period in the New Haven Colony, 1700–1750.   -   -   143

  1. The Fiske - Wildman House, Guilford.

  2. The Caldwell House, Guilford.

  3. The Benjamin House, Milford.

CHAPTER VIII.

NEW LONDON - - - - - - - - - - - - - 158

    1. The Hempstead House, New London.

    2. The Cady House, Putnam.

    3. The Kinsman House, Lisbon.

CHAPTER IX.

CONSTRUCTION - - - - - - - - - - - - 173

    1. Stone - work and Brick - work.

    2. Wood - work and Framing.

        The Frame.

        The Covering.

        The Interior.

    3. Iron - work.

APPENDICES.

I. THE JOSEPH WHITING HOUSE - - - - - - - 279

II. THE WEBSTER HOUSES - - - - - - - - 282

III. THE INVENTORY OF GOVERNOR EATON - - - - - 287

INDEX - - - - - - - - - - - - - 297

LIST OF ILLUSTRATIONS.

————

				PAGE.
Map of Early Connecticut				3
Figure	1.	Development of the Connecticut Plan		6
"	2.	The Cellar		13
"	3.	The Talcott House -	Restored Exterior	14
"	4.	The John Clark House	Exterior	18
"	5.	" " " "	Overhangs	19
"	6.	The Gleason House -	Present Exterior	21
"	7.	" " " -	First Story Plan	22
"	8.	" " " -	Cross Section	23
"	9.	" " " -	Longitudinal Section	24
"	10.	" " " -	Perspective of Framing	25
"	11.	" " " -	Overhang	26
"	12.	The Lewis House -	First Story Plan	27
"	13.	The Cowles House -	Present Exterior	29
"	14.	The Whitman House -	Present Exterior	31
"	15.	" " " -	First Story Plan	33
"	16.	" " " -	Sections	34
"	17.	" " " -	The Drop	35
"	18.	The Moore House -	Restored Exterior	37
"	19.	" " " -	Skeleton Plan	38
"	20.	The Joseph Whiting House -	Present Exterior	40
"	21.	The Joseph Whiting House -	First Story Plan	42
"	22.	The Dorus Barnard House	Exterior	44
"	23.	" " " "	First Story Plan	45
"	24.	" " " "	Attic Floor Framing	46
"	25.	" " " "	Section Thro' Roof	47

				PAGE.
Figure	26.	The Hollister House -	Present Exterior - - - -	53
"	27.	" " " -	First Story Plan - - - -	54
"	28.	" " " -	Cross Section - - - - -	56
"	29.	The Patterson House -	Present Exterior - - - -	58
"	30.	" " " -	First Story Plan - - - -	60
"	31.	" " " -	Cross Section - - - - -	62
"	32.	The John Barnard House,	Exterior - - - - -	64
"	33.	" " " "	First Story Plan - - - -	65
"	34.	The Barrett House -	Present Exterior - - - -	70
"	35.	The Meggatt House -	Present Exterior - - - -	71
"	36.	" " " -	First Story Plan - - - -	73
"	37.	" " " -	Framing Scheme - - - -	74
"	38.	The Sheldon Woodbridge House - - -	Present Exterior - - - -	76
"	39.	The Sheldon Woodbridge House - - -	First Story Plan - - - -	78
"	40.	The Sheldon Woodbridge House - - -	Framing Scheme - - - -	80
"	41.	The Sheldon Woodbridge House - - -	Second Story Plan - - - -	81
"	42.	The Webb House -	Present Exterior - - - -	83
"	43.	" " " -	First Story Plan - - - -	84
"	44.	The Ebenezer Grant House - - -	Present Exterior - - - -	87
"	45.	The Ebenezer Grant House - - -	First Story Plan - - - -	89
"	46.	The Ebenezer Grant House - - -	Detail of Doorway - - - -	91
"	47.	The Gov. Eaton House,	Southwest View, from Lambert -	97
"	48.	" " " "	Restored First Story Plan - -	101
"	49.	" " " "	Restored Second Story Plan - -	106
"	50.	The Henry Whitfield House - - -	Present Exterior - - - -	112
"	51.	The Henry Whitfield House - - -	Exterior from an old Photograph -	115

PAGE.

Figure　52.　The Henry Whitfield
　　　　　　　House　-　　-　　-　　Smith's Drawings　-　　-　　-　　- 116

"　　　53.　The Henry Whitfield
　　　　　　　House　-　　-　　-　　Cross Section, looking east　-　　- 117

"　　　54.　The Henry Whitfield
　　　　　　　House　-　　-　　-　　Present First Story Plan　　-　　- 118

"　　　55.　The Henry Whitfield
　　　　　　　House　-　　-　　-　　Smith's Plans　-　　-　　-　　-　　- 119

"　　　56.　The Henry Whitfield
　　　　　　　House　-　　-　　-　　The North Side　-　　-　　-　　- 120

"　　　57.　The Henry Whitfield
　　　　　　　House　-　　-　　-　　A Restoration　　-　　-　　-　　- 121

"　　　58.　Plan of Sutton Courtenay, Berkshire　-　　-　　-　　-　　- 122

"　　　59.　The Henry Whitfield
　　　　　　　House　-　　-　　-　　Detail of Folding Partition　-　　- 123

Tailpiece.　The Henry Whitfield
　　　　　　　House　-　　-　　-　　The North Sides Before Alteration,
　　　　　　　　　　　　　　　　　from a Photograph　-　　-　　- 124

Figure　60.　The Baldwin House　-　　Present Exterior　-　　-　　-　　- 125

"　　　61.　"　　"　　"　　-　　First Story Plan　-　　-　　-　　- 126

"　　　62.　"　　"　　"　　-　　Cross Section　-　　-　　-　　-　　- 127

"　　　63.　The Thomas Painter
　　　　　　　House　-　　-　　-　　Present Exterior　-　　-　　-　　- 133

"　　　64.　The Thomas Painter
　　　　　　　House　-　　-　　-　　First Story Plan　-　　-　　-　　- 134

"　　　65.　The Thomas Painter
　　　　　　　House　-　　-　　-　　Cross Section　-　　-　　-　　- 135

"　　　66.　The Thomas Painter
　　　　　　　House　-　　-　　-　　Longitudinal Section　-　　-　　- 136

"　　　67.　The Stowe House　-　　Present Exterior　-　　-　　-　　- 137

"　　　68.　"　　"　　"　　-　　First Story Plan　-　　-　　-　　- 138

"　　　69.　The Goldsmith-Cleveland
　　　　　　　House　-　　-　　-　　Skeleton Plan　-　　-　　-　　-　　- 140

"　　　70.　The Goldsmith-Cleveland
　　　　　　　House　-　　-　　-　　Elevation of Outside Wall　-　　- 141

PAGE.

Figure 71. The Moore House - Exterior - - - - - - 142
" 72. The Fiske-Wildman House Present Exterior - - - 146
" 73. " " " First Story Plan - - - - 147
" 74. " " " Overhang - - - - 148
" 75. The Caldwell House - Present Exterior - - - 151
" 76. " " " - Second Story Plan - - - 152
" 77. " " " - Cross Section - - - - 153
" 78. The Benjamin House - Present Exterior - - - 155
" 79. " " " - First Story Plan - - - 156
" 80. " " " - Cross Section - - - - 157
" 81. The Hempstead House Present Exterior - - - 162
" 82. " " " First Story Plan - - - 163
" 83. " " " Cross Section - - - - 164
" 84. The Cady House - Ruined Chimney - - - 167
" 85. " " " - Sketch Plan - - - - 168
" 86. " " " - Plan and Section of Chimney - 168
" 87. The Kinsman House - First Story Plan - - - 170
" 88. " " " - Second Story Plan - - - 171
" 89. Chimney, Whitfield House - - - - - - 191
" 90. " Thoroughgood House - - - - - 192
" 91. " Talcott House - - - - - - 194
" 92. Brick Details, Sheldon Woodbridge House - - - 195
" 93. The Kerf, Scoring, Sawing - - - - - - 203
" 94. Methods of Sawing Timber - - - - - 208
" 95. Posts - - - - - - - - - 212
Plate I. Framing Details, Gleason House - - - - 213
Figure 96. " Scheme, Meggatt House - - - - - 214
" 97. " " Sheldon Woodbridge House - - - 216
" 98. " " Caldwell House - - - 217
Plate II. " Details, Whitman House - - - - 219
" III. " " Baldwin House - - - - 220
" IV. " " Dorus Barnard House, John Barnard House,
Hempstead House - - - - - - 222
" V. Framing Details, Hollister House, Patterson House - 226
" VI. " " Painter House - - - - 227

PAGE.

Figure 99. Chamfers - - - - - - - - - - - 228
"   100. Details of Overhangs - - - - - - - 232
"   101. Drops, Whitman House - - - - - - - 233
"   102. Scale Drawings of Overhangs - - - - - - 234
Plate VII. Framing Details of Overhangs - - - - - 235
Figure 103. The Post-Bracket and the Overhang - - - - 237
"   104. Development of the Hewn Overhang - - - - 238
"   105. Gable Bracket, Moore House - - - - - - 241
"   106. Framing of Gable Overhang and of Cornice - - - 242
"   107. The Froe - - - - - - - - - - 245
"   108. Sash now in Rooms of Connecticut Historical Society - - 254
"   109. Mouldings - - - - - - - - - - 260
"   110. Stair Details - - - - - - - - - 263
"   111. Scheme of Staircase, Patterson House - - - - 265
"   112. The Marsh House, Plan Showing Alterations - - - 268
"   113. Handles and Hinges - - - - - - - - 275
"   114. Lock-Plate, 1657 - - - - - - - - 276
"   115. The Webster Estates - - - - - - - 282

EARLY CONNECTICUT HOUSES.

CHAPTER I.

INTRODUCTION.

THE colonial commonwealth of Connecticut was made up, like its early New England neighbors, of several independent settlements. Hartford, Windsor, and Wethersfield—the river towns, as they were called—formed one group; New Haven, Guilford, and the other settlements around Quinnipiac, a second; while the unsuccessful venture at Saybrook made a third. A fourth—partly independent in character, if not in politics—existed at New London, founded in 1646.

Progress in unity began with the Hartford colony, and did not cease till the whole territory covered by the present State was brought under the jurisdiction of the charter government. Therefore, though there never were between the original components of the commonwealth the strongly marked differences which existed in Rhode Island, there still were joints visible in the political structure of Connecticut; and these were faithfully repeated in the architecture of the first century of the colony's existence.

Hartford, Windsor, and Wethersfield were settled at practically the same time—the spring of 1636. The people thereof were not exiles from Massachusetts. They came voluntarily; lured, indeed, by the rich valley of the Connecticut, but chiefly because they were too democratic to live under the theocracy of Massachusetts Bay. Not closely straitened for this world's goods, settled on some of the most fertile land in New England, they soon pushed their boundaries before them into the wilderness and gave evidence that they were to be the dominating element in the new territory. With the help of Massachusetts they conquered and practically destroyed the Pequots and annexed their territory—thereby acquiring, as they claimed, the title to jurisdiction over New London. They bought Saybrook from Fenwick, and with it, as they asserted, the patent right of the original proprietors under the Warwick grant, and the chance of extending their jurisdiction to Narragansett Bay. Finally, when longer existence without a charter title to the soil was becoming impossible, they sent Winthrop to England; and, on his return with the charter of 1662, they brought their reluctant brethren of New Haven under its yoke with themselves and tried to subject to it the Narragansett country of Rhode Island. Shrewd, far-seeing, careful men, with as much piety as those they left behind in Boston and with less spiritual pride, the founders of the river colony held a calm but sure grip on the things of this world. A quiet, steady people, they stood midway between the persecuting theocrats of Massachusetts and the scriptural republic of New Haven.

The latter colonists were still less exiles from Massachusetts than their Hartford brethren. Settling in 1638 around the mouth of the Quinnipiac river, they gradually acquired the territory toward the north and spread over upon the shore of Long Island Stamford and Branford they sold to seceders from Wethersfield;

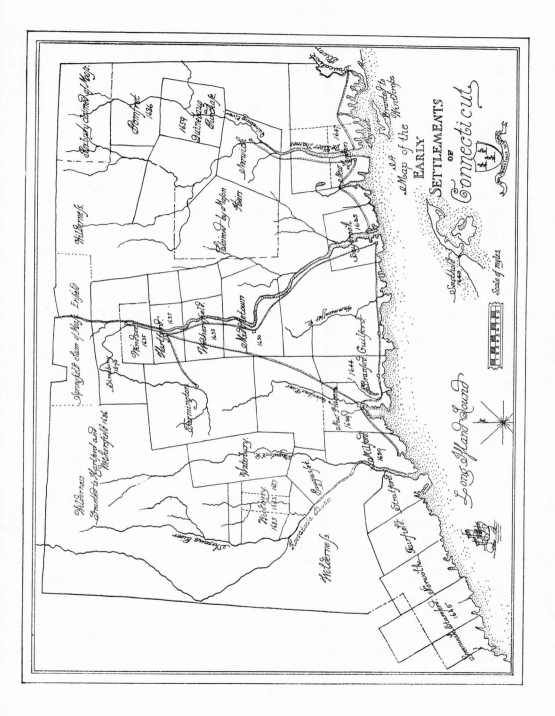

but these were ultra-Puritans like themselves, so that the jurisdiction of New Haven over those towns was not thus impaired, and the confederation formed in 1643[1] stood till the shrewder men of Hartford, by including the territory of New Haven within the jurisdiction given by the charter, forced that colony to join them in the new government.

In 1638, John Winthrop the younger, who had in 1635 been appointed by the English patentees governor of the fort at Saybrook, had made a purchase of land in the old Pequot territory. This, as covering land claimed by right of conquest, the unpatented court at Hartford persuaded the Commissioners of the United Colonies to disallow on rather flimsy pretexts. Winthrop seems to have submitted with a good grace. In 1647 he took from the Hartford legislature his commission as the first magistrate in the settlement which in 1645 and 1646 he had founded at New London.

These three settlements, then, with their dependencies—for the Saybrook foundation was never a factor in the history of the State—were the framework on which hangs the political history of Connecticut.[2] They were all different, yet not sharply so, and the differences are also slight which we find in the schools of architecture that prevail among them. One typical plan will serve for all three. The differences which appear are differences of detail. These came from the constructive preferences of the carpenters and masons who literally founded and built the commonwealth, and who,

---

[1] New Haven, Guilford, and Milford were originally independent.

[2] The map opposite page 2 aims to explain the political history here rehearsed. It does not confine itself to any one period, but gives, in their larger extent, all the settlements or towns where the oldest houses are to be looked for. We may point out that the towns all cling either to the shore of the Sound or to the river valleys which invited settlement, not only by the water and the meadows they offered, but by the fact that their north and south direction exposed them to the sun and gave them thus a pleasant climate. The historical geography of New England is an absorbing subject ; and it is strange that no serious attempt to deal with more than parts of it has yet been made.

through their successive apprentices, handed down their different craft-traditions. In the very beginning the greater wealth of the New Haven men, as compared with that of the other colonists, did make an apparent difference, and perhaps Hartford also may at first have surpassed New London; but in a few years these differences became less prominent in the architecture of the colonies, and we find the general uniformity of which we spoke.

The political relation of the settlements in what is now Connecticut with the other members of the league, which, under the name the United Colonies of New England, was formed in 1643, is also reflected in the architecture of the period; for, as the Connecticut colonies were not isolated from the others in New England—except from Rhode Island, which was left out of the union—so we do not find in them houses which differ greatly from those in Plymouth or in Massachusetts Bay. An apparent exception to this is found in Newport and Narragansett. Between Providence and either of these places there is, architecturally, a chasm of no mean breadth. Between the Newport or the Narragansett house and the house in Connecticut, either at Hartford or at New Haven, the difference, in the seventeenth century, was not great. At Newport this may be explained by the fact that many of the settlers were wealthy men from the Bay Colony; in the Narragansett it may readily be referred to the early dependence upon Connecticut, or to the Massachusetts origin of most of the Atherton partners and of the settlers they gathered.

The wide difference between the work in Providence and the other building fashions in New England, as well as the general resemblance between those fashions as we find them in Connecticut and in Massachusetts, will best be appreciated in Figure 1, where the plans common in the various colonies are set forth.

The typical Connecticut house consists of two rooms with a chimney between them. In front of the chimney is the entry with its staircase. The second floor is carried by a beam called the summer, which runs, in each room, from the chimney to the end

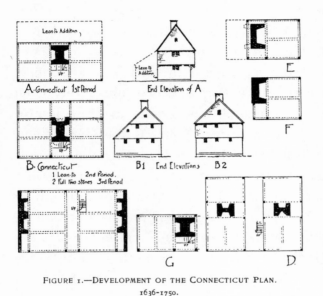

A. Connecticut 1st Period

End Elevation of A

E

F

B. Connecticut
1 Lean-to   2nd Period.
2 Full Two Stories   3rd Period

B1   End Elevations   B2

G

D

FIGURE 1.—DEVELOPMENT OF THE CONNECTICUT PLAN.
1636-1750.

of the house, and which is thus parallel with the front wall of the building. In only one instance, the older part of the Hempstead house at New London, does the beam run across the room.

In Massachusetts Bay we find exactly the same plan, the two rooms with the central chimney. We do not, however, always find the summer running in the same way. It is not uncommon to see it spanning the room from front wall to back wall, and thus parallel to the end of the building (as in *G*, in Figure 1). This is the case in the Roger Williams house in Salem, and in the Fairbanks house at Dedham.

In the Plymouth colony the two-room plan occurs with the summer running as in Connecticut. To this we have seen no exceptions. Side by side with this plan is another, of one room with a chimney standing at one end of it, though generally not appearing on the outside, and with sometimes a lean-to at the end, beyond this chimney, as we have indicated by the dotted lines at *E*.

In Providence, which in the seventeenth century included all northern Rhode Island, the typical plan contains one room, at the end of which is a vast stone chimney which appears on the outside of the house. The summer runs as it does in Connecticut, so that the building, it will readily be seen, resembles the exact half of a Connecticut dwelling.

In Newport and Narragansett this "stone-end" house occurs, but the typical plan is that of Connecticut.

Let us now trace the development of the type of plan which prevailed in Connecticut. Our knowledge of the earliest building in the colony — drawn, in the cases of all three of the original settlements, from the records — shows that, as in Massachusetts and Rhode Island, the craftsmen either were among the original settlers or came soon after them. We can prove that among those who followed Hooker through the wilderness,[1] or who came with Davenport, there were artisans of several kinds; so that we are justified in passing over very lightly the cellars or the log hut and wooden chimney stage of building, and in fixing our type for the first period of the three into which we intend to divide the chronology of the subject as that which we have described above — the two-room house, of two stories, with the chimney in the middle and the staircase in front of the chimney.

In the old Connecticut colony the chimney is usually of stone, and there is, very often, a heavy framed overhang in the second story. This is shown in *A*, of Figure 1. In the New Haven jurisdiction, though the chimney was very commonly of stone, it was often of brick — more frequently so than elsewhere — and the

---

[1] Nicholas Clark, in 1635, before the arrival of Hooker, built for Talcott the first house in Hartford.—*Mem. Hist. Hart. County*, vol. I., p. 263. Francis Stiles, a London carpenter, sent by Saltonstall, was at Windsor in 1635.—Stiles, *History of Ancient Windsor*, I., p. 44.

overhang, when it occurred, was of a different type.   In New London and Norwich the overhang was not so much used as in Hartford, and the chimneys, as in general in eastern Connecticut till very late, were of stone.

We have made the first period extend, as in Rhode Island, to King Philip's War.   The last quarter of the century shows a change in the manner of building which, while it came earlier in one place or later in another, is best marked by the year 1675. Wealth had been increasing during the preceding years.   The older settlers were by this time passing from the stage, and the younger race of craftsmen had come forward, in whom the traditions, brought from England by their fathers and grandfathers and already modified by the new surroundings, were to undergo still greater change.   Accordingly, in the second period, from 1675 to 1700, we find everywhere, except where gneiss, a stratified granite easily split, is abundant, a more general use of brick and an abandoning of many of the older and more traditional forms of construction and ornamentation.   The lean-to also appears; but while in the first period it had been an addition merely, it is now used not only to enlarge old houses, but as an integral part of the enlarged plan which had come to be a necessity in the new dwellings   This enlarged form of the plan is given in *B* and *B1*, of Figure 1.   The added space at the back, used for the kitchen, with a pantry and a bedroom, is covered by the lean-to.

In the river towns these changes are accompanied by the dropping of the great overhang or by the reduction of it to a few inches.   Lime mortar and plaster also come into use in these settlements.

In New Haven, beside the enlargement of the plan, we find less change than in Hartford; but here and in New London the greater use of brick and the lean-to as part of the house may be looked on as the marks of the second period.

The third period lasted from 1700 to as late as 1750, or even beyond. The years after 1725, however, though the old lean-to forms can still be found persisting through them, are really a part of the so-called Colonial time, and nothing but the tenacity with which the carpenters clung to the ancient modes of framing distinguishes such houses as the Webb and the Grant from those of Revolutionary days. The clothing of the frame and the treatment of the details, though rude at times and lacking in taste and skill as classic work, are still those which belong to the Georgian period, or at least to the days of Sir Christopher Wren.

In the early part of this period—what we might call the period proper—the plan does not change. The same disposition which we saw in the second period is still characteristic of this time throughout the State. The great improvement is the abandoning of the long, sloping, lean-to roof, and the building of two whole stories on the plan of the second period. The lean-to has been raised, so to speak, till its "chamber" is no longer a rude garret-like space, but is a room like the kitchen and other apartments below, and of the same height as the front chambers.

During the last two periods houses were built which were survivals of the types in use in the preceding times. The two-room house is common in the second period and lives on even into the third, while the lean-to house of the last quarter of the seventeenth century lingers in the third period as far down as 1750.

The overhang, too, still survives in this third period, though sometimes in a much modified form, and brick supersedes stone except in the poorest districts, or in places like Guilford or Norwich where gneiss was so easily procured as to be the natural material.

Toward the end of the period, after 1730 or 1735, the increased wealth of the colonists and their desire to follow English fashions introduced more elaborate finish.   There appears, too, a most significant change in the plan,[1] the introduction of the central-entry type, which we have shown in the corner plans in the lower row of Figure 1.   Here the old entry or porch, with the chimney behind it, is replaced by a passage running from the front to the back of the house.   There are two rooms at each side of this passage, and the chimneys of these were at first in the end walls of the house and then between each pair in the plan at D in Figure 1, as the chimney once was between the two rooms which anciently constituted the dwelling.   Finally, when this type was fully established, the summer ran as the dotted line in D shows— that is, it followed its old habit and ran toward the chimney—for we have now, as it were, two of the old first period houses placed side by side with a passage between them.   The summer is here, therefore, not really changing and running differently from its old way, though it seems to be doing so.[2]   We still have called it a summer, but it has lost all its former character.   It is now of the same depth as the floor joists, and, like them, is concealed by the lath and plaster of the room.

A later development still is the addition of the ell—often really an older house—to contain the kitchen, which at first, in these houses, was in the room behind the winter parlor, which, in its turn, was at the west or south side of the dwelling, at the opposite end from the summer parlor.

---

[1] Developed, at this time especially, from an older central-entry type which came from England. See Chapter X ; also the Sheldon Woodbridge house, Chapter IV ; and the Whitfield house, Chapter V.

[2] There are some peculiar ways of treating the late summers which we shall explain under the houses in which they occur.

Already, early in this period, if not toward the end of the one before it, the old sharp pitch of the roof had been visibly flattened, and before the end the gambrel had become established — though how or when it came into fashion is an obscure question.

The central-entry plan with either a gambrel or a plain pitched roof held sway till long after the Revolution, and was superseded only at the Greek revival of 1830. About 1800 we sometimes see four chimneys in the outer walls — one chimney for each of the four rooms — but it is not often. Nor are the large three-story houses of Salem and Providence, dating from the years 1780 to 1820, common in Connecticut.

With this general classification of the types and periods of the colonial architecture of Connecticut in mind, let us now study the work of the different time-divisions in each of the original settlements of the colony. We will then, as in our essay on Rhode Island houses, analyze in detail the forms and methods of construction, and study the European origin of the traditions held by the early craftsmen.

CHAPTER II.

THE EARLIEST PERIOD IN THE CONNECTICUT COLONY.

1635–1675.

THE adventurers, as they were called, who laid the foundations of Hartford, arrived at Suckiaug in the spring of 1635. They came from what is now Cambridge, Massachusetts, and were followed in the fall of the same year by a larger party of about sixty, which included women and children. In the following June—that is, in 1636—arrived the well-known body of settlers under the leadership of Hooker and Stone. During the same year the people from Watertown and Dorchester completed the settlements which we now know as Windsor and Wethersfield.

Of the original houses built by these first settlers there seem to be no remains. We have, however, much documentary evidence—most of it contemporary—considerable tradition of more or less value, and some of the houses built within a few years of the settlement, from which to reconstruct the appearance of the ancient towns.

According to a tradition,[1] supported by descriptions in early deeds, the first dwellings, at least among the poorer class, were

---

[1] *Mem. Hist. Hartford Co.*, vol. I, p. 224.

what were called cellars. These were so named, no doubt, because they were constructed in exactly the same way as the outdoor cellars used for a long time in all the colonies for the storage of vegetables, even after cellars in our modern sense of the word had been built under the houses. These cellars were made by digging a shallow pit in the ground, preferably in a bank, and then lining the sides of the excavation with stone walls carried above the ground enough to give a height of about seven feet, or by setting against these sides upright logs long enough to give the same height. These stone or wood walls were then

FIGURE 2.—THE CELLAR.

banked high with earth on the outside, as is shown in Figure 2 and were roofed over either with logs laid close together and plastered with clay, or with bark or thatch on poles. The probability is that the roofs were of considerable pitch and were thatched.

None of the well-to-do among the settlers made use of these cellars except for the first few weeks, or perhaps months, of their stay; and the frame house made its appearance at the very beginning of the settlement. John Talcott, one of the adventurers who came in 1635, had a house built for him by Nicholas Clark, who must have been a carpenter. His son, Lieutenant-Colonel John Talcott, has left us this information, with a very brief account of the building[1]: " The kitchen that now stands on the north side of

---

[1] Memorandum book of Lt. Col. John Talcott, Jr., quoted in *Mem. Hist. Hartford Co.*, I., p. 263.

the house that I live in was the first house that my father built in Hartford, in Conn. Colony, and was done by Nicholas Clark, the first winter that any Englishman rought or built in Hartford, which was in the year 1635. my father and mother and his family came to Hartford in the year 1636, and lived first in said Kitchen, which was first on west side of chimney. The great barn was built in the year 1636, and underpined in 1637, and was the first barn that was raised in the colony. The east side of this house that we live in, and was my father Talcott's, deceased, was built with the porch that is, in the year 1638, and the chimneys were built in 1638."

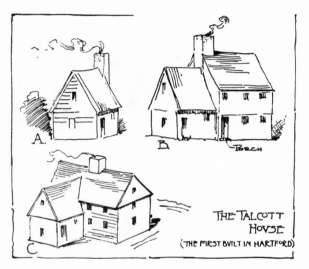

FIGURE 3.—THE TALCOTT HOUSE RESTORED.

This first house was no doubt a frame affair one story, or at the most a story and a half, in height. From the fact that the chimneys[1] were built in 1638 it looks as if this original dwelling, which stood near the present corner of Main and Talcott streets, had its gable turned toward Main street and only a chimney of wood at its eastern end. In 1638 a stone chim-

---

[1] The use of the plural "chimneys" does not mean more than one chimney in the sense in which we use the word. When Talcott wrote this, the word "chimney" had not yet lost an earlier meaning of *flue* which had belonged to it. Compare the expression "a stack of stone chimneys in the midst" in the town order about the minister's house at New London, June 1, 1666, quoted by Miss Caulkins in her *History of New London*, pp. 139, 140.

ney replaced the wooden one, and another half of a house was added toward the east, thus making a building with two rooms, one on each side of a central chimney. The reference to the porch is obscure. It is best explained, as we show in Figure 3, by supposing it to refer to what was generally called the porch and assuming that Talcott meant that the space containing the stairs was built in front of the new chimney when that chimney was built, so that while the chimney-stack was outside the old kitchen it was within the new east end. To account for the new position of the old kitchen on the north of the house we must suppose that Talcott moved it round to that position to serve as a kitchen when he replaced it by a western addition in keeping with the new eastern end and porch, which were probably two stories in height. The old kitchen was very likely incorporated into the other constructions by a lean-to roof.

It would seem, then, that there was a class of houses which consisted of one-story or of one-story-and-a-half structures, with either two rooms and a central chimney or one room with an end chimney, which, however, seems always to have been covered over or included by the frame of the house. Only two examples of a stone chimney placed at the end of the house and showing on the outside are known to the writers, and both of these are outside of the Hartford colony—the one at Saybrook, the other at Guilford. The one-room, end-chimney type does, however, seem to have appeared in the early houses of Hartford as an inferior or temporary dwelling. How long it survived it is impossible to say. No ancient example is known to us, and it would be untrue to give it a place as a type of the colony work in the way in which we give a place to the "stone-ender" type in Providence.

The presence of carpenters, like Nicholas Clark of Hartford

and Francis Stiles of Windsor, would lead us to expect that the dwellings of the wealthier settlers — such men as the Reverend Thomas Hooker, Governor Haynes, and the others who were addressed by the title of "Master"—would be somewhat elaborate, and would express the traditions, modified by what the craftsmen had seen or learned in the Bay, which the carpenters had brought from England. We have further warrant for this belief in the fact that George Wyllys, one of the wealthiest of the original settlers, sent his steward, William Gibbons, to Hartford in 1636, with twenty men, to build him a house and to make other preparations for his coming.

These dwelling-houses of the better sort during the first period in the Connecticut colony were of a well-marked type, the plan and the end elevation of which we have given in *A* and the view beside it in Figure 1, and which we have already described. They were sometimes a story and a half high, but generally of two stories. The second story, where there were two, presented the same plan as the first, but the rooms were larger, for the wall of this story generally projected about eighteen inches beyond that of the one below and thus formed an "overhang" which, with the stone chimney, and the absence of the lean-to except as a later addition, is a marked characteristic of this first period.

No example of a story-and-a-half house of this time has come down to us, though we know that they existed. Thomas Nowell of Windsor, who died in 1648 and left an estate worth £368, had such a house, for his inventory,[1] after mentioning the parlor and the kitchen, speaks of the "parlor loft" which contained a bed worth £5, and of the "Kitchen Lofts and Garrits."

---

[1] *Conn. Col. Records*, vol. I, p. 507.

The summer, in each story of the more common two-story dwellings, ran, as we have already explained, parallel with the front of the house.   The walls were of studs, the space between which was filled with clay mixed with hay, while upon these studs, on the outside, clapboards were nailed without any intermediate boarding. The roofs were steep, and were sometimes shingled and sometimes thatched.

In Hartford itself there is now standing only one house which belongs to this early time.   There are, however, in the neighboring towns several examples of the better class of dwellings, and from all these we shall be able to see the original aspect of the valley settlements.   Let us take them up in the order of the dates, as nearly as these can be ascertained — except that we shall put the two houses without overhangs in a class by themselves — and make of each a separate study.   The houses, then, which can claim to belong to the first forty years of the Connecticut settlements are :

I.   THE JOHN CLARK HOUSE, FARMINGTON, c. 1645.

II.   THE GLEASON HOUSE, FARMINGTON, c. 1655.

III.   THE LEWIS HOUSE, FARMINGTON, c. 1660.

IV.   THE COWLES HOUSE, FARMINGTON, c. 1660.

V.   THE WHITMAN HOUSE, FARMINGTON, c. 1660.

VI.   THE MOORE HOUSE, WINDSOR, c. 1664.

VII.   THE JOSEPH WHITING HOUSE, HARTFORD, c. 1650.

VIII.   THE DORUS BARNARD HOUSE, HARTFORD, c. 1660.

CLARK HO
FARMINGTON.

I.   THE JOHN CLARK HOUSE.

This house, often called the Porter house, stood until the year 1880 on the corner of High street and the Hartford road in the village of Farmington.   It was built before 1650 by Robert Wilson or by John Steel, and was bought in 1657 by the John Clark whose name we have given it and in whose family it long remained.   The external appearance of it, as shown in our drawing, with the overhang on the ends as well as on the front and with the bracketed overhang in the gable, marks it as one of the earliest of an early class of houses.   While there were, at the time this dwelling was destroyed, three examples of the bracketed overhang group[1]—the oldest form of the overhang type—this old building was without doubt the most venerable of them all.

From the hands of Erastus Porter—from whom it obtained the name of the Porter house, though it was not long owned by the Porters[2]—the house passed into those of John Riley, who after using it for some time as a barn pulled it down. The destruction of it is the more to be regretted as it was the oldest house in the colony, and since, except the Hollister and the Patterson houses, there seems to be no example remaining of so strong an end overhang in connection with one on the front. The combination of bracket and drop in the overhangs is not common; and an arrangement such as the end overhang makes necessary when both bracket and drop are used, as we have shown in Figure 5, is unique. The drop is quite elaborate—more so than any other we know. The form of the bracket on the front we are not quite so sure of, as we had to make the drawing from a small photograph. The essentials are, however, correctly given. In the chapter on Construction the reader will find an explanation of the method of framing this overhanging corner.

The walls of this house are of the stud construction typical of

FIGURE 5.—OVER-HANGS, PORTER OR CLARK HOUSE.

---

[1] The Gleason and the Cowles were the other two houses. They are still standing (1897).

[2] For the history of this property, from the deed to Clark in 1657 down, we are indebted to Mr. Julius Gay of Farmington. The earliest entry which he found in the town records concerning the house is as follows:

"Jan. 1657 to John Clark. One psell on which his dwelling house now standeth with yeardes or orchardes thearein being contan by estma Ten acres be it more or less yt wheare of he bought of John Stell & ded sum tyme belong to Robberd Willson, Abutting on porke brook on the East & on William Smiths land on the West & on John Stells land on the South and on the highway on the North"

The estate was, therefore, well enough established to be provided with orchards.

the colony.   These studs are covered on the north end of the
house and in the north gable with wide, overlapping "weather-
boards," the original of the clapboards which cover the other sides
visible in the photograph as we have reproduced it in Figure 4.
In the second story, however, whatever may have been the case
in the first, the clay filling is lacking.   There is no intermediate
boarding under the clapboards such as we find in a modern house.

The windows of the house, as it appears in the drawing, are
not original.   The chimney, which rises through the roof a little
in front of the ridge—an unusual position—may be as old as the
house.   It is apparently of red sandstone, laid up in small blocks.
It has a thin projecting course for a cap, and another, just below
it, for a necking, while a third, close to the roof, serves to shed
the water and to prevent it from running down the face of the
stack into the house.   The thinness of the mass in proportion to
its length or size in the direction of the ridge—a trait which is
characteristic of these early chimneys—is quite noticeable here.
The lack of a lean-to is also very conspicuous in the photograph
and the drawing.   There may have been one, added after the
house was built, which does not appear in the view we have.

GLEASON HOVSE
FARMINGTON

II. THE GLEASON HOUSE.

Another old dwelling—which, after reaching the condition of a
stable, that last stage of existence through which the Clark house
passed, is now waiting a similar destruction—stands in the rear of
Mr. Porter's house on the east side of the main street of Farmington, about a hundred yards south of the Hartford road. It was
built, no one knows by whom, somewhere between 1650 and 1660.
Originally it stood facing west on the main street, but some eighty
or a hundred years ago its chimney was taken down and it was
moved back a hundred feet or so and turned with its face to the
south. It is a fact which may be noted here, in passing, that
while in Rhode Island the earliest houses invariably face the south
no matter what their relation to the street may thereby become,
so that it is safe to question the pretensions to age of any house

which does not so face, the earliest dwellings in Connecticut and in New Haven pay more attention to the direction in which the street runs, and face south only when they can front decorously upon a highway which runs east and west.

A glance at the first-story plan, which we give in Figure 7, will explain both the original arrangement and the present condition of the house. At its present west end, the north end as it stood upon the street, was the parlor—years ago turned into a wagon-shed—with its summer *G*, its end girt *H*, its back girt *K*, front girt *L*, and chimney girt *M*.

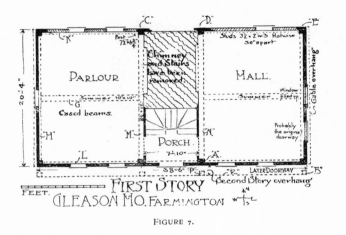

FIGURE 7.

All the beams overhead are cased, and the ceiling is plastered. Some of the posts[1] at this end have lost their casing and have been patched at the bottom, while the end sill and all of the original floor are gone. The side walls are lathed and plastered over the old matched and moulded boards of the horizontal "wainscot" which originally covered them. The plastering of the ceiling is also an addition contemporary with the casing of the beams.

The original stairs have disappeared along with the chimney, but the width of the porch or entry is given by the space between the chimney girts *M* and *N*.

---

[1] The letters at the posts are referred to in the framing details given in Plate I. in the chapter on Construction.

The original hall at the eastern end—the southern, of course, when the building stood on the street—is now taken up by empty stalls for horses and cattle. It shows the same constructive arrangement as does the parlor and, like that room, has its beams cased and its walls and ceilings plastered. A door, which has on the outside a casing of a late colonial type, opens from the original southwest corner, now at the southeast.

This old room, the descendant of the hall in the old English manor house, was the kitchen as well as the living-room of the dwelling. More constantly occupied in winter, it would naturally be put at the southern end of the building. The statelier parlor— the name of which came into domestic architecture from the monastery, where, as the word itself implies, it was the room in which the monks were allowed to converse—was, when not employed as a

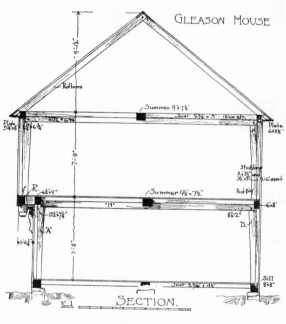

FIGURE 8.

sleeping room, used for a dining room or for notable gatherings like weddings or funerals.[1]

---

[1] The parlor of our early houses is the direct descendant of the *solar* of the Saxon and Norman house. See the chapter on The Relation of Colonial Architecture to English Work.

Upstairs, in the hall chamber—the parlor chamber has its walls wainscoted, but at the time of our visit was half full of hay—can be seen the rough and almost careless construction of the old house, which is shown in the sections, Figures 8 and 9. All the floor joists and the boarding of the original attic floor are gone.

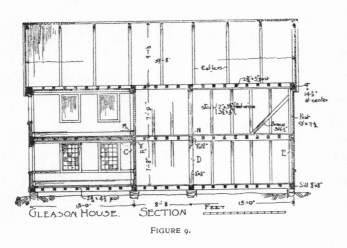

GLEASON HOUSE.   SECTION

FIGURE 9.

The summer in the hall chamber is in strong contrast to the rest of the work, is well smoothed and cleanly chamfered with plain stops, and shows few axe marks. It looks as though it had belonged to an older house. The end girt in this room is cambered—that is, is deeper in the middle than at the ends. The braces run from near the top of the posts down to the end girt in the second floor, which is just the reverse of what we see in Rhode Island. The walls in this room are studded and are covered with clapboards nailed directly to the studs with neither outer boarding, clay filling, nor inside wainscoting. As we have just said, the workmanship, except in the summer, which may have come from a still older building, is rude in the extreme.

The roof, though old, cannot be original; for the Connecticut carpenters preferred roofs of a pitch even steeper than forty-five degrees. They were not accustomed, moreover, so early as this, to do away with the collar-beams, which this roof lacks.

We urge the reader to study carefully the plans and sections of this house and especially the perspective of its framing, which we give in Figure 10. The names of the rooms, which occur constantly in the old inventories, and the terms " summer," " girt," " plate," " rafter," and so on, which will often appear in these pages, are there clearly indicated ; so that by a little study the reader will obtain a clearer idea of the typical house and of the construction of it than he could gain from many pages of text and from much repetition.

The present appearance of the house is given in Figure 6. It lacks its chimney and is rather dilapidated, but is still picturesque. It has an overhang on the front and one in each gable, but none at either end in the first story as has the Clark house. In the underside of the plate, which projects to receive a barge-board

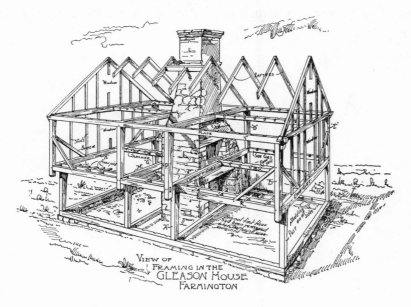

FIGURE 10.

long since departed, there may still be seen at the southwest corner of the house the mortise for a former bracket like that in a similar position in the Clark house.

The very disrepair and ruin of the house were of the greatest service to us, for we were thereby enabled to study the framing with considerable ease. In Figure 11 we give a drawing of the present southeast corner — showing the overhang as well as the bracket and the end of the post. There is no drop here, and it is hardly probable that there ever was one. The four little gouge-cuts on the lower edges of the tapering block in which the post ends are interesting. They do not seem to be common. The bracket is of quite a common form. A geometrical drawing of it, with measurements, will be found in the chapter on Construction.

It will be noted that this house had no lean-to, and we think we shall show that during this period the lean-to, although it appears early in the inventories, is always an addition to the original house.

FIGURE 11.—OVERHANG.

III.   THE LEWIS HOUSE.

Few visitors to the Elm Tree Inn at Farmington are aware
that a house of about 1660 is concealed at the centre of the mass
of buildings which forms the present hostelry.   At the end of the
long hall which runs back from the entrance we come upon the
stairs—of comparatively modern date—just in front of which runs
a passage at right angles to the entrance hall.   These stairs occupy exactly the place of those in the ancient house.   The present
smoking-room is the
original hall, as the
summer overhead and
the oven—probably
built into an older
fireplace—still pro-
claim.   The parlor is
now absorbed in the
dining room of the
inn, but the summer
still traverses a part
of the ceiling of the
new room.   As you
stand in the passage

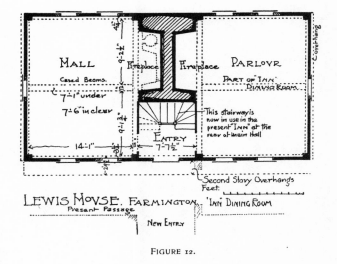

FIGURE 12.

in front of the stairs, you are in the entry of the original house;
and if you face toward the door, with your back to the stairs, you
will see above you, with its soffit flush with the rest of the ceiling,
the ancient overhang, which shows even the edges of the bottom
board of the second-story front.

There is also an end overhang, as the plan shows, which can be seen on the outside of the present smoking-room. It is small, however, and there are no brackets now remaining under it.

Who built the house we do not know. It may have been Captain William Lewis, whose son — also named William Lewis, one of the schoolmasters of Farmington — undoubtedly lived here in 1704.[1] It belongs somewhere about 1660.

---

[1] "Schoolmaster William lived in a house which stood on or very near the site of the Elm-Tree Inn, and was one of the seven houses which the town, on the 31st day of March, 1704, ordered to be fortified and supplied with powder, lead bullets, flints and half-pikes."—Julius Gay, *Schools and Schoolmasters in Farmington in the Olden Time*, p. 21.

COWLES HOUSE, FARMINGTON

IV. THE COWLES HOUSE.

This house, or rather one half of it, stands on the western side of the main street on the little rising ground just north of a brook at the extreme southern end of the village. As our drawing shows, it is a house of the class which includes the Porter and Gleason houses—that is, it has a bracket at each post under the overhang. Two only of these brackets now exist, the third is not in its place, and the fourth was, of course, on the northern half of the house which was cut away many years ago and moved a few feet further north, where it now stands as a separate tenement—a rather exaggerated reminder of the colonial fashion of bequeathing the different halves of a house to different persons. The entry still remains on the southern house, but the chimney and stairs disappeared when the building was cut in two. The present chimney in each of the houses is new.

The roof of the house as it is at present is also new. The ancient ridge was parallel to the road, and originally the building must have closely resembled the Gleason house as that dwelling appeared in the early days when it stood on the main street.

The bracket under the overhang here is almost exactly the same—indeed in pattern it is the same—as that in the Gleason house. There is no drop here either, though it is not safe to say that none ever existed.

The date of this house we can fix only approximately by comparison with the other houses of its class. It belongs, with the Gleason house, in the decade between 1650 and 1660.

WHITMAN HOUSE.
FARMINGTON

V. THE WHITMAN HOUSE.

On High street in Farmington, about three hundred yards south of the spot where stood the Clark house, is the sober-colored dwelling, the last of the three ancient houses, all possessing overhangs, which, within the memory of men not yet old, looked westward from the eastern side of the thoroughfare.[1] The date of this building, now known as the Whitman house, it is impossible to fix by any documentary evidence.[2] As in the case of the Gleason house we fall back upon experience and careful comparison of its construction and details with those of other buildings. A good guide

---

[1] These three houses were the Clark house already described, now destroyed, the Whitman house, and the Joseph Porter house, burned January 15, 1886, which stood south of the Whitman, "on the northeast corner of the intersection of High street with the road to New Britain."—Julius Gay, *Old Houses in Farmington*, p. 19.

[2] The first record of this house is 1720, when John Stanley, Senior, sold it to Captain Ebenezer Steel.—*Ibid.*

in our earliest colonial work is the way in which the traditions brought from England by the oldest carpenters became modified— diluted, as it were—as the lapse of time and as the changed envir- onment begin to work upon them.   The Clark house is among the original dwellings of the settlement.   Next to it — if not actually contemporary with it — is the Gleason, which lacks one tradition, the end overhang in the second story.   And just after the Gleason comes this house, which lacks three traditional features—the bracket under the gable, the end overhang in the second story, and the bracket under the second story on the front.   The date of the building, then, is about 1660.

Though not the oldest house in the Connecticut colony, it is, at least, one of the best preserved, for it is still inhabited and retains nearly all its original appointments intact.   The clapboard- ing has been renewed, the first story has been plastered, the present windows, as the marks in the second-story wainscot show, have re- placed older and smaller ones, and the lean-to has been added with its fireplace, the flue whereof has been built up against the back of the older chimney and has been topped out with the present brickwork—a modern renewal—above the roof.   The brown-stone top of the old stack is itself a rebuilding with lime mortar.   The roof of the main house is also a renewal, contemporary with the lean-to.   Otherwise the venerable house is in the shape in which the carpenter and the mason left it, even to the two flights of stairs which ascend from the first floor to the garret, and the stone steps from the hall by which you may still reach the cellar under the parlor.

The plan of the first floor, which we give in Figure 15, will show how closely this house resembles, in its arrangement and even in its dimensions, all the others of its time.   In fact, one plan would almost suffice for all the dwellings in the colony. It is to be noted, also, that one of the rooms, the hall, is almost always longer than the other, the parlor, even if by a few inches only, an arrangement much exaggerated in Rhode Island in 1730, when the builders there began to use the central-chimney plan. The summer in this hall is not cased—a sure proof that the plas-

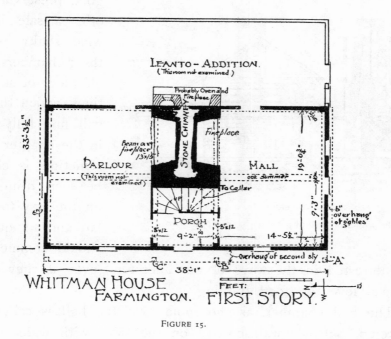

FIGURE 15.

tering there is not original—and it has a filleted quarter-round for its chamfer. The door to the cellar opens from the hall, and this door, as well as that which leads into the entry, is original and is well worth study. Each door is composed of vertical boards of white pine, which are grooved and tongued together and are secured at the back by two moulded "battens" or strips of pine. The boards themselves, of the doors as well as those of the whole partition across the fireplace end of the room—a partition which is constructed the same way as are the doors—have a strip of moulding worked on their edges.

The steps to the cellar are of stone and are not very steep. They are wider, also, than those in southern Rhode Island, as are the stairs to the second story, which, in their original form and in good preservation, still offer a safe if somewhat shaky ascent to the "chambers." The old mode of supporting them, which the reader will find fully detailed in the chapter on Construction, is clearly to be seen from beneath on the way to the cellar, and its quaintness should commend it to

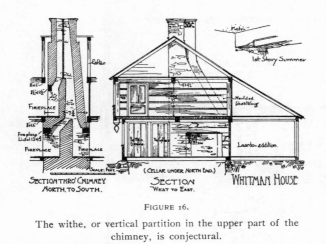

FIGURE 16.

The withe, or vertical partition in the upper part of the chimney, is conjectural.

all interested in the ways of our ancestors, even if they have no especial love for good framing.

The hall chamber, as the room over the hall is called, is not plastered, but is "wainscoted" on the sides with wide horizontal boards of white pine, tongued and grooved and moulded, as in the Gleason house. In the front or western wall, on each side of the present window, are the marks which show the filling-up of an older opening, wider and lower, though higher from the floor of the room. This was probably the original window of the house, for there are cases where these old frames—not the sash—have been taken from buildings within forty or fifty years, and the size of it shows that it was a double window, separated by an upright wooden bar or mullion.

The chimney below the roof is of field stone, well selected, generally flat. The peculiarity of it, which strikes quite forcibly one familiar with the work in the other New England colonies, is that the stones are laid not in mortar of lime, even of the kind called "shell lime," but in clay mixed with hay after the fashion of the old English plasterers.

The house at present, as the drawing shows, has a lean-to. That this is a later addition is proved by the way in which the flue of the lean-to fireplace is built up along the back of the old stone chimney. If anyone requires further proof, let him look between the chimney—which is not sheathed at all on the stairs—and the partition which shuts off the hall chamber, where there is no fireplace. He will see, if it is not too dark—and if it is, let him climb over, as we did, on the back of the chimney—the original outside wall on the back of the house, on a line with the hatched wall in Figure 16, with its clapboards, still in place, nailed directly to the studs, exactly as in the Gleason house.

There is a small overhang in the gable of this house, but none on the end at the second-floor level. That on the front, how-ever, ranks as one of the best that remain to us, and is one of the very few which have all the drops intact. There are no brackets, an omission which marks the house as later than the others we have been discussing. The shape of the drop, which is given in Figure 17, is very elegant, and the workman-ship of the quaint old forms is very good.

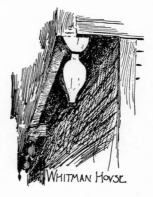

FIGURE 17.—THE DROP.

Those who are interested in the wood-work of those times may compare the effect with the means used to attain it by referring from this drawing to Figure 102, which will give a measured drawing of the drop, and to Plate VII, where the framing of the whole overhang in the Gleason house is analyzed.

The chimney above the roof is, like that of the Clark house, of red sandstone—or, as it is roughly called, brownstone—laid in small blocks, with wide joints filled with lime mortar. It is a rebuilding, for the present roof is of too low a pitch to be the original covering. There are three projecting courses at the top of this chimney for a cap, but there is no necking. The stack is low, and, in its original form, without the present brick stack behind it, was much longer in plan than its width. Unlike the Clark house chimney, the bulk of it is behind the ridge, as the face of the stack, with the projecting strip or water-table, is only a few inches in front of the peak of the roof. This projecting "dripstone," as it may be called, is clearly visible in the drawing of the house.

MOORE HOUSE
WINDSOR

VI. THE MOORE HOUSE.

The Moore house, one of the oldest in Connecticut, and one which after sundry migrations has finally taken its place as a tenement house somewhat west of its original situation, stood, when it was built, on the west side of Broad-street Green in the pleasant old town of Windsor.

Stiles' *History of Windsor* attributes the house to Deacon John Moore, who is said to have given it to his son at the latter's marriage in 1690.[1] The house, however, though it was no doubt given to the young man, as averred by the historian, is, on the architectural evidence, far older than 1690. It is one of the early type of

---

[1] Stiles, *A History of Ancient Windsor*, vol. I, p. 431. In volume II, p. 501, the date of this marriage is given as February 8, 1693-4, and the John then married is called the grandson of Deacon John.

frame houses in the colony, and belongs in the first period.   It
was probably built by John, junior, or by his father, the Deacon,
for him—whence the tradition that it was a gift—at the time of
the former's marriage, September 21, 1664.

It has the overhang and the drop under the second-story posts,
and ranks with the Whitman and the other houses in Farmington
as one of the patriarchs of the Connecticut river settlement.

We give a plan in Figure 19, and in Figure 18 a restoration.
Two only of the drops remain.   One, at one end, was sawn off
when the house was abutted against another to form an ell.   The
other, at the other end, was cut off only a short time ago by a
curiosity-hunter.   Those that remain are beautiful specimens, different from any others we know.   Figure 18, in which the drop is
given in perspective, may be compared with the measured drawing
in Figure 102.

The alterations the house has just undergone have changed its
appearance considerably from that which it presented when on the
main street; but its present owner[1] has kept the main lines, and
the house can still be studied.   To his great credit he has kept
the old gable overhang on the south and has put back the original
brackets which were under it.   To his kind assistance are due the
measurements we give of these, which, in shape, resemble the examples preserved in the museum at Deerfield, Mass., which were
taken from the famous Sheldon house in that town.   These in
Windsor are the only gable brackets we know of now existing in
Connecticut.   There were brackets, it will be remembered, under
the gable of the demolished Clark house in Farmington, and the
mortise for one still exists in the projecting plate of the Gleason

---

[1] Mr. Horace C. Clark.

house, though the
bracket itself has dis-
appeared. It will be
seen, in Figure 105,
that the Windsor ex-
ample is superior in
contour to that in the
Clark house, which is
of the same general
outline as the form

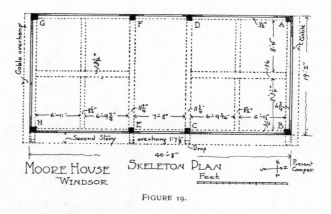

MOORE HOUSE   SKELETON PLAN
WINDSOR   Feet

FIGURE 19.

used in that house and in the Cowles and the Gleason for the
second-story overhang on the front.

In the migrations of the old building the chimney has disappeared. Probably two successive stacks — the earlier of stone, the
later of brick — have been demolished. The brick chimney is
shown as of herring-bone work in the sketch which Stiles in his
History gives of the house. Though this drawing seems to have
been from memory and is inaccurate in several points, the herring-
bone is very likely to be correct. Still, we have restored the stone
top as that of the original stack.

The inside of the house is extremely interesting from the fact
that we have here one of those rare examples of crossed summers,
the only instance we know of in the present territory of Connecticut, and one of the very few which exist in all New England.
The regular summer, that parallel with the front of the house,
runs through entire. The other is in two halves, framed into this
main one, and is of smaller size. All are of hard pine, as is the
rest of the frame in this house.

VII. THE JOSEPH WHITING HOUSE.

We have neglected the strict line of chronology in the treatment of the last houses we have been discussing, in order to follow the development of the framed overhang through its various examples. Let us now turn back and consider a house which, though the second story of it does not project, is, and for a long time has been, the oldest house in Hartford — a house which can rank with the Clark in the first half of the seventeenth century, if, indeed, it do not date from the very first years of the settlement on the banks of the Little River.

Not all the two-story houses in the Connecticut colony were built with the overhang. The existence of that feature depended partly, perhaps, on the personal taste of the owner and on the memories he had brought with him from his old English home.

It depended far more on the carpenter the owner employed and on the part of England in which that carpenter had learned his trade. A town-bred craftsman, for instance, was more likely to use the overhang than was one trained in the country, where projecting upper stories were not so common.[1] Perhaps Francis Stiles, who came from London and who very soon had apprentices here, was responsible for the overhangs of the houses we have been studying. His apprentices would naturally follow his ways. Again, the overhangs in different parts of England vary; so that, fully to account for the use of the overhang or of the straight front in any case, or for the use of one kind of overhang in preference to another, we must know who our earliest carpenters were—whether they came from Shropshire or from Kent, or from one district or another, and whether they were townsmen or rustics.

Captain Joseph Whiting, Treasurer of the Colony of Connecticut,[2] a man of considerable importance in the public life of his day, once dwelt in the old house which now stands on the east side of Main street in Hartford, next north of the building on the corner of Charter Oak avenue. It has sadly descended since that day. The lower story has been converted into a store for liquor, at present, while above are tenements accessible from the street by a flight of steps along the original front of the building; for this house—unlike most other old Hartford dwellings—does not face upon the street. Probably it never did, but always looked out toward the south upon the garden which lay between it and what was then the highway to the South Meadow.

Although treasurer Joseph Whiting owned this dwelling, he did not build it. He bought the estate in 1682 from Zachary

---

[1] S. O. Addy, *The Evolution of the English House*, p. 102. This is a very interesting book.
[2] Under the Charter, from 1678 to 1717. He was a son of William Whiting, Senior.

Sandford, who had acquired it in 1667 from Francis Barnard, who, in turn, had purchased it in 1650 as part of the estate of Andrew Bacon. It was Francis Barnard who built the house, if, indeed, it was not standing when he bought the land. His dwelling, with gardens, is mentioned in the record of the land belonging to him, and each succeeding record of the property, down to Whiting's title, names the dwelling-house or messuage thereon.[1]

As the reader may judge from the brief description and from the drawings, the house has been greatly altered both outside and in. The windows are new, and have over them quite elaborate pediments which date from the time of George the Third. A lean-to has been built on, as is evident from the change of pitch in the roof— a change made also on the front to accommodate the larger

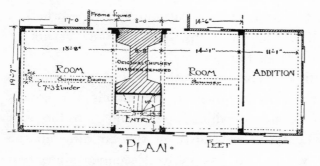

FIGURE 21.—THE JOSEPH WHITING HOUSE.

and higher windows. The old front door has been closed up— though, of course, this was done in our own day; and at some early date an addition was built at the eastern end. The fact that this east end is much plainer than the west, because it was kept away from the street, shows that the house, if it has been moved at all, was turned from the street before the new windows with their ornamented heads were put in. The original floor in the first story is probably gone. The old framing is intact; but

---

[1] See Appendix I.

the chimney and the front stairs have been taken out to gain space for the store. The roof, though repaired, is original. It is very steep, and retains its collar-beams.

Joseph Whiting's inventory, taken February 26, 1716–17,[1] mentions the following rooms : the parlor, the dwelling room—the hall is meant, the old word was going out of use—the kitchen and the little bedroom. The kitchen shows that the lean-to had been added before Whiting's death, as the little bedroom shows that the addition at the eastern end of the house, an addition which has no summer in the first story, is also earlier than 1716. The little chimney room it is not easy to place. It was perhaps one of the rooms at one side of the kitchen, as we shall see in later plans, with an added chimney in it.

In the second story are : the parlor chamber, the little chamber —probably over the little bedroom—the middle chamber—which was over the dwelling room or hall, and which, by its very name, shows that it was the parlor, and not the hall, which was toward the street—the lean-to chamber, and the kitchen chamber. This unusual naming of two rooms where, in the seventeenth century, there was but one, shows that the space under the lean-to roof had been divided.

The garret and the cellar are also mentioned ; and, outside the house, the workshop and the "old shopp."

Of these rooms only the hall and the parlor belong to the original dwelling. Whiting had added all the others.

From one entry we know the value of the property : "The Mantion House and homestead one rood with the barn stable and out houses £155."

---

[1] *Hartford Probate Records*, vol. IX.

DORUS BARNARD HOUSE.
HARTFORD.

VIII. THE DORUS BARNARD HOUSE.

There was—till lately—another house in Hartford which was built in the first period, and built without the overhang. This— the Dorus Barnard house—stood on Retreat avenue, opposite the Retreat itself, and thus on the northern side of the street. It was built in 1659 or 1660 by Robert, son of Governor John Webster. It took its present name from Captain John Barnard's son Dorus, who owned it in the early part of this century. It was demolished in the summer of 1899.[1]

As the perspective shows, the old roof had been replaced by one of much lower pitch, and the windows were large and of late date. There was no lean-to when we saw the house, though some

---

[1] For a complete history of the property, kindly communicated to us by Dr. Henry Barnard of Hartford, see Appendix II.

late sheds have been built up against the outside wall on the back
of the dwelling, probably to replace a lean-to which Dr. Barnard
says existed within his memory; and there was, as we have especially noted, no overhang.

Inside the house, in the south room—the original hall, which
is so designated on the plan in Figure 23—the beams were cased
and the ceiling and parts of the walls were plastered. A wainscot
—not of the early type as we have it in the Whitman house, but

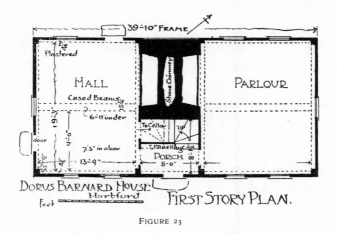

FIGURE 23

one with wide panels—covered three sides of the room to the
height of the window-sills; while the fourth side, that which
contained the fireplace, consisted entirely of panelling of a very
good design. The difference we have just noted between this
panelling and the archaic "wainscot" in the Whitman house
renders it certain that the panelled work was not so old as the
building.

The girts had been cut out for the window-heads, which shows
that the openings and sash shown in the view were not original.
Few people realize how small ancient windows were.

The plastering, too, which fitted around these windows, was contemporary with them and not with the house. Both plaster and panelling, which was of a very old form, were put in at the same time during the first third of the eighteenth century.

The cellar was under the north room—the original parlor—and it was reached from the hall by a flight of stone steps in front of the chimney. It is noticeable that the door to the cellar, so far as we have seen, very rarely opens out of the front entry or porch —a thing extremely common in Rhode Island.

The chimney of this house was built of stone up to the level of the second floor. Above that the original stone stack had been replaced with brick. This must be quite an early example of the

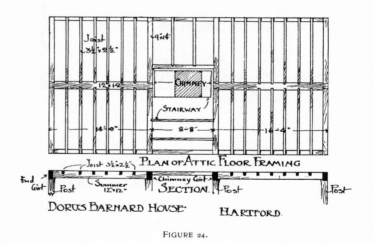

FIGURE 24.

use of this material; for the brick, which were of large size—and this is itself a sign of early date—were laid in a mortar made not of lime and sand, but of yellow clay mixed with hay.

The stone stage of this stack had a peculiarity which, in a two-room house, we have never met elsewhere. The back of the chimney, as will appear in Figure 23, was on the outer line of the building; so that, instead of hiding behind the wooden wall, the stonework showed on the outside of the house. The lean-to covered it, of course, but it was the original disposition or a restoration thereof, otherwise it would have had a fireplace. This lack of a fireplace shows, unless there was one which has been filled up, that the lean-to was a very late addition.

In Figure 24 we give the framing of the garret floor. It resembles in construction what is left of that of the Gleason house, with the tops of the girts rising above the tops of the plates, and the usual dovetail joints with which the summers are framed into the chimney girts. It is peculiar in that the floor joists rest upon the plates, instead of framing into them with the tops of both the plates and the joists on the same level.

The roof, both in frame—Figure 25—and in covering, is comparatively new.

The frame of the building—unlike that of its ancient fellow, the John Barnard house—seemed sound and strong; and there was no structural reason why the house should not have been preserved for many years.

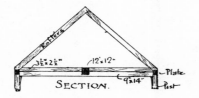

FIGURE 25.—DORUS BARNARD.

We have now the type of the well-to-do houses in the Connecticut colony during the first period—the years, that is, from
1635 to 1675.   With the restorations in mind which we have
placed before our readers, we can easily picture the appearance
of Hartford, Windsor, and Wethersfield—the old valley settlements
—and of the newer towns which spread eastward and westward
from them.

We can now proceed to study the changes which time, the
new problems, and the waning of the older traditions brought
about in the architecture of colonial Connecticut.

CHAPTER III.

THE SECOND PERIOD IN THE CONNECTICUT COLONY.

1675-1700.

LTHOUGH Connecticut suffered little, directly, from King Philip's War, yet the colony, which had shared with the others the danger of extermination, and had sent to the winter campaign its quota of troops, shared the relief which the Swamp Fight brought to all southern New England. In Rhode Island, and in parts of Massachusetts, much rebuilding had to be done as the result of Indian forays; and this contributed something to a change of style, or gave an opportunity for it, since it would have come in any case. Thus, in Connecticut, where no villages or farm houses suffered much from fire in Indian hands, we find that the causes which tended to make the year 1675 a milestone in our architectural history were at work as in the other colonies.

All divisions in architectural history are arbitrary. Styles progress gradually and steadily, if slowly; and any year which is taken as marking a change of fashion must be considered as an average of several on either side of it. The causes at work operate under

better conditions in one place than in another.   In this district
imitation hastens progress ; in that district conservatism retards it.

So it is with our date of 1675.   The last quarter of the seventeenth century shows work different from that of the first forty or
fifty years after the settlements ; and this is true of all New England.   The dates of the houses, as nearly as those uncertain facts
can be ascertained, point to this year as a good average for the
change.

We have already hinted at the causes which worked to bring
about these changes.   They were, principally, increased wealth and
changed habits of life and work.   The former operated to encourage
the enlargement of the houses, the addition of more rooms, a more
uniformly comfortable style of living.   Without it no change would
have been probable, for the house plan of the earlier time survived, as we shall see, into the period of which we write.   The
other causes — the changes of habit — were inevitable in the new
country.   Life was necessarily different from what it had been in
England ; and the new generation which had come up took to the
new existence with no homesickness and with less struggle than
its elders had endured.   The direct English tradition was somewhat weakened.   The older settlers were passing away, and the
current of migration from England had slowed or stopped.   A
new way of living — though not a startling change — drifted in,
which suited those of the new generation — men who had never
seen old England.

With the increase of wealth there had been also a growth of
the community, and this brought new buildings and new — or, at
least, different — problems.   And the changes in the colonists
brought new ways of meeting these problems.   The old carpenters
were dead, and the new work had to be done by their apprentices

and by the apprentices of these apprentices, who, in the new en-
vironment—which was all they had ever known—had ceased to
cling to some traditions which, to their old masters, were of the
essence of the craft.

Again, the union of the whole State under the Charter may
have done something to lessen the differences in construction and
in design which had marked the formerly separate settlements.

These changes of which we have spoken were not great. We
shall see that clearly. But the old framed overhang stops entirely.
Another form in which the projection is hewn out of the post
comes in from New Haven.[1] In many cases—more than in the
first period—the overhang is not used at all. Brick came into
use during this period;[2] and we see the stone chimney, except
in remote places, gradually give way before the new material.
Lime appears, also, during this time,[3] and with it the plastering
for which, rather than for mortar, it seems principally to have
been used. Plastering was at first confined to the wealthier
houses, and to the side-walls of these. It can hardly have been
widespread until late in this period and early in the next.

The great change in this time, however, was in the plan. It
consisted in the addition of a kitchen and of other rooms at the
back of the two rooms of the older type of plan—an addition
covered by a lean-to roof and built, rooms and roof, as an integral part of the house, and not, as in the previous period, as a
later construction.

The existence of this enlarged plan appears very clearly in the

---

[1] See Chapter IX, under " Overhang."

[2] In 1685. See Chapter IX, under " Brick." The material was older than this, but it was not
in general use.

[3] In 1679. See Chapter IX, under " Lime."

inventories,[1] but it is only from actual examples that we can see that the lean-to of this time differs from those of the previous period in that it is built with the house.   Nor is it always easy to see this; for the old type, one room deep, survived into this period also, and the lean-to was added to it in this time as before, and, as the construction of the incorporated lean-to does not differ in Connecticut—as it does in the Benjamin house, Milford, for instance, in the New Haven colony—from that of the added lean-to, we have to be quite careful in deciding what the character of any example may be.

The houses we shall discuss in this period are:

I.   THE HOLLISTER HOUSE, SOUTH GLASTONBURY, c. 1680.

II.   THE PATTERSON HOUSE, BERLIN, c. 1680.

III.   THE JOHN BARNARD HOUSE, HARTFORD, c. 1680.

---

[1] JOSEPH NASH, September 3, 1678.—Parlor, parlor chamber, east chamber over the haule, garrets, leantoe chamber, kitchin, 2nd cellar, shop.   Estate £419.

JOSEPH HAINES, Hartford, December 4, 1679.—Parlor chamber, porch chamber, hall chamber, parlor, closset, hall, kitchen, inward cellers, outward cellers, cheese chamber, little chamber, garret. Homestead with house, barns, etc., £250.

JAMES EGLESTON, December 1, 1679.—Upper chamber, inner chamber.

JAMES RICHARDS, Hartford, June 11, 1680.—Parlor, hall, space room (sic), kitchen, green chamber, parlor chamber, porch chamber, space chamber (sic), kitchen chamber, parlor chamber (mentioned again?), garret chamber.   Estate £7385 06s 10d.

—Hartford Probate Records, vol. IV.   MS.

I. THE HOLLISTER HOUSE.

All the houses of the first period in which the second story projected have represented a single type of overhang, and that has been what we may call the framed type. We have now to consider two houses—so far as we have seen, the only specimens of their kind now standing in the Connecticut colony—which, while otherwise they do not vary from the house of the second period in this jurisdiction, belong, so far as the overhang is concerned, to quite a different family. These dwellings—the Hollister, which was built with a lean-to, and the Patterson, which is a survival of the older type with the lean-to added—represent what we may call the hewn type of overhang, a type in which the projection is in the post itself, and is obtained by hewing that post into the required shape.

The Hollister house stands, facing east, on the west side of the street, just below Roaring Brook, in South Glastonbury. It is said to have been built by a Hollister in 1675.[1] It is probably a little later than that. It is a very interesting example; and, while it is of the same type as the Patterson, it is peculiar in the carving of the brackets under its overhang.

The house has been changed somewhat on the outside. Upon the old clapboards furring strips have been laid, and to these new

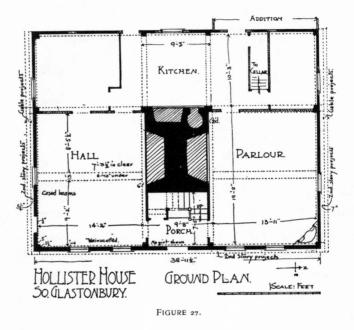

FIGURE 27.

clapboards have been nailed. This adds a thickness of nearly two inches to the walls, and covers somewhat the bottoms of the brackets. The carpenter who did this new work wanted to hew off these old brackets, which were in his way, but the owner right-

---

[1] It is now owned by Mr. James B. Killam.

eously refused to hear of it. The present windows, as well as the covering of the house, are new.

The lean-to, in this example, was built with the house. The low pitch of the roof, which is original, is one proof of this. The fact that the second floor is level throughout, instead of dropping in the lean-to chamber, is another proof—though this is not a sure sign. A dropped floor in the lean-to chamber may occur, as in the Painter house, West Haven, and in the Pulsifer house, South Glastonbury, where the lean-to is undoubtedly original. A level floor is not so likely to occur in an added lean-to house, for it is so much easier to frame the girts of the lean-to into the backs of the old posts below the mortises of the main house girts instead of on a level with them, and it is so much better for the house.

In the entry, which is very wide, there is a good left-hand stair —one with the rail on the left as you go up—and under this stair is that rare and rather late feature, a door to the cellar, which is reached by a flight of solid wooden steps. Between this door and the newel-post, as the plan explains, there is a seat. This whole stair, however, with the wainscoting and the casing of the beams in the rooms, is later than the house.

The chimney is of brick, on a stone foundation which rises to the first-floor level. The cellar wall is of the same kind of masonry—flat stones, largely of gneiss, perhaps from the river bank— and is pointed, and seems to have been originally laid, with good lime mortar.

The cellar extends under the lean-to, and there is no sign of patching in the masonry. A heavy stick like the sill on the front, shown in the section, here runs across on the line of the partition between parlor and kitchen; and the framing, as the section displays it, changes suddenly. The joists of the kitchen floor run, as is natural, across from the back wall to this beam.

In the garret the chimney shows none of that patching for the kitchen flue which is the surest sign of an added lean-to. The rafters of the main roof—which, as we have said, is original—are completely finished; and the ends of them project, as on the front,

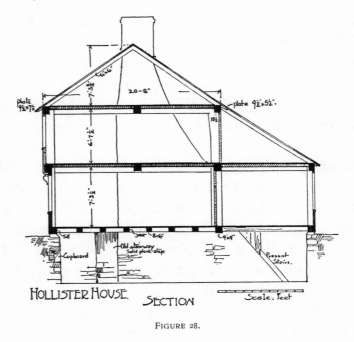

HOLLISTER HOUSE.   SECTION   Scale. Feet

FIGURE 28.

over the plate which crowns the wall between the chambers and the lean-to. Upon the same plate rest the ends of the lean-to rafters. There are no collar-beams, a characteristic of this period, though not an especially common one, which seems to have come up from New Haven.

In the partition wall which we have just mentioned the posts and braces are in place, with the studs around them. The intermediate studs are gone, but the mortises for them remain. The timbers are very clean — one stud is quite dark — but nail holes exist in them, which testify to the former presence of clapboards or of boarding put on in the lean-to chamber for the sake of warmth — a device not uncommon in these original lean-to houses. The stains from the nails are not strong enough to have been made by the weather. They are caused simply by the gallic acid of the oak, which acts on the iron.

The shape of the bracket under the overhang of this house, as given in Plate VII, is peculiar. It is unlike any we have seen elsewhere, and seems to be a union of the hewn-bracket idea with the curious double curve of circular contour which was used under the overhangs in the Gleason house and in the Cowles house in Farmington.

PATTERSON HOUSE
BERLIN

II.   THE PATTERSON HOUSE.

What is called the Patterson house stands just east of a little
stream which runs northward into the Mattabesett river.   It faces
eastward upon a road which has some appearance of having been
bent around in that direction to accommodate the dwellers in the
house.   It is on the edge of the meadow land, just at the foot of
the hill on which stands the village of Berlin.

The choice of such a site would of itself mark the building as
the home, or the successor of the home, of an early settler, even if
the house were unsatisfactory; but in this case the sunken, twisted,
weather-beaten veteran—which still faces the visitor who passes
under the shadow of the trees which darken the door-yard—leaves
nothing to be desired.

The house is said to have been built by Isaac Hart in 1721.
This we cannot believe.   Isaac may have added the lean-to, but
the house is of a type which belongs to a time before his day.
If it is not so late as this, it cannot, on the other hand, be earlier

than 1670. The house belonged, probably, to some settler attracted to the neighborhood by the presence of Richard Beckley,[1] and was built in the decade which began with 1680.

The house as it now appears — Figure 29 — has at the back a lean-to, which a very slight investigation shows to have been a later addition. The building stands upon a foundation of rough stone concealed, except at the back of the lean-to, by the settlements which have taken place in the walls. Under the parlor — the more northern of the two rooms which the house originally possessed — there is a cellar which may once have had windows, but which is now absolutely dark.

The porch or entry — see the plan in Figure 30 — contains the original staircase, which is almost exactly like that in the John Barnard house, both in the plan, with its steps all winders, and in the construction, with the peculiar device for carrying the treads — a device which appeared also, it will be remembered, in the Whitman house.

In the hall the ceiling has been plastered, but the walls, which have been papered, still retain their old "wainscot" or sheathing of horizontal boards. Summer and posts have been cased. There is, in front of the old fireplace, which has been filled with a later one and with an oven, a hearth of brownstone in three pieces. Under the stairs is the descent to the cellar, reached by the usual wide door opening from this room. The steps are of solid timbers. Over the fireplace in this room, and in the parlor also, is the common wooden lintel, each end of which rests — at the end visible on

---

[1] The pioneer in this region — once the southwest corner of Wethersfield — was Sergeant Richard Beckley a carpenter from New Haven, from whose name the territory east of the Farmington line in this neighborhood was called the Beckley Quarter. This house seems not to have been within the grant made to him by Wethersfield soon after his arrival in 1668.

the cellar stairs, and no doubt at the other end also in the original scheme—on a 6×6 oak stick embedded in the chimney and reaching from one face thereof to the other. This is a wise precaution, both as a tie and as a bearing for the heavy lintels, which are liable to roll with the least settlement in a chimney which, like this, is laid up in nothing but the ordinary clay so common in the Valley settlements.

The parlor differs little from the hall. It has never been plastered. It still retains in its northeast corner the "boffet," as

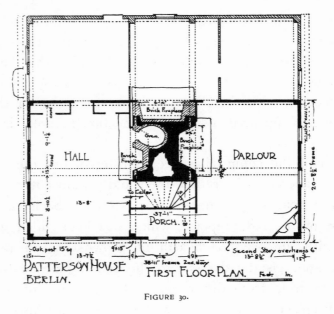

FIGURE 30.

the old inventories sometimes spelled the word, which tells of a time when it was the dining room of the mansion—a position it assumed at the time when the lean-to was added. This boffet, then, makes it probable, from its date, that Isaac Hart built the lean-to in 1721.

The lean-to contains a kitchen with a very wide stone fire-place; and it has a small chamber at each end. There is no crane in the fireplace, and the original arrangement of long "tram-mels," hanging down from bars across the flue, is still to be seen. There is no oven here—a proof of what we have constantly noted, that the old stone chimneys nowhere have them, and that they came into common use when brick was plenty. They are, there-fore, especially in these remoter houses, always additions built into an older fireplace—here that of the hall. It would look a little from this as if the lean-to came later than the building of the oven, which dates from the time when the hall was still the kitchen also of the house.

The second story contains little of note, except the construction of the stairs which lead to the garret and the framing which ap-pears in the lean-to chamber. The stairs we shall illustrate in the chapter on Construction. The framing which can be seen in the lean-to chamber is evidently that of the outside wall of the original house. Posts, braces, and studs are all in place; and, though the clapboards are gone, certain weather stains on the frame show where they once were. The flue added to the chimney when the lean-to was built is plainly visible. There is no fireplace in the parlor chamber; that in the hall chamber has been built up with a smaller opening. The flooring in this story is of hard pine, and the floor boards are halved together instead of being tongued and grooved.

In the garret the patching of the stone chimney is even more apparent than it is below. The framing of the roof is intact. There are four pairs of principal rafters—one pair over each girt crossing the house, in the usual way—with purlins; but there are no collar-beams—a touch which seems to indicate New Haven in-

fluence.   Above the roof the chimney is of brick, and the present
topping-out is quite modern.

To return now to the outside of the building.   We find its
most striking characteristic in the overhang of the second story.

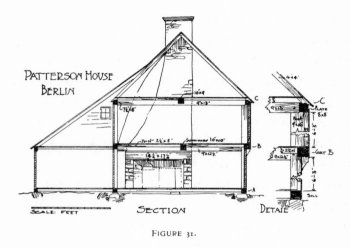

FIGURE 31.

This, we have said, is of what may be called the hewn type ; that
is to say, the posts — corner posts and all — are of one piece of
timber throughout their length.   The size is taken in the second
story, where the corner post, for instance, is fifteen inches square,
and then the bracket which apparently supports the overhang is
hewn out of this excess, so that the post is thus reduced in size,
in the first story, to the ordinary square section of about seven
inches.   This scheme, it will be seen at once, is quite different
from that used in the Farmington and Windsor houses we have
studied, and exactly like some examples we shall meet later in the
New Haven jurisdiction.   It points to a tradition which must have
descended through another line of craftsmen than those who
wrought the overhangs so much more common in the Connec-

ticut colony. We shall try, in the chapter on Construction, to which we refer the reader for the details of this method, to suggest the origin and the history of the type.

The gable overhangs at each end of the house. At the south end there still appears, in the under side of the projecting plate, the mortise for a bracket which has now departed.

This house gives us the only opportunity we have had to see a complete cornice of this date in its original condition. The rafter-ends project nearly a foot, and are so cut on the under side as to be heavier at the ends than where they leave the plate—a very artistic touch.

The old place has not many more years of existence. Its roof is tight, and that will keep it for some time yet; but it is abandoned, and it is very strange how fast a house goes down when once it is out of touch with humanity.

JOHN BARNARD HOUSE HARTFORD

III. THE JOHN BARNARD HOUSE.

This house, which had no overhang, and which was a survival of the type of the first period, stood also on Retreat avenue, several rods north or east of the Dorus Barnard mansion. It was built by Robert Webster for one of his sons, or possibly by that son for himself on his father's land, about 1673. Matthew Webster, great-grandson of Robert, sold it in 1762 to Jonathan Bigelow. In 1765 it came from Bigelow into the hands of his son-in-law, Captain John Barnard, from whom it took the name it bore till it was pulled down in June, 1898. From Miss Lavinia Barnard, granddaughter of Captain John, it descended to its last owner, Mr. John Barnard Cone.[1]

The building, while not quite so old as the Dorus Barnard — which, in some dimensions, it very closely resembled — had retained

---

[1] The history of this house will also be found in Appendix II.

the ancient sharp-pitched roof over its original rooms, and thus had preserved more of its primitive appearance. It had also suffered severely from decay, and looked, as it stood just before destruction, to be the older house of the two.

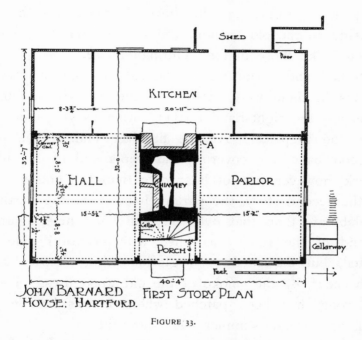

JOHN BARNARD   FIRST STORY PLAN
HOUSE: HARTFORD.

FIGURE 33.

The lean-to which appears in the drawing was not original, nor was it even an early addition. It was built, tradition says, by Captain Barnard, about 1767. The chimney had a T-shaped top, which shows a rebuilding, very clearly seen in the garret, to accommodate the new fireplace in the kitchen of the lean-to. At the back of the lean-to, in a sort of extension, was an old door, which looked as if it had once served as the front door of the house. It was boarded vertically on the outside, horizontally on the inside; in the fashion, remembered but seldom seen, which the settlers brought with them from England.

Within the house we find, at the south end, the hall, with a door at the side of the fireplace—a door which, if we open it, discloses the stair to the cellar beneath the parlor. The stairs to the second story, under which the cellar stairs went down, were, as the plan in Figure 33 will show, all winders, with a partition at the side, in the old fashion, and with no rail. The steps were constructed like those in the Whitman house.

Both hall and parlor were plastered on walls and ceiling, and the beams in them were cased. In the hall was a buffet in the usual place—the right-hand further corner as you stand with your back to the fireplace. At the fireplace end of the parlor was some good panelling, covering the whole end of the room. All this work, however, was of later date than the house.

In the second story, the parlor chamber, at the north end, was more elaborate than that over the hall; and here, again, the fireplace end of the room was filled with beautiful pine panelling, unpainted, but darkened to a glorious tint, almost like that of Spanish cedar, by the smoke of the old wood fires. The end girt in this room had been patched where it was broken under the summer, and a new summer had been put in.

The roof was original and, in the garret, showed manifestly that the lean-to roof built up on the main rafters was an addition. The chimney, as we have already said, showed the patching—or rather the adding—made necessary by the new kitchen flue which rose along the back of the old stack with a plainly-visible vertical joint between them. The old chimney was of brick laid in mortar of clay, and probably replaced an earlier stack of stone.

There was a quaint charm about this house—a picturesqueness, nay, even a beauty of line and of pose. It made a powerful appeal for simplicity in architectural design.

CHAPTER IV.

THE THIRD PERIOD IN THE CONNECTICUT COLONY.

1700–1750.

E have seen that the houses of the earliest period were of two rooms—one at each side of the chimney—on each floor. As more room became necessary a kitchen was thrown out behind the chimney; and this kitchen, with other rooms which later were added to it, was covered with a lean-to roof. We saw, also, that in the second period, while in many houses the early type of plan survived, this modification, brought about by the added kitchen, was taken up and made an integral part of the house from the beginning of its construction, and that, therefore, the lean-to appears in this second period as a part of the original fabric.

In the third period the builders went one step further. The old lean-to chamber, as the room under that roof and above the kitchen was called, was of very little account. To make this part of the floor-space of some value, the craftsmen abandoned the lean-to and raised the back of the house to the same height as the front. They made a two-story house on the same plan on which they had previously built the lean-to. The lean-to survived, indeed, well down into the third period; but the distinguishing mark of the time is the "upright" or full two-story house, with its kitchen and kitchen-chamber behind the parlor and hall, with the chambers over them.

Other marks of advancement also appear. The front stairs become more elaborate, and are constructed in a manner different from that of the older flights. Lime mortar is the rule. Brick and even cut stone appear in the underpinnings. Classic details come in also; and toward the end of the period—which lasts twenty-five years longer than in Rhode Island—there is nothing on the outside of the house, or, except the summer, on the inside, to distinguish the work of this period from that of the years just before or just after the Revolution.

The overhang still appears very often; but it is used with much less projection, and with neither bracket nor drop. The constant encroachments of plaster, and the desire to keep the new plastered ceilings free from the old-fashioned beams, led, toward 1750, to the abandonment of the summer. The old beam still exists, as it did in the Rhode Island houses; but, as in them, it was now of less depth, that it might, on the under side, be flush with the joists, now made larger, and so might be plastered over and concealed—only making itself known by the persistent crack which the shrinkage of it brought about in the plastering.

The plan changes again toward the end of the period. This change may have been, due, like the introduction of the classic orders, to English influence, but it had its root in an old type of plan more common in Virginia than in New England.[1] The hall

----

[1] See Chapter X for an explanation of this type.

or passage through the house from front to back, with the stairs at one side of it, now came into fashion, and to this innovation a change in both the number and the arrangement of the rooms was due. We can trace this admirably, as we shall show, in the old Connecticut colony, where it appears in the Sheldon Woodbridge house on Governor street, Hartford, and in the Burnham-Marsh house and the Webb house at Wethersfield. All these are steps in the line of development—in which the Sheldon is very close to the old type—which led up to the final result as we see it in the Belden-Butler house, Wethersfield, and the Butler-McCook house, Hartford, where the summer has disappeared.

In studying the house of this period, we shall consider first those which are survivals of the preceding period—those, that is, which have original lean-tos. We shall then take up those which in form are typical of this time, and finally examine those which may be considered as transitional — as leading to the four-room, central-hall type of Revolutionary and later date.

The examples we have to discuss are:

  I.   THE BARRETT HOUSE, WETHERSFIELD, c. 1730.

  II.   THE MEGGATT HOUSE, WETHERSFIELD, c. 1730.

  III.   THE SHELDON WOODBRIDGE HOUSE, HARTFORD, c. 1710.

  IV.   THE WEBB HOUSE, WETHERSFIELD, c. 1752.

  V.   THE EBENEZER GRANT HOUSE, SOUTH WINDSOR, 1757.

BARRETT HOUSE

I.　The Barrett House.

This old dwelling stands backed up against the railway on the road which leads south from the west side of the lower end of Broad-street Green. It is another lean-to house, contemporary with the Meggatt house, which it also resembles in the staircase. Which is the earlier stair it is hard to say. They are almost exactly alike, left-hand turn and all, except that the Barrett stair has balusters while the Meggatt has not. We are inclined to think the staircase later than the house, which seems older than the Meggatt. It is in fair condition. The door-handle, of which we give a drawing in Figure 113, while some years later than the rest of the house, is very artistic. It is more ornate than the one we give of the Meggatt house, with which it should be compared.

MEGATT HOUSE

II. THE MEGGATT HOUSE.

Wethersfield is full of old houses—the greater number of them skilfully adapted to modern, or at least later, requirements, but still retaining under their disguises the framing of the seventeenth or the early eighteenth century. There are, however, as we have seen, a few dwellings which have been suffered to remain without addition or alteration of any account, and though these are all of the third period, and late at that, they are very interesting. Noteworthy among them in size and interest is the dilapidated old house we have now to study.

The Meggatt house stands on the main street of Wethersfield, below the church, and almost directly west of the great elm on Broad-street Green. It is in a terrible condition as to roof and walls, though most of the frame is still sound, and it could be made quite habitable. It was built we do not know when or by whom, but certainly not far from the year 1725.

The house, which faces east, consists, as the plan in Figure 36 shows, of the central porch on the front, with the hall on the south and the parlor on the north. Behind the central chimney is the kitchen, at the north of which are a chamber and the present back-stairs, and on the south of which there is another chamber. We have here, then, the complete scheme in the plan, and, as the perspective shows, in the elevation also; for this is a full two-story house.

The underpinning is of good brick laid in lime mortar, as is the topping-out of the chimney. The material of the chimney itself below the attic floor was not to be seen; but it is no doubt of brick, since the underpinning is. The fireplaces are of brick. That in the kitchen is flanked by the oven and the wood-box under it common to this period.

The walls are built with studs. On the north the spaces between them are filled with hand-made brick laid in the red clay of the district, which has now a fine chocolate color. In the first story, on this north side, the clapboards—of white pine, only a very little thicker at the lower edge than at the upper—are nailed directly to the studs. In the upper story, on this side, boarding appears. The whole clapboarding of the house is late—when the traditional use of oak had died out—and the boarding an added repair. On the west the bricks do not appear, and in the centre of that side the whole wall is broken away, so that the mortises in the sill and in the girt to receive the studs are plainly visible. Here, at the south end of the side, there is pine boarding in the first story, joined with beveled edges, and the clapboards fail. In the second story and in the north end of this story they appear again. In the boarding just described there is the opening of a very old window. On the south end the clapboards are still in

place, and the brick filling is probably intact.   It is so on the
front.

The second story overhangs the first about three inches all the
way around the house, as in the Fiske house at Guilford; but
there are no brackets, nor do any signs appear that there ever
were any.

The roof we have not at this writing examined.   It appears to
be original.

The front door opens into the usual porch or entry, which contains a fine staircase — Figure 36 — with a heavily moulded string,
a moulded rail, caps with moulded tops, but no balusters.   The
panelling under the string, and the seat, with a panel on its riser,
are excellent.   It is
probable that all this
work is original.   This
is another left-hand
stairway—that is, as
the plan shows, the
visitor turns to his left
to ascend, and keeps
the rail on his left
hand.   Moreover, the
door to the cellar is
under the upper part,
as the plan again will
show, and forms part
of the panelling under

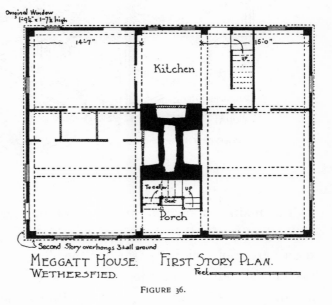

MEGGATT HOUSE.   FIRST STORY PLAN.
WETHERSFIED.

FIGURE 36.

the string, while in most houses — especially in those of the earlier
periods — so far as we have seen, the descent to the cellar is from
the hall.   The explanation of this change, which agrees with the

later practice in Newport and Narragansett, may perhaps lie in the fact that the hall is in this period no longer the kitchen.

In the parlor, or north room, there is a cased summer in the usual position, and the usual corner post on the front. There is no post in the northwest corner; but the second summer—the descendant of the old side girt—is framed into the end girt just

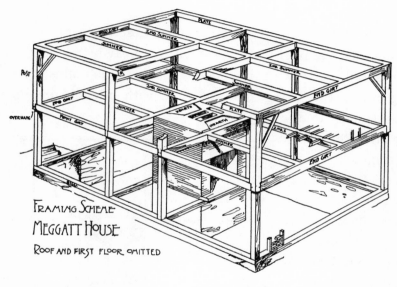

FIGURE 37.

as the main summer is, and it is of the same, or almost the same, size—just as in the Benedict Arnold house at Newport. That is, there are only eight posts in the house, as the plan will show, instead of ten, as in the house where the lean-to is part of the original house, or where, as in the Providence houses of this period, the logic of framing had not gone so far. It is a concession to the lightening of framing timber, and it foretells the death of the old heavy fashion of construction. The bottom of the summer, indeed, is almost exactly flush with that of the end girt, although this has a tremendous span—twenty-eight feet—and carries two summers instead of one.

There is some good panelling on the fireplace end of this room. A partition under the second summer separates the parlor from a chamber which opens out of it on the west. Another door leads to the kitchen, between which and the chamber there is now a back staircase—a very common addition to all these older dwellings. In the kitchen, which probably included originally the room now given to the stairs—though there may have been a pantry there—is a brick fireplace with the usual oven and wood-box.

In the hall, or south room—the living-room of the house—the work is rougher. The beams are bare, though the end of the room around the fireplace is elaborately panelled, as in the hall of the Dorus Barnard house. This combination of panelling with uncased beams is an argument for the later date of all the panelling in the house, and of the staircase as well.

The floor in the kitchen—at least the upper floor, for even then floors were double—is of hard pine. Of course it is impossible to say how many times it has been renewed.

So far as present indications go, the house will soon be a thing of the past. This speedy end is to be deplored, as the building is a valuable monument.

III.   THE SHELDON WOODBRIDGE HOUSE.

Perhaps the most interesting house now standing in Hartford, certainly the most interesting of those in the period we are studying—a house unique, so far as we know, in the whole Connecticut colony—is that which, known to the older residents of Hartford as the Sheldon Woodbridge, after a former owner, stands on the eastern side of Governor street, a few doors from Sheldon.

The house, which faces west, is a very large one, and is very striking in appearance. Built probably by a Mr. Sheldon in 1715,[1] it has neither the central nor the two lateral chimneys, but one at either end of the long ridge, and of these that at the northern end is exactly what we find in a Providence house of the same date,[2] and what we do not find elsewhere in Connecticut.

---

[1] Dr. Charles J. Hoadly.

[2] The John Crawford House was built in 1715.—*Early Rhode Island Houses*, p. 51. The date 1710 for that house—*Ibid.*, p. 94—appears, on later study, to be doubtful.

The whole house, except the addition on the back, was built at one time. The north end, just referred to, is a solid brick wall. The south end had once a door and three windows. The windows remain, the door has been built up and a fourth window cut near it. This difference between the north and south ends is to be accounted for, if it is original, by the desire to admit the southern sun and to exclude the northern wind. There is little doubt that the difference was always present. The only arguments against it are the large size of the windows, with the use of flat, instead of segmental, arches in the heads, and the iron tie-anchors which, in the second story, cut through the belts, and which do not appear on the north end.

The north end has, beside the resemblance of its unbroken brick wall, a strong analogy with Rhode Island work—showing how close, after all, was the connection between the New England colonies. This is in the use of blue "headers," or bricks with their ends burnt to a dark blue-grey color and sometimes vitrified, and then laid with these ends outward in the face of the wall. Two courses laid in what is called Flemish bond—where the headers and "stretchers" (brick with their long sides in the face of the wall) alternate in the same courses—have their headers of blue color, and, as from the bond the headers come over the stretchers, and *vice-versa*—see Figure 92—the effect is excellent. In Rhode Island, English bond—a course all headers alternately with one or with several all stretchers—is preferred, and the headers are alternately red and blue. This Hartford scheme, however, occurs in the projecting belts of the old Israel Sayles house near Saylesville, R. I. Above these two courses, in the Sheldon house, come five of the ordinary color, then two more of the pattern. The belts are two courses high; but the color scheme, contrary to what we should expect, does not prevail in them.   In the gable is a panel of herring-bone work, as it is called.

The chimneys are L-shaped in plan above the roof, as are all those in Rhode Island which have these fireplaces in the end wall. There is no panelling, nor are there any pilasters; but two string courses run around each stack, one just above the ridge, the other near the top.   The bricks are very large—8 × 4 × 2½.

There is no color pattern in the south end of the house.   At the base of the north chimney is a beveled water-table of brownstone.

The entrance to the house is in the center of the front, and the usual two windows appear on each side.   These windows are

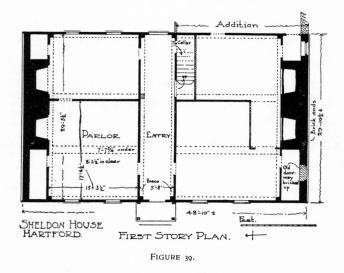

FIGURE 39.

probably later than the rest of the building—though the cornice is not, but is one of the earliest cornices we have.

Inside the house we find ourselves in a wide entry, as it was called, which runs straight through to the back of the house, where it has a door corresponding to that on the front.   The stairs, which probably once took up half of this entry, are not now there in the first story, but are, like those of the Burnham-Marsh house, in a separate case at one side, as the plan in Figure 39 will show. The attic stairs are now between the girts which form the sides of the entry; but they were not so originally, as we can see by the girt at the south of the passage in the attic floor—for this girt still shows the mortises of the old floor-joists which were taken out to make room for the stairs.

At the north of the entry, or long passage, are the parlor and the chamber which opened from the parlor on the east.   On the south a part of the front room has been partitioned off; but the arrangement was substantially the same as it is on the north. The front room was the hall and the back room probably was the kitchen, or else the hall was used as a kitchen and there was a chamber out of it on the east.

In either end each room has its fireplace with a closet beside it, as the plan will show.   The framing is of the same kind as that we saw in the Meggatt house.   The second summer, which is on the chamber side of the partition, though a cornice appears in the parlor, is spaced with the main summer so as to divide the width into three parts—see Figure 39; but there is no post under the chimney end of it.   There is now, under the other end, a post which appears in the passage, but it is not original.   The girts show in the hall, or one of them—the north one—does.   The other projection is very likely only a cornice; and under each end of this north girt, which spanned without support the whole width of the house, is a mighty brace, in rather an unusual place for it. In fact, the appearance of this brace led us first to imagine that there was before us a genuine "brick-ender" of the Providence pattern, of the end wall of which this girt formed a part, and to which the south end had been added. Further examination con-

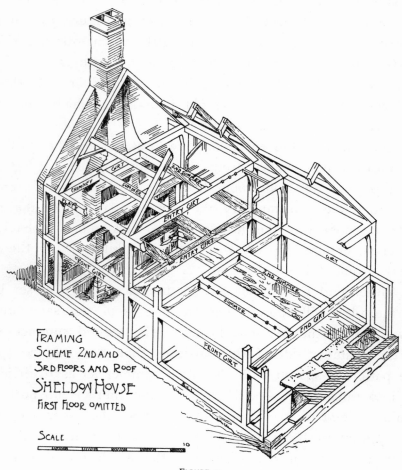

FRAMING
SCHEME 2ND AND
3RD FLOORS AND ROOF
SHELDON HOUSE
FIRST FLOOR OMITTED

SCALE

FIGURE 40.

vinced us that this was an error, and that the house was, as we have stated, built all at one time.

There is some good panelling in the parlor, and a good mantel considerably later than the house. The doors, one panel wide, are possibly of that date, and the hinge — of which we give a drawing in Figure 113, Chapter IX — almost certainly is. It is almost exactly the same as the English specimen from Oundle, Northamptonshire, which is given in Gotch's *Architecture of the Renaissance in England*.[1] Though not necessarily a very old example, it is of a very old type.

All the casing of the beams is probably later than the house, while the plastering may or may not be — at least in the front

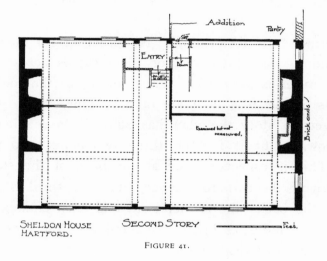

SHELDON HOUSE   SECOND STORY   Feet.
HARTFORD.

FIGURE 41.

room. The outside brick-work is laid in lime mortar. There are traces of clay on the inside of the north chimney in the garret.

The roof is original and is interesting. It consists of four sets of heavy principal rafters, resting one on each girt — the extreme ones on the chimney girt, the two intermediates on the girts at the sides of the central passage. These girts form the tie-beams;

---

[1] Part I, p. 11. The specimen before us may have come from Gov. Hopkins' house, which stood here.

there are no collars.   Between these principals—we might really call them trusses—purlins are framed on each side of the roof. The purlins between the two central pairs of rafters are dropped a little below the others, to avoid cutting the rafter too much where the two mortises would come in a line.   Those purlins which frame into the extreme rafters—those next the chimneys—are connected with the principals by a brace.   Over these purlins run the common rafters, the backs of which are flush, or nearly so, with the backs of the principals.   This description will be explained by Figure 40.

The dormers are not original.   No provision for them was made in the framing, and where one of them comes across a common rafter, that rafter is sawn off.   The framing of the roof is of oak. The boards of the attic floor are of hard pine.

In the second story the plan has suffered more alteration than it has below, to fit it for the three tenements into which it is divided.   This is especially true at the head of the stairs and in the southern of the two front tenements—the third is in the later addition at the back—the former front and back chambers over the hall.   The plan indicates briefly the relation of the present arrangement to the original disposition.

WEBB HOUSE.

IV. THE WEBB HOUSE.

This—also known as the Welles house—is the most famous house in Wethersfield. It stands on the western side of the main street, just south of the old church. It was once Joseph Webb's tavern, and, as the place where Washington and Rochambeau held the council which decided on the Yorktown campaign, it is renowned all over the country. At the same time it is—especially in its plan and framing—of surprising interest.

The house consists of a rectangular main building with brownstone underpinning and steps, columnar porch, and gambrel roof, and of an ell at right angles to the southwestern corner of this main block. The ell first claims our attention, for it is the oldest part of the building. It originally occupied the place of the present main house, and has been moved back and turned around, or at least one half of it has, for only one end and perhaps the old stair-porch now remain, so that it faces now at right angles to its original aspect. A glance at Figures 42 and 43 will make this plain. It has its summer and end girt, and one chimney girt with a brace under one end thereof, but it was never more than one room wide. The ancient overhangs, of three or four inches, still exist on the outside wall on the north and on the south.

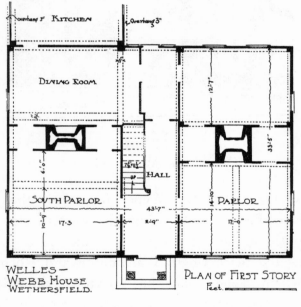

FIGURE 43

The summer, with the whole second floor, is now on the level of the second floor of the main house—or at least very near it—so that, as the rooms of the front house are very high in the clear, the first floor of the ell is most likely a new one. The whole ell is set upon an underpinning of brownstone, which, while contemporary with that under the main house, is not so elaborate — in fact is perfectly plain.

The form of the overhang would put this ell in the third period. It must be remembered, however, that there are two lines of development in the Connecticut colony — one which dropped the overhang in the second period, and another which clung to it while it diminished its amount. This second school is a descendant of that at New Haven, and for years was powerful in the Connecticut valley. From the single-room depth of this ell, and the absence of any lean-to, it may be that we have here an instance of this class, and that we may justify ourselves in putting this remnant of a house in the second period.

Now, what is the date of the main house? The late Sherman W. Adams, in his article on Wethersfield,[1] says that Joseph Webb bought the lot with a house on it from Wolcott in 1750, and that this house Webb presumably tore down, and built the present one. He gives no authority for his statement; but he needs no better argument than that furnished by the old ell which we have just described. This ell measures the extent of the tearing down; the main building shows the amount of the new work.

The interest of the house, however, lies not in the ell, but in the main block. This has a dignified, well-proportioned exterior, and an interior which, to ordinary observation, presents only the usual central-entry and staircase type with the details of the period. The house is, however, not only the earliest of its kind which we know, but it shows in a remarkable manner the transition from the earlier to the later mode of building. In actual plan the house is precisely like the other central-entry houses — among

---

[1] *Mem. Hist. Hartford Co.*

which in one sense it belongs. With its chimneys each in the centre of the back wall of a front room, it is a step in advance of the Sheldon Woodbridge, and on the same lines as the Belden-Butler in Wethersfield or the Butler-McCook in Hartford.

In its framing, however, the house is only half a step beyond the Sheldon Woodbridge. For one end is framed in exactly the same way as is that house. In the other end, the north, the carpenter changed his scheme, and fitted it more closely to his chimney—adopting the arrangement used, without showing the summer, in the later central-entry houses. The framing in the south end is logical for a central-chimney or an end-chimney house; it is not so for this house. That in the north end is logical.

We have here, then, what we shall find again in the Grant house—a last attempt to adapt the summer to the new plan and the new finish before the old-fashioned beam was abandoned altogether.

V. THE EBENEZER GRANT HOUSE.

This dwelling, now standing at East Windsor Hill—though it is one of the most elaborate in the colony, as well as one of the best known — is, from its date, outside the strict limits of our work. We venture to include it, however, for several reasons. It is framed in the old-fashioned way, though planned entirely in the new ; in many ways, also, it is curiously like the Webb house ; and it has an absolutely certain date, based on the contemporary building accounts which are still extant. The house consists of a main building, built by Ebenezer Grant in 1757 and 1758, and of an ell, said to have been built in 1697 by Samuel Grant, 2d, grandson of old Matthew Grant, the famous Recorder of Windsor. This ell, it is said, was built as a house, and was

moved back for use as a kitchen when the larger and more im-
posing mansion was erected.

The view of the exterior shows the extent and the elaborate
character of the dwelling.   The doorways are well proportioned,
and the details, though somewhat rough, are very interesting in
showing some strongly Elizabethan touches.   The mouldings are
not of good classic profile, but are beak-like, and rather sharply
undercut.   The capitals of the pilasters of the front door show
foliage strongly resembling that on some of the old chests still
preserved in the neighborhood of Hartford, while the treatment of
the pedestals is almost the same as in Elizabethan and Jacobean
work.

The plan of the house — Figure 45 — is of the type becoming
common at this time — that with the central passage and the two
rooms at each side.   The chimneys stand one at each side of the
passage, between the front end rooms, which differ considerably in
size.   They are carried on foundations pierced from east to west
— the house faces east — with brick arches, or rather barrel-vaults.
This construction we have never met elsewhere in Connecticut
— though it occurs in Newport and in Warwick, Rhode Island.
The cellar walls are of excellent masonry, of the brownstone of
the district, which appears on the outside in underpinning and in
the steps.

The entry or passage contains the staircase, which does not
run up and land without a turn as in the Webb and the Belden-
Butler houses, but which has, at about two-thirds of its height, a
landing and a half-turn, with the rail so arranged about the opening in the second story as to produce a very pleasing effect.

In the southern pair of rooms the summer runs in the old-
fashioned way—that is, as it would run in a lean-to or an upright

house.   The chimney is west, or outside, of the "second summer" of the old plan—see Figure 45.   Then, behind the chimney, there is another girt which carries the ends of the floor-joists over the narrow room at the back.   The regular back girt carries the other

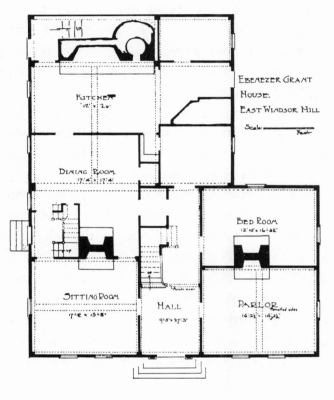

KITCHEN
12' x 20'

EBENEZER GRANT
HOUSE.
EAST WINDSOR HILL

Scale: Feet

DINING ROOM
17'4" x 17'4"

BED ROOM
12'10" x 16'2½"

SITTING ROOM
17'8" x 15'8"

HALL
9'5" x 27'3"

PARLOR
panelled sides
16'2½" x 14'2½"

FIGURE 45.

ends of these.   It will be noticed that here, as in the Webb house, the chimneys do not align, but that one is nearer the front of the house than the other,

In the northern pair of rooms the framing is different, and reminds us strongly of the remarkable difference to be seen in the Webb house—though, it will be seen, the scheme is not the same, and we cannot trace any hesitation in the construction.

Here the chimney is a little further forward; but the summer runs, as in one end of the Webb house, from the front girt to the girt in front of the chimney—the old second summer. This second summer has a post under it, and there is no girt at the back of the chimney in the first story, though one appears in the corresponding plan upstairs.

The ell is, in appearance, of the old type, with a lean-to—only part of which is an addition. There is a tradition, which we have already mentioned, that this ell was an older house moved back from the post of honor upon the street.

A little study of the ell, however, will reveal certain peculiarities which render it doubtful whether this part of the house was ever independent, and make it look as if the whole building was put up at one time. The plan lacks one end, for no apparent reason; and, while the chimney is in its natural place, the space between the two chimney girts is so narrow that it would have been difficult to place there the regular form of staircase. Again, the stairs now in the back room of the main house—apparently an old flight which may have come from an older house—certainly have never stood in the narrow space between those chimney girts. Further, the end girt of the ell — speaking of it for the moment as if it were an older house — is also the back girt of the new house, that is, the same stick serves for both. This incorporation of an older building is rare, for, generally, it cannot be accomplished.

In the large chamber of the ell is some very fine panelling of pine, beautifully wrought, still unpainted, and splendidly colored by age and the smoke of the wood fires. This panelling is not necessarily older than that in the front of the house; neither are the

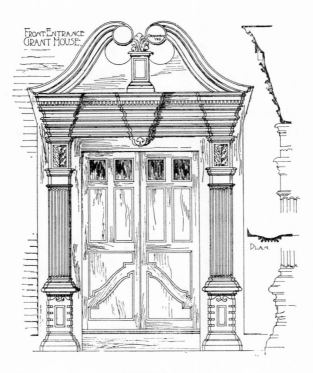

FIGURE 46.

stairs, of which we have spoken, at the south end of the front. These may have been simply of a type which was at that time out of fashion, and which was therefore chosen as suitable for the back stair, which here is quite prominent.

Another argument there is which does not appear upon the plan. It is to be found in the garret of the ell, where the top of the plate is visible. The upper inside corner of this plate is chamfered—a thing unheard of in the annals of colonial carpentry —and the chamfers have stops. There are also some old mortises which, like the chamfers and their stops, have no relation to the present construction. The plate is simply an older beam, perhaps, and, indeed, quite probably a plate, turned upon its side and used again. This makes it look as though the house which Samuel Grant built in 1697, of which this re-used plate was a part, had been pulled down sixty years later, and the timber in it worked over in the ell of the new and higher-storied house.

CHAPTER V.

THE EARLIEST PERIOD IN THE NEW HAVEN COLONY.

1638–1675.

HE influence which the wealth or poverty of the earliest settlers had upon their architecture finds a notable illustration in the New Haven colony. If we consider the planters of Providence the poorest body of men that ever founded a New England state, it is certain that the proprietors of Quinnipiac were the wealthiest, as a whole, that ever began a plantation north of the Hudson. In this conclusion tradition and the documents agree.

We should, therefore, expect to discover in New Haven a school of craftsmen accustomed, in the first place, to the English houses of the larger class, and granted, in the second place, through the opulence of Davenport, Eaton, and others, an opportunity to build such houses in the new town. And this is just what tradition, amply supported by records and inventories, shows us as actually existing.

The colonial records of New Haven are very full and explicit on matters of building, much more so than those of Rhode Island. Indeed, they surpass even the town records of Hartford for that

early time. From these documents it appears that carpenters, as
well as other craftsmen, were among the earliest comers; but a
great deal of building was to be done, skilled labor was in demand,
and wages were forced up, as they always are in a new country.
This was before the day of Adam Smith; and, therefore, to the
fathers of New Haven, who knew far more of the statutes of
Moses than of the law of supply and demand, this action of the
craftsmen, in taking all the wage they could get, seemed outra-
geous.   Accordingly, they passed a law to restrain such rapacity
and to fix the amount due for all kinds of labor. They even—with
sublime disregard of the state of the market—fixed the price for
all building material.   This same course, familiar in English legislation from the time of the Black Death, had been taken by the
authorities of Massachusetts Bay; but the laws were soon repealed.
In New Haven the action of the court seems never to have been
formally annulled.   It probably fell into disuse and consequent
oblivion.   In spite of the bad principle underlying it, we cannot
be too thankful the old law was passed; for it sheds more light
than all other documents put together on the architecture of the
New Haven settlements.

From these enactments, supplemented by other notices not a
few about building and material, scattered through the records, we
learn that the people of Quinnipiac could have lime mortar and
brick, could have their houses plastered—both walls and ceilings
—and could even have paint if they were so minded.

Plaster and paint, and even brick, however, were only for the
wealthy.   Through the records of the same court, which had the
unfortunate habit of directing, by its legislation, all the concerns—
spiritual and temporal—of the people, we learn that many of the

poorer class, single men at least—and indeed others, as we know from Michael Wigglesworth—lived in cellars as the same men did at Hartford. Again, the oft-repeated action as to the chimney-viewer, while it does not, necessarily, in this colony, imply the existence of the wooden chimney, does tell us, in so many words, that story-and-a-half houses existed side by side, as in Hartford, with the more pretentious dwellings. Both the one-story houses —whether of one room or two—and those of two stories were of the same type as those we have just been studying in the Connecticut colony; that is, the plans of both, setting aside a few special examples for separate study, are identical. In some details of construction the houses of the two settlements differ, showing two different lines of tradition from old England; for it seems certain that the small overhang—which, as we have said, characterizes the western part of the present State after the heavy Hartford form dies out—had its root in the training of the New Haven carpenters.

In the second period we find that, while the early forms survive, the incorporated lean-to is characteristic.

In the third period this lean-to form, as well as the old type, survives; but the "upright" house comes into fashion, as in the Connecticut colony.

There was, however, in New Haven, during the earliest period, a class of houses which seems not to have existed in Hartford or, indeed, elsewhere in New England—with perhaps one or two exceptions in Massachusetts. We refer to the four large dwellings —almost manor houses, as that phrase is generally understood— of the Reverend John Davenport, Governor Theophilus Eaton, Mr. Thomas Gregson, and Mr. Isaac Allerton.

We shall begin our study of the examples with one of these houses, and shall set forth, so far as we can gather it, what is known of the mansion of Governor Eaton.

Beside this house, which was destroyed more than a century ago, we have, in striking contrast to what we could say of Hartford, only two buildings of this early date to offer.

We shall discuss, then:

    I.   THE THEOPHILUS EATON HOUSE, NEW HAVEN, c. 1640.

   II.   THE HENRY WHITFIELD HOUSE, GUILFORD, c. 1640.

  III.   THE BALDWIN HOUSE, BRANFORD, c. 1650.

FIGURE 47 —SOUTHWEST VIEW OF EATON HOUSE. (*From Lambert.*

I.   THE THEOPHILUS EATON HOUSE.

There are two sources from which we obtain all that we know of this house.   The first is an old woodcut published in 1838 by Lambert in his *History of The Colony of New Haven*, with the statements which Stiles and Lambert, in their writings, have made about the building.   The second source—the only one from which there is no appeal—is the inventory of the Governor's estate, " taken, and apprized by Mathew Gilbert, Jo: Wakeman and Richard Miles in the twelveth moneth: 1657."

We give, in Figure 47, a fac-simile of Lambert's " Southwest view of Governor Eaton's House."   In describing the building he says[1] : . . . . " Gov. Eaton built his house on the spot which is now the north corner of Elm and Orange streets.   It was built in

---

[1] Edward R. Lambert, *History of The Colony of New Haven*, p. 52.   We do not know Lambert's authority for this view, but he was a painstaking antiquary, and probably had access to traditions and descriptions and perhaps drawings now lost.

the form of a capital E, was large and lofty, and had 21 fireplaces. Mr. Davenport had his house on the west side of Elm street, near State street, built in the form of a cross; with the chimney in the center.   The common houses at first were small, of one story, with sharp roofs, and heavy stone chimneys and small diamond windows."

Stiles says: " Mrs. Sherman, aged 86, ... born in Gov. Jones's[1] or in Gov. Eaton's house, which had nineteen fireplaces, and many apartments; . . . . that Mr. Davenport's house also had many apartments, and thirteen fireplaces, which indeed I myself well remember, having frequently, when a boy, been all over the house."[2]

The drawing shows five chimneys.   If, therefore, Lambert is correct, we must allow four fireplaces in each of four of the chimneys and five in the fifth.   If Stiles is right, we must assume four fireplaces in each of four chimneys and three in the fifth. It is evident that one of them must be in error.   We think we can make it appear that, unless there were many out-buildings which had fireplaces, or unless great additions had been made since the Governor's time, neither writer is accurate.

The " E " plan, as it is called, on which the house is laid out, was a very common form in the manor houses and even in the larger cottages of the England of Eaton's time.[3]   It was also a very old form, dating from the thirteenth century, if not from the twelfth, or even earlier, and it had, in its long career, come to be the expression of a regular and well-recognized arrange-

---

[1] This same house is meant.   Governor Jones married Governor Eaton's daughter Hannah.

[2] President Ezra Stiles, *History of Three of the Judges of King Charles I.*, p. 63.

[3] Ralph Nevill, *Old Cottage and Domestic Architecture in Southwest Surrey.*

ment.   The great hall—which at this time had just lost its full
height into the open roof, and was divided into two stories by
a floor[1]—occupied the central block, and thus formed the con-
necting link between the two wings.   At one end of the hall—
the ancient dais end—and thus in one of the projecting wings,
had been placed, from time immemorial, the private rooms of the
house.   At the other or "screens" end, and thus in the other
projecting wing, had been for a long time the "offices," as the
English call them—the buttery and the pantry, as also the kitchen
after the cooking ceased to be done in the great hall or in a
separate building in the courtyard.   The servants' hall was in
this wing.   This grouping, which can be very clearly seen in
Hambleton Old Hall, Montacute, and other great English houses
of which Mr. Gotch gives plans,[2] must, almost certainly, have prevailed in Governor Eaton's mansion.

Let us now consider the inventory, and see whether it would
conflict with the scheme we have outlined.   According to this
document, which we give in full in Appendix I, there were in the
house—we follow the order of the text—the "greene chamber,"
the "blew chamber," the hall, the parlor, Mrs. Eaton's chamber,
the chamber over the kitchen, the "other chamber," the garret,
the counting-house, and the brew-house.   The kitchen is mentioned only in this indirect way, and no pantry or buttery is
spoken of, though the cooking utensils are all inventoried.   Possibly the brew-house may have included the pantry, though it
may, more probably, have meant a separate out-building.   Atwater,

---

[1] This change occurred about 1550.—Blomfield, *Hist. Ren. Arch.*, II, p. 354.

[2] J. Alfred Gotch, *Architecture of the Renaissance in England.*   For Hambleton, see Part I,
p. 11–12, Plate 21.   For Montacute, see Part II, p. 7.

in his explanation of the plan,[1] conjectures that the "study" mentioned by Mather was the same as the counting-house of the inventory, and this is no doubt correct.

There is nothing in the list of rooms to indicate the relation of one to another, except that, before any rooms are mentioned at all, but after the list of kettles and the item of 253 pounds of pewter, there comes, just before the item of a "cheny bason," a "clocke & a brass candlestick at Parloue door." This might look as if, in spite of the fact that no room is named, the parlor was next to the kitchen, in which the clock, a small one with a short pendulum, was fastened to the wall. It seems so strange, however, to put in the kitchen an article rather rare in the colony, to say the least, and valued, with the accompanying candlestick, at £3 12s 6d, that we have assumed the clock as ticking in the hall and the parlor door as opening out of that apartment.[2]

In the centre of the house, then, is the hall; and at one end of it are grouped the private rooms, the parlor and the study or counting-house, with the main staircase leading to the principal chambers on the second floor. At the other end are gathered the kitchen and the pantry; the buttery, if there was one; the brew house, if it was under the main roof; and the summer kitchen, if such a room existed. Here, too, were the back stairs, with probably an outside door.

In Figure 48 the reader will find a plan of the first story of Governor Eaton's mansion, worked out upon the theory given

---

[1] E. E. Atwater, *History of The Colony of New Haven*, pp. 116, 117.

[2] Rev. Mr. Hooker's clock was in his new parlor. Inventory, April 21, 1649.—*Conn. Col. Rec.*, vol. I, p. 501.

James Richards, of Hartford, in 1680, left a clock in his parlor. The clock of Rev. Joseph Rowland, Wethersfield, November 24, 1678, was in his kitchen.—*Hartford Probate Records* (MS.), under those names.

above. There is nothing in existence to give us even approximate sizes for the rooms. We have assumed that the amount of furniture in a room is a rough guide to its area in proportion to that of the others. The hall, which, of course, was the largest room on the floor, we have made twenty feet wide—a trifle more than

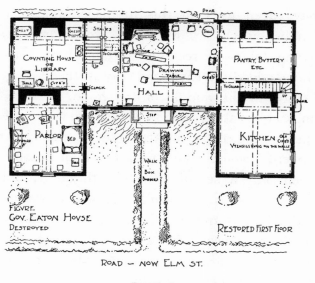

FIGURE 48.

that in the Roger Williams house, Salem.[1] For the length we have taken twenty-six feet. We are justified in assuming these dimensions, if not even greater ones, by the furniture which, in order to bring the life of the time, as Governor Eaton lived it, more vividly before the eye, we have drawn on the plan—each piece in the place it probably occupied.

---

[1] This is, nearly, nineteen feet seven inches wide. The hall chamber, where measurements can be taken, is twenty feet and one-half inch wide, and twenty-one feet four and one-half inches long. The second story, however, overhangs seventeen and one-half inches.

The hall fireplace we have put opposite the entrance door, which, to complete the " E " shape of the plan, may have been provided with a porch, though Lambert does not show one.   Two sets of andirons are inventoried among the contents of this room. Probably only the "great brass Andirons," with the "doggs" which held the back-log, belonged here.   The "small Andirons," though they may have been used in this fireplace, were usually kept in the blue chamber, where no fire-irons are recorded.

The drawing table—a rectangular table with leaves beneath it which could be added at each end[1]—was the dining table of the family, and stood in the middle of the room.

The round table valued with it—the two were rated at £1 18s —we have put in the alcove at the right of the chimney.

The "cubberd" would stand near the door to the kitchen.   It may have been only a set of shelves with doors, but it probably served more or less as a sideboard.   It was worth only about ten shillings, as the long forms rated with it were hardly worth more than two shillings apiece.   It had a cloth upon its top.   These two forms, or benches, are shown in the plan—the one drawn up to the table, the other before the fire.

The "great chaire wth needleworke," Governor Eaton's special seat, stood at the corner of the fireplace, just as its ancestor, the heavy, almost immovable, oaken seat of the mediæval merchant had stood.

The two "high chaires setwork"—a sort of woven pattern— would stand, with the four high stools with setwork seats, at the side of the room, for they were rather expensive for ordinary use.

---

[1] Dr. I. W. Lyon, *Colonial Furniture in New England*, p. 218.   Atwater quotes Mather as saying that Eaton's household sometimes numbered thirty persons.   If this were so, the immediate family

The four "low chaires setwork," each worth a little over a third of the value of one of the high ones, are shown around the fire and at each side of the entrance door.

The two low stools with setwork seats are near the fire.

Two Turkey carpets may have been used on the floor or may have been spread over the tops of the tables. There is nothing in the word itself by which the use can be determined. Together they were valued at £2.

The clock we have hung on the wall next to the parlor door. It was a small affair, placed near the ceiling, where its short pendulum could not interfere with the people moving about the room.[1]

The six "high wyne" stools would be scattered about, near the walls and the fireplace. They were probably a plain high stool.[2]

There are several cushions in the room. Some of these were for the forms, others for the plain wooden stools, as needed, or for the floor; we should now call them hassocks. The high chairs of that day presupposed foot-stools or cushions on account of the cold air along the floors.

The stair, placed at the left of the hall, we have shown as an open-well flight.

At one end of the west wing of the house is the counting-room or study, with a chimney. None is mentioned in the inventory, but Lambert shows one in his view. At the other end is the parlor, which also has a fireplace.

In the parlor we have:

---

followed an old custom and dined at the round table next mentioned, while the domestics and dependents sat at the great drawing table.

[1] Dr. Lyon, *Colonial Furniture*, cited above, pp. 233, 246. All the furniture here named can be admirably studied in that work.

[2] Were these stools used in taverns, and so called because they would not be injured by the wine spilt on them?

A livery cupboard. This was like our sideboard or like a what-not. It was, as it appears in the colonies, of two stages—the lower open, the upper partly closed.[1]   This one was valued at ten shillings, very nearly the worth of the cupboard in the hall.

A bedstead and a trundle bed. This use of the parlor for a sleeping-room is characteristic of early New England. Just what was the appearance of the bedstead we have no means of knowing, beyond the fact that it was a four-poster. We have no examples of colonial bedsteads of that early date, and those generally illustrated as English types were much more elaborate than this could have been, for it, with the trundle-bed and a short table, was considered to be worth only £1 2s 6d.

A set of curtains and a valance, together with the feather bed, the blankets, and the rest.

A high chair, six high stools with green and red covers, a low chair, and two low stools.

Great brass andirons, dogs, fire-pan and tongs.

The furnishing of the counting-house or study is, as the reader can see by consulting the inventory, somewhat obscure. We have assumed that there belonged in it:

A cupboard with a chest and drawers valued at £4. This was all one piece of furniture, and was much like the combined desk and high bookcase which came later—that is, it was a set of drawers with a shelf over them, and above this shelf a cupboard like that of the livery cupboard. We doubt, however, if the Governor used this for writing. For this he employed the next pieces on the list:

A square table and a chair.

---

[1] Dr. Lyon, *Colonial Furniture*, pp. 44, 46, 47, *et seq.*

Two iron-bound chests contained perhaps the plate, valued at £107 11s, part of which reappears, valued at £27, in the Jones inventories.

Books, a globe and a map, valued at £48 15s—quite a sum in those days. These could hardly be in the brew-house, as the inventory, literally followed, might make us think. They are mentioned between an item of "2 steele malt mills" and another of "one Cart with wheels," etc., a location which, by its analogy, goes to show that the clock of which we spoke was not necessarily in the kitchen.

In the other wing we have: in front the kitchen, in the rear the "offices"—we have no guide to them, but have left the rooms blank—with the back stair between.

In these two rooms—or perhaps three—was disposed the following array of kitchen furnishing—very large compared with that of the ordinary households, and remarkable even as against that of Rev. Mr. Hooker of Hartford. There were in the fireplaces or on the walls of the rooms, either hung or on shelves:

Two pairs of racks [spit racks]; three spits; a jack. This was a machine for turning the spit. It was sometimes run by the draft of the chimney-flue.

Tongs; bellows; fire irons; smoothing irons.

Four gridirons; a frying-pan; three dripping-pans; five pans; a little brass pan.

A fish plate; an apple roaster; a still.

Nine trays; two platters; a salt; a galley pot.

The last was "a small earthen glazed pot, especially one used by apothecaries for ointment and medicine.[1]"

---

[1] Murray's *Oxford Dictionary.*

Fourteen earthen pots.

A great brass kettle; a lesser kettle; a little kettle; a little brass kettle.

An iron posnet; two little brass posnets; chafing dishes. A posnet was a dish shaped like a porringer, but used, as the metal shows, for cooking.

A great iron pot, weighing fifty pounds; a little iron pot, ten pounds; a brass pot, thirty-one pounds.

Four brass ladles; three brass skimmers; four brass candlesticks.

Three little baskets; a "voyder" or large basket for table waste.

In pewter two hundred and fifty-three pounds.

For other furniture there were: a chopping-board, a little wheel, an old cupboard, and a plank on "Tressills."

In Figure 49 we give a conjectural restoration of the second story.

FIGURE 49.

The chief chamber of the mansion, the green chamber, we should naturally place over the hall. We are prevented, however, by an item in the inventory of Governor Jones, which we give in part in Appendix I. Here we find the green chamber, with its hangings, mentioned again, and, along with it, the "hangings of the middle chamber." [1] This must, of course, have occupied the main body between the two wings, and, as it was not the same as the green chamber, we are forced to put the latter over the parlor and the chamber of Mrs. Eaton over the hall. It is possible that the hall was two stories high in the Governor's day, and that the floor for the middle chamber was put in later. It is not probable, however.

The green chamber contained, as the plan will explain:

A cypress chest, in form like those still possessed by many families of Connecticut. [2]

A cupboard with drawers; what was called also a "press cupboard." [3]

A bedstead and all its paraphernalia.

A couch, "with the appurtenances."

A short table; six low stools; a looking-glass; brass andirons; fire-pan; tongs; dogs.

There were also a tapestry carpet, probably for the floor, worth £4; the hangings for the walls; six cushions; and a long window cushion.

A great chair and two little chairs.

All this, like the presence of the bed in the parlor, harks back to the time when the bed room was a sitting room and when people received their friends therein. [4] For it must be remembered

---

[1] It is interesting to note that in Eaton's time the green hangings were considered worth £2 15s, the blue worth £1 10s, and those of Mrs. Eaton's chamber, with the window curtains, £1. 10s. In Jones' time the green hangings are rated at £2, and those of the middle chamber at 30s. In Mrs. Jones' inventory appear only "green curtains in the middle chamber," valued at £1 10s. See Appendix 1.

[2] Dr. Lyon, *Colonial Furniture*, pp. 2, 6, 8, *et seq.*

[3] The same, pp. 50, 52, 53, *et seq.*

[4] Compare the king's levée.

that it was not the parlor that became a bed room, but the bed room, with its carpet—whence the term "carpet knight"—which became a sitting room and finally took the monastic name of parlor.

Over the hall was Mrs. Eaton's chamber, so-called, probably because she, "with her watchers," occupied it as a sick room at the time of her husband's death.[1]

Here, beside the bedstead and its furnishings, and several cases for bottles, there were:

A little cupboard, with drawers; two chests; a desk; a little table.

This table held the desk, which was a small portable affair.

Two chairs; two "high wyne" stools; three low stools.

A pair of brass andirons; dogs; fire-pan; tongs; fire iron; poker.

An iron back. This was a cast-iron back to the fireplace, of which a few other instances occur.

There were also hangings and window curtains in this room.

The blue chamber, over the counting-house, was used as a sort of linen closet. There was little furniture there except the bedstead. The inventory gives merely:

A cupboard with drawers. This is the press cupboard again, this time worth £3 6s against £2 15s for that in the green room.

A short table; two trunks and an iron-bound case; a looking-glass.

No fire tools are mentioned. Perhaps, as we suggested, the second pair of andirons in the hall belonged here.

In the chamber over the kitchen was a bed and what is distinctly called a press.

---

[1] Atwater, *History*, p. 414.

The other chamber, which would seem from this expression to have been in the same wing, contained only a "half headed bedsteed," a trundle-bed, a chest, and a stool.

The garret held a half-headed bedstead.

We think it will be evident from the plans that it would be impossible for the house, as it stood at Governor Eaton's death, to contain twenty-one fireplaces, or even nineteen. There were not fire irons, indeed, for all the hearths we have shown, and those have reached only the comparatively modest number of ten.

What additions the house underwent we have now no means of knowing. To judge from Lambert's wood-cut, which must show the building as it looked—or was said to have looked—just before it was pulled down, the only possible way of adding rooms must have been at the back, behind the hall and the projecting wings.

The ground in front of the mansion, extending forward to the street—the "front yard" of our common speech—was treated as a "fore court," with its walk, grass plots, and hedges. The existence of the hedges is betrayed by the garden shears of the inventory. We are also justified in imagining, on one side of the house, the western, it is most likely, a box-bordered garden, with its walks of clean gravel or of grass, and its flower beds filled not only with gillyflowers and other quainter blooms, of which the names sound oddly to our ears, but with mint, rue, lavender, and other herbs.

What finally became of this house we do not know. It was destroyed in some way before 1730, for Stiles, who, when a boy, was familiar with Mr. Davenport's house, claims no personal knowledge of this mansion.[1]

---

[1] A map of New Haven, drawn in 1724, and another dated 1748, assign Governor Eaton's home lot to the Rev. Joseph Noyes, who became pastor in 1716. The house which in this view occupies the lot does not resemble Lambert's picture of the Eaton mansion. This may mean nothing, as all

The houses of the Reverend John Davenport, Isaac Allerton, and Thomas Gregson are said to have been as fine, or nearly as fine, as that of Governor Eaton, but we know less about them.

Davenport's house, Lambert says, had thirteen fireplaces, and was built in the form of a cross, with the chimney in the center. There must have been at least four chimneys for that number of fireplaces, and it is not easy to see how the central chimney was used.[1] Davenport's inventory does help us solve the riddle. He died in Boston, and his effects were not listed in rooms.

Thomas Gregson's inventory is a little better for our purpose. He had a parlor, a hall, and chambers; an arrangement which requires nothing more elaborate than the two-room, central-chimney plan.

Allerton's inventory tells us nothing, but we learn a few details about his house from the traditions which Stiles collected in his search for evidence in regard to the regicides. In speaking of the story that Mrs. Eyers, Allerton's granddaughter, concealed the judges there,[2] Stiles says, quoting his informant, Mrs. Sherman:

"Mrs. Eyers had on one side of the room a large wainscoted closet, which she has often viewed and admired; it had cut lights at top, full of pewter and brass, and a wainscot door, which, when shut, could not be distinguished from the wainscot, and all over

---

the dwellings in New Haven, according to the artist, were very nearly alike, and therefore we can not trust the drawing implicitly. Both maps are given in Atwater's *History of The City of New Haven*, p. 24 and p. 30. This work is not to be confused with the same author's *History of The Colony of New Haven*.

[1] If we trust the map of 1748 this house had two low wings or additions. These, with a porch and a lean-to, would give the cross shape. Stiles had no way of discriminating the ages of the different parts of the building. The plan was originally, perhaps, of the ordinary central-chimney type.

[2] Atwater has shown that this tradition, in the form in which Stiles gives it, can not be true. *History of the Colony of New Haven*, pp. 434-5, note.

the door, and on the outside of the closet, was hung braizery and elegant kitchen furniture, that no one would think of entering the closet on that breast work. . . . her father[1] was Mr. Isaac Allerton, of Boston, a sea captain, who . . . . built a grand house on the creek, with four porches, and this, with Governor Eaton's, Mr. Davenport's, and Mr. Gregson's, were the grandest houses in town. The house highly finished; he had a fine garden,[2] with all sorts of flowers and fruit trees, ..."

Stiles further says: " Captain Willmot, aged 82, remembers the story of their being hid in Mrs. Eyers's house. . . . . He remembers the old house, that it was grand, like Mr. Davenport's, which he also knew, and all of oak and the best of joiner's work. There was more work and better joiner-work in these houses, he says, than in any house now in town. He is a joiner, and helped to pull down Mrs. Eyers's house.

" Judge Bishop . . . . remembers Mrs. Eyers. . . . . He remembers her old house, which he says was one of the grandest in town, like Mr. Davenport's, and fit for a nobleman."[3]

It is strange that any one of these four mansions, which seem to have made so great an impression on the minds of men from the days of Hubbard,[4] the Massachusetts historian, to those of President Stiles and his informants, should ever have been pulled down. It is also a distinct loss to New Haven, and, indeed, to all New England.

---

[1] Grandfather. Atwater, *History*, pp. 434–5, note.

[2] This, as Mrs. Sherman's own reminiscence, cannot relate to the garden of the older Allerton. It may describe that of his son.

[3] Stiles, *History of The Judges*, cited above, pp. 64, 66. The book was published in 1794.

[4] Born 1621.

II.   THE HENRY WHITFIELD HOUSE.

The stone house which bears this name stands some distance south of the Green at Guilford, on the present road to the railway station.   It was built, tradition asserts, by the Reverend Henry Whitfield, in 1639.[1]   As the settlers of Guilford did not arrive at New Haven till the summer of that year,[2] the building must have proceeded with reasonable dispatch if it was finished before cold weather.   It probably was not occupied till 1640.

---

[1] Smith, *History of Guilford.*   Palfrey, *History of New England*, II, p. 59, note.

[2] Atwater, *History of New Haven*, p. 160, *et seq.*   Rev. Thomas Ruggles, in his *MS. History of Guilford*, says that the settlers went at once to their new lands, "though it was almost winter." *Mass. Hist. Coll.*, vol. IV, p. 184.

The house, in its present condition, consists of an L shaped block, which faces southwest. The internal arrangement shown in our drawing, Figure 54, gives little or no clue to the ancient plan. In fact, except the chimney and the walls shown in black in the main part, with perhaps the foundations of the walls and of an other chimney shown in black in the ell, there is nothing original about the building. The whole ell is new. The southeast gable has been rebuilt, the walls of the main part have been raised, and the stonework has been concealed by a coat of stucco. The roof is new, while the floors and the interior woodwork are all later than Whitfield's time.[1] In fact the house which Whitfield built can hardly be said to exist, save as a shell which would with difficulty be recognized by its reverend owner.

It may, to many readers, seem strange that, as this house is of stone, it should have suffered from alterations so much more than the wooden houses. This, however, is almost always the case. The Bull house at Newport, a stone dwelling of the same date as this house, is almost unrecognizable. It is much easier to take out and rebuild a floor in a stone house than in a wooden one, for the walls will stand while you are at work, and, as the ends of the beams rot in the masonry, there is more reason for the repairs. If the roof leaks, moreover, the upper part of the stone wall suffers as much as the occupants of the house, and it is easy to take down the work and to rebuild it wholly or in part. An examination of this house will convince any one that nothing remains of the original interior construction.

If, therefore, we had to take the building as it stands, the restoration of Whitfield's original abode would be fully as difficult as

---

[1] Traces of fire are said to have been found during the last repairs.

that of Governor Eaton's mansion, for we have here no inventory to help us.[1]

Fortunately, however, there are several old views and a set of plans of this house which enable us to go back another step in the history of the building. Barber, in his *Connecticut Historical Collections*, published in 1828, a very valuable book, gives a view of the exterior. Lambert, in his *History of the Colony of New Haven*, gives practically the same picture in 1838. Several years later, in 1860, Palfrey, in the second volume of his *History of New England*, gives three plans of the house, made by Mr. Ralph D. Smith, of Guilford, and two views of the exterior, together with a description furnished by Mr. Smith. All these last-named drawings appear again in the history of Guilford, which was compiled from Smith's manuscripts after his death. They appear once more in Atwater's *History of the Colony of New Haven*. A view of the front of the house is also given in an early number of *St. Nicholas*.[2] An old steel engraving of the north side of the building shows the ancient chimney of the ell. Mr. Samuel Adams Drake, in his book, *Our Colonial Homes*, has published a half-tone from a photograph of this drawing.

Let us consider first the views of the outside. They agree, substantially, with the drawing we give in Figure 51, which we have made from an old photograph—a stereoscopic view dating from the early sixties at least. They show that the old northwest chimney has not been seriously tampered with; that the present chimney near the center of the ell roof replaces one formerly at the end of

---

[1] The house was sold September 20, 1659, to Major Robert Thompson, whose inventory mentions the dwelling, but specifies no rooms. Mrs. Cone, the present owner, tells us that "the acknowledgement of deed was from his (Henry's) brother, Nathaniel Whitfield," who was a "merchant of London."

[2] *St. Nicholas*, vol. II, p. 706.

that ell, which then was much shorter than it now is; that the present chimney at the southeast end of the main house is new; and that the easternmost of the three windows in the second story of the main front is a late insertion. None of the drawings show clearly the texture of the wall. The older ones do not pretend to notice it. Neither Smith's drawing nor that in the *St. Nicholas*—

WHITFIELD.

FIGURE 51.—WHITFIELD HOUSE. (*From an old photograph.*)

which was evidently taken from a photograph—explain it. The old photograph shows some sort of plaster over the masonry, apparently whitewashed or painted white, which must be that coat, or a renewal thereof, which Barber, in 1828, said was put on "15 or 20 years since."[1] The present covering of cement, which is quite dark

---

[1] J. W. Barber, *Connecticut Historical Collections*, p. 211.

in color, is not the same as that shown by this old stereoscopic view, but dates from the repairs of 1868.

Smith's drawings differ from the photograph in one respect. They show in the south corner of the second story, in the main house, a curious window occupying the extreme edge of the angle ; and give a huge, Dutch-looking wall-anchor of iron next to the window on the gable end.   This opening is a loophole which Smith says had existed at that point, but which had been built up when he wrote, though the stone floor of it still remained.   Barber and Lambert, in their drawings, which are older than this we refer to, show the wall-anchor, but not the loophole, which they do not even mention.   In fact, the so-called loophole is a restoration by Smith,

FIGURE 52.—SMITH'S DRAWINGS.

and an incorrect one at that.   For the old photograph which we have followed in Figure 51 shows very distinctly a walled-up window at that corner, but not at the edge as Smith's drawings claim. Instead of this, it is back from the edge just the thickness of the gable wall.   It is not a loophole at all, but simply one of the original windows, with possibly a mate to it on the other face of the corner, leaving the solid pier between.   Smith must have found the mark of the old jamb on the inside wall, and have mistaken the side of it on which the opening had been.   Some large stone at the floor line, or at the level of the window-sills, made him think that the window, which he says was only about a foot wide, was at the corner; a most unlikely place for any sound constructor to put it, and a place where there would be no special advantage in having a loophole, with almost the whole northern side of the house unprotected.

The windows now in the house can make no claim to be original. Smith says they were filled with leaded glass within the memory of people living in his day, but even those were not the sash of the original windows, which, as this old walled-up opening shows, were very much smaller.

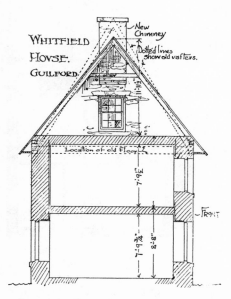

FIGURE 53.—CROSS SECTION, LOOKING EAST.

Smith says, in the account he gave Palfrey, that the pitch of the roof was sixty degrees. The present roof, which is slated, is not so steep as that, though the angle of it is more than forty-five degrees. A glance at our section in Figure 53 will show, however, that the old roof, the plate of which was lower—the old walls were only fifteen feet high—could not have been of that pitch even had its cornice been just above the old windows unless its ridge were just below the old chimney cap. It is not possible that this could have been the case, for the old photographs show no such height of ridge. The evidence they give refutes Smith's statement.

Let us now consider the plans. That which we give in Figure 54 shows the house as it was in 1896, and dates only from 1868.

If we turn now to the plans as Smith gives them, we see, in

Figure 55, a disposition which, though earlier than that now to be
seen in the house, is far from being that of the ancient dwelling.
Some change is evident, for instance, in the passage at the head
of the stairs in the second story. The stair scheme is older than
the partitions contrived about the head of the flight, but the house
is older than the stairs.

There was, according to Smith, a
hiding-place arranged at the end of
the garret in the ell, on either side of
the chimney. What seemed to be the
wooden gable was not such, but was
merely a partition two or more feet
inside the true gable which overhung
the stone end of the house. A glance
at the attic plan in Figure 55, and at
the sketch of the old north side of the
house, in Figure 56 — redrawn from a
photograph of the same view which
Mr. Drake used — will explain what
Smith meant.[1]

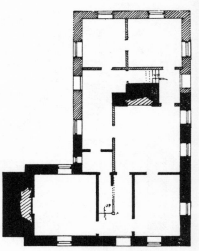

FIGURE 54.—WHITFIELD HOUSE—THE
PRESENT PLAN.

If these plans of Mr. Smith's can not show us the arrangement of Mr. Whitfield's house they are still very valuable, and
they give us a clue to work upon; for the walls they show are
undoubtedly those built in 1639–40, or are on the same lines.
These lines it would be difficult to recover, in the ell at least, if
these old drawings did not explain them.

In fact, Smith's plans show an arrangement which dates from

[1] In reply to our question Mr. Drake courteously referred us to Mr. H. S. Wedmore, of Guilford,
who furnished the photograph.

some repairs made between 1769 and 1795. Thompson's heirs seem to have neglected the building; for Rev. Thomas Ruggles,[1] in his historical sketch of Guilford, says that the house, "with a comparatively small expense, might be made the most durable and best house in the town." Ruggles' MS. was dated February 3, 1769. The editor, in behalf of the Massachusetts Historical Society, which in 1795 published the history among its *Collections*, interpolates, in brackets, the statement: "That house has since been handsomely repaired." Thompson's descendants sold the

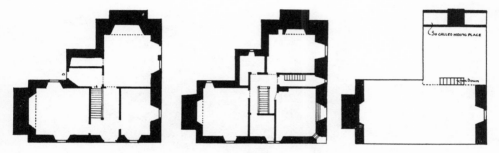

FIGURE 55.—WHITFIELD HOUSE—SMITH'S PLANS.

estate to Wyllys Eliot, October 21, 1772. He, in turn, deeded the property, November 8, 1772, to Joseph Pynchon, whose son Thomas sold to Jasper Griffing, May 27, 1776. The tenure of the first two was rather short for much repairing, though Pynchon may have done somewhat. As Griffing owned the house till 1800, it is fair to assume that he was the one who "handsomely" restored the old building. His descendants have held the estate since his death.

Just how much of the arrangement shown by Smith goes back

---

[1] The MS. was printed in *Mass. Hist. Coll.*, vol. IV, p. 182; vol. X, p. 90. Mr. Ruggles was settled at Guilford, March 26, 1729.

of 1769 we can not say. His plan, however, represents in its disposition an old type which we find in the Sheldon house at Hartford, and which certainly dates from at least the early years of the
eighteenth century, when the house was still owned by Thompson's descendant's. For there is a tradition that, before Griffing
bought the house,[1] another chimney, which stood at the south end
of the main building, had been taken down. If we restore this
chimney we come at once to a typical form—principally confined

FIGURE 56.—WHITFIELD HOUSE—THE NORTH SIDE.[3]

to Virginia, but with some examples in New England—the house
with the central entry and stair, and the chimney at the end of
each room at the side of the passage.

---

[1] For the history of the property and for the traditions connected with the house, we are indebted to the courtesy of Mrs. Sarah B. Cone, of Stockbridge, Mass., a descendant of Jasper
Griffing, and the present (1899) owner of the house. The wall-anchor is said to have been put in
when this chimney was destroyed.

[2] See Chapter X of this book.

[3] This view we have redrawn from a photograph of a steel engraving which appeared about

Another step brings us to the original plan of the house given in Figure 57, which is based on tradition, inherent reasonableness, and likeness to old English examples.

According to a tradition handed down in the Griffing family, the front part of the house was originally one large room, open to the roof, and thus without any second floor. There was a chimney at

FIGURE 57.—WHITFIELD HOUSE, A RESTORATION.

each end of this great hall, which was used as a meeting-house, it is said, as well as a parsonage, and which, in its two story height, followed the halls of mediæval England. In fact, as we

1862 in the *Ladies' Repository* of Cincinnati   Mr. Myron B Benton, now of Leedsville, N. Y., made the original drawing. He has authenticated the view, with certain corrections which are embodied in our drawing.

Since this book went to press we have received from the Rev. Dr. William G. Andrews. of Guilford, a print from an old negative of this same view of the house. A half-tone of this unique view, which confirms the accuracy of Mr. Benton's drawing, we print, by the courtesy of Dr. Andrews, at the end of this article.

have already said, it was at about the middle of the sixteenth century that these high walls were divided in two two-stories by a new floor.   In the eastern ell was the kitchen with the chamber over it.

The stairs in this arrangement could only have been in the small square space in the re-entrant angle between the two parts of the building.

All this is perfectly reasonable,   It represents one type of manor-house in use in England as early as the twelfth century; for though the chamber was generally at the opposite end of the hall from the buttery, yet there were no doubt many instances, of which the manor at Padley[1] is one, in which the chamber was over the offices.

There are also in England instances which will show how common an arrangement in stone houses that must have been which we have assumed—the L shape with the stairs in the re-entrant angle. At Sutton Courtenay, Berkshire, is a fourteenth century manor-house of the L plan, which, as Figure 58[2] will explain, has its stair in precisely the position to which we have assigned the flight in this restoration of Whitfield's house. The plan of Little Wenham Hall, Suffolk, which also

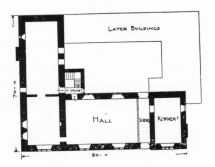

FIGURE 58.—SUTTON COURTENAY, BERKSHIRE.

has the L shape, though it is built of brick,[3] is another example of the re-entrant angle as a place for the stair.

---

[1] Sydney O. Addy, *The Evolution of the English House*, p. 140.

[2] This Figure has been redrawn from Turner and Parker, *Some Account of Domestic Architecture in England*, etc., vol II, p. 272.

[3] *The same*, vol. I, p. 152–3.   This house is of the thirteenth century.

The reason for the size of the hall we have already hinted at in saying that the dwelling was, it is said, a meeting-house as well as the home of the pastor. In order to reconcile these two uses, Whitfield employed, tradition says,[1] movable partitions wherewith to divide the enormous room. These, of which we give a drawing in Figure 59, were a sort of Venetian blind on a large scale, of horizontal wainscot, with each board hinged to its neighbor above and below, and strung at each end upon a rope. Two lengths of board, and thus two sections in each partition, were needed to reach across the room. When not in use they were drawn up by the ropes and fastened to the tie-beams of the roof. When in use they were lowered and bolted to the floor. How many of them there were we do not know. Probably there were two, perhaps only one. If there were two, as the two fireplaces seem to indicate, the central entry scheme, with a room at each side, was the original idea of the builder, an idea made permanent by the partitions set up by some descendant of Major Thompson — if not by the major himself — and transmitted to our own day by the present partitions in the main part of the house.

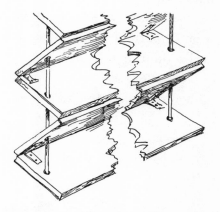

FIGURE 59 — FOLDING PARTITIONS. WHITFIELD HOUSE.

Let us now sum up the history of the house as we understand it.

As built by Whitfield, it consisted of a two-story hall with an ell which contained a kitchen and a chamber.

Some descendant of Major Robert Thompson put in the two

---

[1] Mrs. Cone, who received the tradition from her grandmother, born in 1767.

floors and divided the house by a central entry in which he placed the stairs. This was about 1700–10. He thus had in the front part two rooms, each with a fireplace,[1] and in the ell a kitchen, with a pantry, or more probably a bedroom, where the stairs had been. Upstairs he had three chambers.

Lack of light induced some later descendant to take down the southeast chimney and to put in the windows which old drawings show in the south gable. Jasper Griffing repaired the house at some time between 1776 and 1795, and to him is perhaps due the arrangement which Smith's plans show. Jasper's son, Nathaniel, who inherited the house from him in 1800, plastered the stone walls on the outside.

In 1868 Mrs. Cone, who had inherited from her mother,[2] took down the old ell and rebuilt it in its present condition, raised the walls about two feet and a half, and put on a new roof. She also put in the third window in the second story of the front—the others probably date from Jasper Griffing's repairs—and built the present chimney on the south gable, nearly in the place of that which was originally there.

THE NORTH SIDES BEFORE ALTERATION. (*From a photograph.*)

[1] If we accept the traditional fireplace in the south end wall.

[2] "Frederick Griffing inherited from his father, Nathaniel, 1845. Mary G. Chittenden inherited from her brother. Fred R. Griffing, 1852. I inherited from my mother, Mary G. Chittenden, in 1868." Letter of Mrs. Cone.

BALDWIN HOUSE.
BRANFORD.

II. THE BALDWIN HOUSE.

This is an ancient affair recently abandoned and now going to ruin, although it is the oldest house in Branford, and is of great interest and value to the student of colonial work. It stands on the outskirts of the village, on the road to New Haven. It was built, we do not know when or by whom; but its date, judging from the many examples with which it can be compared, can not be later than 1650. It may be much older. It possesses the sill projecting into the rooms, a feature which, however common it may once have been when more of the oldest houses were standing, we have so far found in but three houses in New England, in two of which the documentary evidence for an early date was convincing; the Hempstead house, New London, 1643; the Roger Mowry house, Providence, 1655; and the Shadrach Manton house, Manton, R. I., which documents carry back to 1680, but which must be far older than that.

We have in this house a clear case also of an added lean-to, another good sign of early date, for the ancient clapboarding can still be seen on the back wall of the main house in the lean-to chamber, as the section shows.

The house faces south. All the rooms in the main part of it are plastered. In the east room, the parlor, the summer has been cased, and there is a very good buffet, or corner cupboard. The

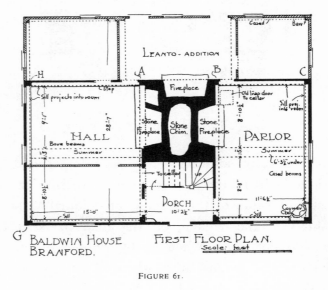

BALDWIN HOUSE BRANFORD.   FIRST FLOOR PLAN.

FIGURE 61.

whole side of the room around the fireplace is covered with panelling of later date than the house.

The porch or entry is very wide here, as in the Fiske house, and, indeed, in most of the houses in the New Haven colony. The stairs, which are left-hand, have no balusters, but are enclosed by a wooden partition.

They are built with winders at the bottom, and these tenon into a finely wrought oak post, three inches square, which runs to the ceiling and to which the string of the straight run above is fastened. The steps are constructed like those in the Whitman house, with a slight difference of detail. Beneath these stairs those to the cellar go down from the hall, which was also the kitchen. The cellar steps are of six-inch rise and twelve run, and are of solid pieces of oak, except at the bottom, where a rough stone step serves as a foundation to the whole.

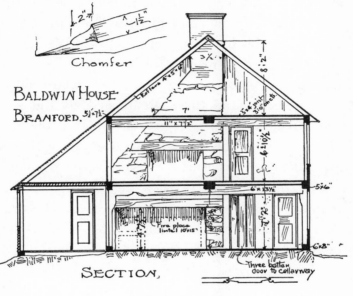

FIGURE 62.

The cellar is under the parlor only. It has one outside entrance and only one window. The masonry, of the red sandstone of the district, is excellent. The mortar appears to be of a clay mixed with shell lime.[1] The chimney is of stone to a point just below the roof, and there are signs that it had once been stone

---

[1] For an analysis of this mortar see Chapter X of this book.

above that point, and that the present brick topping-out is a much later addition.

In the hall the stone fireplace is quite large. The summer, here uncased, shows its beautiful chamfer-stop of an old form, clearly cut, and the girts and posts are also bare. The posts here do not, in the second story, flare from the bottom, as in many cases, but have a regular projection at the top, which, curiously enough, is turned, not in the usual direction across the house in the line of the chimney and end girts, but lengthwise of the house in the direction of the front and back girts. We have never seen another instance of this in any of the Connecticut settlements.[1] In the first story the posts have bracketed heads, also, which is a very old arrangement; and these are turned, as the section shows, in the usual direction, with the girts and across the house.

In the second story the stairs go to the attic with the same construction and arrangement which we saw below, even to the diminished height of the top step in each flight.

In the parlor chamber the summer is cased. In the hall chamber it is not. In the lean-to chamber, as we have said, the old outside clapboarding is still to be seen.

The kitchen fireplace is, like the lean-to which contains that room, a later addition to the chimney. There is no clapboarding at the back of the chimney in the second story, for it was pulled off to allow the masons to put the new flue into the chimney when they built the new fireplace in the kitchen.

The roof is original and is well framed, without either collar-beams or the purlins so common in the New Haven jurisdiction. The garret floor is of oak.

---

[1] It occurs, about 1715, in the Spencer house, East Greenwich, Rhode Island.

As this very interesting and important house was deserted, we had an excellent opportunity to examine it thoroughly and to study its arrangement and construction. The plan and the section given above will show both the one and the other more clearly than many pages of description. For the more technical details of the framing we refer the reader to the chapter on Construction.

The presence of a small window in one of the wooden partitions of the building, and the intricacy of the later dividing partitions, makes us think that the house may at some time have been a tavern; while the width of the entry and staircase, and especially of cellar stairs, makes it possible that such may even have been its original vocation.

CHAPTER VI.

THE SECOND PERIOD IN THE NEW HAVEN COLONY.

1675-1700.

THE last quarter of the seventeenth century was marked in all the New England colonies by an enlargement of the area of settlement. The outlying territory of each of the older towns was now safer for habitation; and the increase of the population, whose main support was still in farming, drove the younger men to dwellings at some distance from the old centers. Immigration from England had ceased, in any great amount, long before, and the colonists had now to develop the country by their own resources. Commerce had not attained the vast proportions which good Governor Eaton hoped for, and for which he and Davenport laid out New Haven on so grand a scale. Here, as in Hartford, the settlers of the older generation were nearly all dead, and their grandchildren were already coming upon the stage as men and women.

All these facts had a levelling influence upon the houses of the colony. In material possessions the people stood between the wealth of the original settlers and the accumulating riches of the early eighteenth century. We see no more great houses like those of Eaton, Davenport, Gregson, and Allerton. The dwellings are more uniform in size and in appointments. The carpenters, too, have changed somewhat in their methods. They have accommodated themselves to new needs and to a new climate, and have lost some of their old English traditions.

The lean-to comes into use in this period, sometimes even yet as an addition to accommodate a growing family, but often now as a part of the original dwelling; a concession to the need of more apartments in the house, and of a better separation between the different parts of the household. We have the kitchen no longer in the hall, but in the new lean-to.

The stone chimney still remains in the center of the house. Brick may be used, but it is still rare and is mostly confined to the topping-out above the roof, which in some cases may be of this date, though most of the examples are later.

The parlor is used as before. The hall, as we have remarked, is freed from the cooking, but either room may still contain a bed. The chambers are the same as before, for the lean-to chamber is little more than a lumber-room, with perhaps a bed for one of the apprentices or servants.

The overhang, always of the hewn type in the New Haven jurisdiction, must have existed during this period, though we have no certain examples of it. It is common in the period beyond.

In New Haven itself there seems to be but one house of this period which is still standing. This is the Trowbridge house, on George street, which dates from 1680.

The examples we have to study are in the other towns of the original confederation.   They are:

I.   THE THOMAS PAINTER HOUSE, WEST HAVEN, c. 1685.

II.   THE STOWE HOUSE, MILFORD, 1685–90.

III.   THE GOLDSMITH–CLEVELAND HOUSE, SOUTHOLD, c. 1680.

SMITH-PAINTER-HOUSE
1685.

I. THE THOMAS PAINTER HOUSE.

West Haven has its " Green," like the other old towns of the colony. East of this central rectangle, on the north side of Main street, stands the house which Thomas Painter bought of Morrison in 1695, and which Morrison built in or about 1685. The building has undergone some alterations, but it has been well cared for, and it is very easy to restore the original plan.

The house has a lean-to, built as part of the original fabric. Otherwise it is of the regular central-chimney type, with no overhang.

The entrance porch is very wide, a trait characteristic of these New Haven dwellings, which possess nearly two feet more of width in their porches than, in general, do the houses of the Connecticut people. The staircase, which may be original, though we think it is not, is a very fine one with moulded string and rail—see the chapter on Construction—and with turned balusters, which are

of double curve, and thus of the same profile above and below
the center. A half-baluster is placed against the square post. All
this woodwork is of oak. It is to be noted that we have never
yet seen in Connecticut, west of New London, the flat balusters
with sawn contour which are so common in Newport and in the
southern parts of Rhode Island.

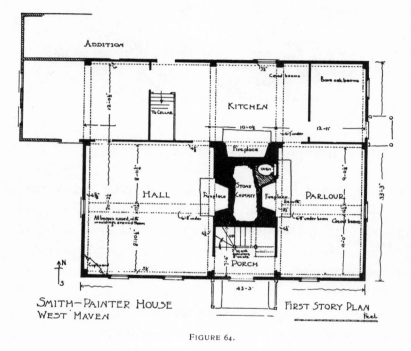

SMITH—PAINTER HOUSE
WEST MAVEN

FIRST STORY PLAN

FIGURE 64.

The cellar is under the hall—the western room—only. It is at
present reached by stairs from the kitchen, as the plan will show.
It is whitewashed, but the original mortar was of shell lime. Some
of the original square-hewn joists in the first floor can still be seen
overhead. The others have apparently been replaced by newer
sticks of rougher make.

The hall has a cased summer, posts, and girts, and some fine panelling at the fireplace end. It contains also a very good buffet or corner china cupboard. The parlor is very much like it, but is a considerably shorter room.

In the lean-to chamber can be seen the framing of the wall between that chamber and those in the front of the house. Here the studs are still in place, but the clapboards, and even the nail-

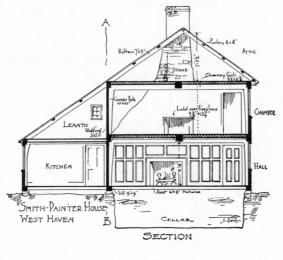

FIGURE 65.

marks which would betray the former presence of them, are wanting; and the fact that the pins of the joints in the northwest post had never been cut off close to the wood proves that this was only an inside wall and that the lean-to could not have been an addition.

The chimney, up to a point just below the roof, where the later brick top begins, is of stone laid in clay. The roof is original and is of a kind very much in fashion in this colony. There

are no collar-beams and the boarding, which is vertical, that is,
from plate to ridge, is nailed to purlins framed between the rafters. All the framing, as well as the roof and floor boards, is of
oak.

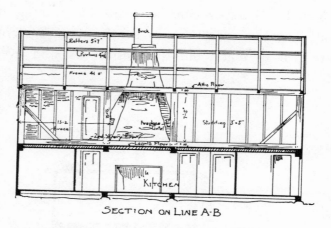

SECTION ON LINE A·B

FIGURE 66. THE THOMAS PAINTER HOUSE.—LONGITUDINAL SECTION.

II.   THE STOWE HOUSE.

The present sedgy harbor of Milford was once of sufficient commercial importance to warrant a town wharf, which still exists on the same site, and which is reached by an ancient thorough-fare now called Wharf street.   Upon the western side of this, nearly at the water-side, stands the Stowe house, famous in the Revolutionary annals of the town.

It is one of the most interesting houses in all the colony, though it has undergone considerable alteration.   As it now stands it has a lean-to which was original.   It also possesses a central passage or entry and two chimneys, neither of which are of the same date as the house.

A glance at Figure 68 will show how peculiar the plan is. According to all analogy the chimney should be, and perhaps originally was, in the central passage where now a very interesting and artistic flight of stairs is backed up against the wall which separates the front rooms from the lean-to.   The southern chimney, standing behind the summer, appears on the outside above the ridge. The northern, which cuts away the girt at the second floor level as well as one of the original braces in the back wall of the northern chamber of the second story, goes through the roof in the lean-to and does not, in a front view of the house, appear against the sky.

The roof is old, built with the purlin and ridge scheme already mentioned as characteristic of the New Haven colony. It can hardly be original unless the peculiar position of the southern chimney is also original, for there are no signs of patching after the removal of a central stack. If the south chimney is original, how could the north room be heated? For the north chimney is certainly a late addition. The clearest solution lies in assuming that the old stone chimney in the present entry was taken down

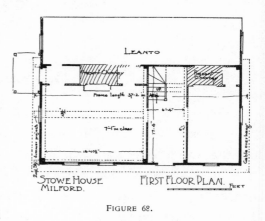

FIGURE 68.

and that, as it was desired to make two tenements of the building, the two separate chimneys were put in. This must have been done before the Revolution, for the stairs, which we give in Figure 110, are of an old type and belong to at least the first quarter of the eighteenth century. They are the only dog-legged[1] stairs we have ever seen in these old houses.

The northern end is most probably an addition. The house was originally a single-room building with an end chimney where

---

[1] A stair in which there is only one post at the turn and in which the rails are over each other is called dog-legged.

the stairs now are, and with a small entry in front of that chimney, so that the door was in the same position as that which it now occupies.

The extremely great projection of the cornice, attained as the section shows, see Figure 106 in chapter on Construction, is interesting, but is rather late.

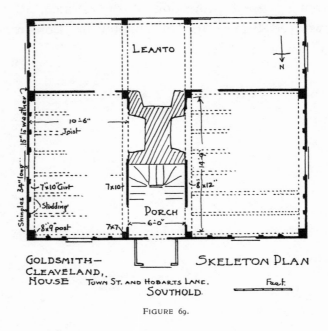

FIGURE 69.

III.   THE GOLDSMITH–CLEVELAND HOUSE.

The people of Southold came from the county of Norfolk in Old England.   They were, Atwater thinks, the passengers in a ship which Davenport, in a letter to his friend Lady Vere, says was expected shortly to arrive.[1]   The settlement which they made at Yennicook, as the Indians called Southold, Long Island, was at first directly under the control of New Haven, and it remained a part of the New Haven group until 1662, when it went over to

---

[1] Atwater, *History of New Haven*, pp. 162, 163, note.

the Charter government of Connecticut.[1] In 1665, after the capture of New Amsterdam by the English, it was, in the boundary adjustment, brought under the "government of his Royal Highness the Duke of York."[2]

There is one house still standing in Southold which belongs to this period. It has been moved from the main street to a lane which runs from that street toward the north. It is a single-

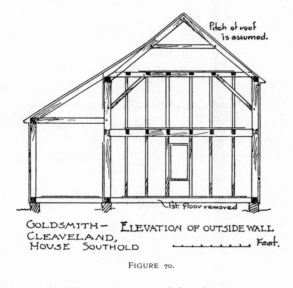

GOLDSMITH-CLEAVELAND, HOUSE SOUTHOLD ELEVATION OF OUTSIDE WALL

FIGURE 70.

room, story-and-a-half structure, with the summer and girts, and it once had an end chimney which never appeared on the outside, and which was taken down when the house was moved. The work is very rough and is of little interest.

All the other houses, and there were several of considerable interest, among which the Barnabas Horton and the Goldsmith-Cleveland ranked with the best, have been destroyed.

---

[1] Atwater, *History*, pp. 463-4.
[2] Palfrey, *History of New England*, II, p. 595.

The people seem to have preferred a low, small dwelling, generally of one story, like the Moore house in Figure 71.

Of the Goldsmith-Cleveland house we give a plan and an elevation of the frame of one end. These drawings will explain very clearly what was left of the building in 1894. The bearings, it will be seen, were rather short, a fact which accounts for the peculiarity which the house shows in having no summer.

MOORE HOUSE
SOUTHOLD.

FIGURE 71.

CHAPTER VII.

THE THIRD PERIOD IN THE NEW HAVEN COLONY.

1700–1750.

THE lean-to house which we saw in the second period in New Haven went over into the period we have now to study. It seems to have been a favorite form which persisted side by side with the later type characteristic of the first half of the eighteenth century, and it probably even survived into the years closely preceding the Revolution. The full two-story house, two rooms deep, appears here as in the north during this period, and side by side with it still lives on the old type of one room in depth. The former type here, as in Hartford, is a direct development from the central-chimney lean-to house; and with that house it undergoes a curious transformation not apparent elsewhere, which marks very clearly the slowness of the transition from the old framing to that in vogue in later times. This peculiarity consists in leaving out the summers in the first story and retaining them in the second. The advent of plastering is responsible for this. The desire to keep the plastered ceiling level led the carpenters, in the new houses, to lessen the depth of the old beam in the down-stairs rooms so that the bottoms as well as the tops of the joists it carried were flush with it, and the lathing could be nailed over the whole. The cracks in the ceiling, caused by the shrinking of the stick or by the springing of the floor which it was not stiff enough to hold firmly, show that this was the case.

In the Fiske house and in the Caldwell house, both in Guilford, we have examples of this in two-story houses. In the Benjamin house, Milford, we have an instance in a house with a lean-to. In two of these cases the summer appears, as usual, in the second story, in the ceiling of the chambers.

The next step, of course, was the abandoning of the summer in the second story also. This took place about 1750, some twenty-five years later than the first step. Here, in contrast to what we find in Rhode Island, the southern settlements seem to have been very little, if any, more conservative than the northern and to have clung little, if any, longer to the old framing. The New Haven carpenters had left the summer out of the first story of their houses before the craftsmen of Connecticut dropped it altogether. In that case they might be considered as in advance of their northern neighbors, who, when they changed, suppressed both summers at once.

Connecticut Hall, which is now the oldest building of Yale University, and which bears the date of 1750, has the summer system of framing in its floors, though its walls are of brick. The beams, too, are panelled on their soffits in exactly the same way as the summer in the south parlor of the Webb house.

An overhang of small dimensions, often only one inch, and never, so far as we have seen, exceeding six inches in its projection, is quite characteristic of houses of this period. Its occurrence on the ends of the houses in the second story is a good guide to the date in lean-to houses. If it occurs, the lean-to is generally an addition. If it does not, the lean-to may usually be looked on as a part of the original house.

The two-story house once established, the development of the plan produced the four-room house, with central passage and two chimneys, which here are very commonly at the end of the house, as in the Sheldon Woodbridge in Hartford. Later on, after the Revolution, the large square house with hipped-roof and wall-chimneys appears, a type which does not confront us in Hartford and which somehow rather seems to be a sea-board creation to be found at Salem, Providence, New London, and New Haven, with, of course, characteristic variations in all these places.

The use of brick in this period, while more common than in the others, was not universal. We still find many chimneys of stone in Guilford. Many stacks are of stone with brick topping out. The brick houses so common north of the city of New Haven, houses with gambrel roofs and with one chimney or two in each end wall, are much later than this period.

We have three houses to discuss:

I. THE FISKE–WILDMAN HOUSE, GUILFORD, c. 1720.

II. THE CALDWELL HOUSE, GUILFORD, c. 1740.

III. THE BENJAMIN HOUSE, MILFORD, c. 1750.

FISKE-
PARISLEE-
HOUSE GUILFORD.

I.   THE FISKE–WILDMAN HOUSE.

Guilford was laid out around a rectangular "Green." From the south end of this, continuing the street which bounds the open space, runs the New York and Boston stage road, the colonial post-road, a prolongation, along the Sound, of the old "path which leadeth to Pequot," which ran from Providence to New London.

On this Boston road, perhaps an eighth or a quarter of a mile from the Green, stands the Dr. Fiske house, to give it a familiar name,[1] one of the largest as well as one of the most picturesque dwellings in Guilford. It is a wooden house, with a central chimney topped-out with brick, and it has a long lean-to in the rear. This lean-to, though very old, is not original, and, if we

---

[1] It is the property of Mr. F. J. Wildman.

consider the plan, where the oldest work is shown in black, we shall see that we have here a survival—a house of the old two-room, hall-and-parlor type.

From a view of the house it would not seem possible that it could have been built as late as 1720,[1] but, on closer study, we

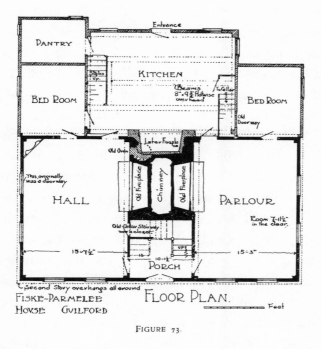

FIGURE 73.

must admit that the evidence in support of that date is very powerful.

In the first place, the great width of the house, nineteen feet or thereabout, in the clear, and the considerable height of the two stories, argue very strongly for the late date.

In the second place, the summer does not appear in either of

---

[1] The builder is said to have been Ebenezer Parmelee, the clockmaker.

the lower rooms. We might suspect that they had been hewn away, especially as there are two parallel cracks in the ceiling which betray the presence of a beam flush with the floor joists. This suspicion, however, receives a heavy blow in the second story, for the summers are lacking—to all appearance—even here, nor have they been hewn off, since they are still to be seen in the attic, the bottoms of them flush with those of the floor joists, the tops projecting above the garret floor.

If it were not for the treatment of the summers in this house and in another like it, to be described later, we might be inclined to ignore the width of the rooms and the height of the stories;

FIGURE 74.—THE OVERHANG.

for the Roger Williams house in Salem, which dates from 1634-40, is almost as wide in the clear as this building, and the stories of it are nearly, if not quite, as high. Moreover the Fiske house has on all four sides of the original dwelling, an over-hang[1] which, at the first sight thereof, would make us claim an early date for the mansion. For this projection is of the hewn type employed elsewhere in the New Haven jurisdiction, and used in the Hollister and Patterson houses in the Connecticut colony, the type, that is, in which the lower half of the post is hewn away to let the upper half come forward. But the overhang is not exactly like that in either of the houses we have mentioned, nor, indeed, like any example we have seen in the present State of Connecticut. The brackets, instead of being double-swell affairs like those in the Hollister house, or plain bevels like those in the Patterson, have a reversed curve,

---

[1] The overhang appears on the front and on each end. The existence of it on the back—which is really a sign of late date—is proved by the distance at which the posts of the lean-to stand from the back wall of the main house.

as the drawing shows, and the outer edges of the girts which these brackets appear to support are beautifully chamfered with a cyma reversa filleted above and below, and stopped with a double curve.[1] This is not, however, the real mediæval curved chamfer-stop into which the mouldings all curve and die away. That stop we have, so far, seen but once in New England, on the edge of the lintel over the fireplace in the old Arthur Fenner house, in Cranston, Rhode Island, where it dated back to 1655.[1]

These chamfered beams, in fact, can be only copies of older work which has disappeared. They seem isolated because the forerunners of them have been lost with the destruction of the houses, or have been covered up by later boarding. The brackets, too, are rare because older examples have been hewn away in many cases to make easier the work of renewing the clapboards, or because the houses have been built out in the lower story to conceal the overhang, as was actually done a few years ago with the Burnham house at Ipswich.

While the hewn overhang has other less elaborate examples in the New Haven colony—where we believe it originated, as far as the Connecticut settlements are concerned—these chamfered speci-mens can not be considered as necessarily earlier than those that are plain. The chamfers occur at Ipswich, in the Colony of the Bay, in two houses, the so-called Saltonstall, which is very old, but the date of which is still under investigation, and the so-called Cobbett, which is undoubtedly as late as 1701. The other im-portant houses with overhangs, in Ipswich: the Howard house, with no brackets, and the Norton house, with brackets of the same shape as those on the Fiske house—though there are no

---

[1] *Early Rhode Island Houses*, Plates 9 and 54. Any collection of photographs of French or English half-timber work will show the form.

double ones on the corners — are also late examples. Neither of them has the chamfer.[1] We have, therefore, to abandon our first thought that here we meet an early chamfer, the work of some old craftsman fresh from the same kind of moulding in his English home.

The final argument for the late date of the house is the existence of another dwelling of almost exactly the same kind, which stands on the same road a little further east. This, the Caldwell house, which we shall describe a little later, has the plan and all the marks of the third period and can hardly be earlier than about 1740. It has the overhang, with exactly the same form of bracket, but without the chamfer.

To return briefly to the interior of the Fiske house. The joists in the second floor of the lean-to, which has no plastered ceiling, run lengthwise of the kitchen, and are remarkable for their length and for the quality of the work bestowed upon them.

The roof is no doubt original. It is framed with principal rafters and purlins which carry the common rafters. Collar beams, as is common in this colony, are wanting.

In the entry, which is wide, as in all New Haven work, there is a very interesting stair with a box string heavily moulded, and with turned balusters of very good contour. The moulded rail will be found in Figure 110.

---

[1] A theory of the curious resemblance between the houses in Ipswich and the work in the New Haven country is propounded, as the old records would put it, in Chapter IX, under Overhang.

CALDWELL HOUSE

II. THE CALDWELL HOUSE.

This dwelling, built about 1740, stands on the south side of the Boston road, at some distance from the " Green," at Guilford. It has the plan of the later period, that is, it is two rooms deep, and it is of two full stories.

The house has a gable overhang at each end and one in the second story on the front and on each end, but not apparently at the back which is now covered in part by an unimportant one-story addition, and in part by a two-story ell. The second story overhangs have, at the point where the posts come, curved brackets precisely like those in the Fiske-Wildman house, but the girts of the second story show no mouldings.

There is now, inside the house, a hall-way or entry which runs, as in the later pre-Revolutionary plans, entirely through the building, with two rooms on each side of it. Between each of the two rooms of each pair there now stands, as in the plans of the type referred to, a brick chimney. This arrangement, however, seems to date only from about 1815.[1] Originally the house had one central chimney, of stone, like all the others of its time, and must have much resembled the Mygatt house, Wethersfield, to which, in dimensions, it almost exactly corresponds. In the first story there is no summer in either of the front rooms, though the girts show

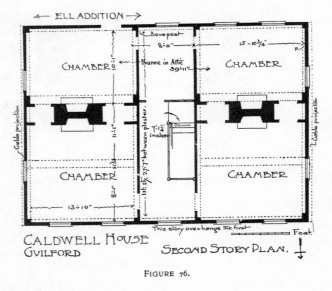

FIGURE 76.

all around the room, and the ceiling shows the presence of a beam in the place of the summer—a beam very likely still called by that name. The new chimneys which replaced the old stone stack are built, as the plan shows, in front, that is, north of the girts which bounded the hall and parlor. This story, as the section will show, is very high, as high as that in the Fiske house.

---

[1] Miss Griswold, of Guilford, gives us this information.

In the second story, in the little passage partitioned off at the head of the present stairway, are still to be seen the two posts of the rear wall, with the chimney girts they carry. One of these girts is chamfered on both sides. The posts also are chamfered, and the whole is well wrought, better than is usual in this colony, though the work here surpasses that in Hartford. The summer

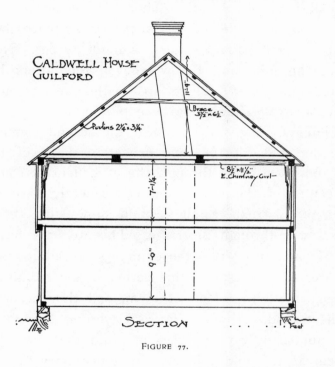

FIGURE 77.

exists in the parlor chamber, and in the hall chamber as well, though both summer and girts are cased.

In the attic we found no traces of patching and repairing such as would have been necessary after the change in the plan we have spoken of. The roof is therefore probably not original. Very likely it dates from 1815, the time of the alterations. It has been strengthened, since it was built, by the introduction of collar beams; for the rafters at first spanned the whole house and carried vertical boarding on purlins, with no tie except at the floor framing. The danger of failure, however, as it proved, was not in spreading—and the result was a justification of the old builders' scheme in that regard—but in the bending of the rafters at the middle of their length. Therefore, as section shows, the joint is so cut as to make the new sticks act as braces between the weak points of each pair of rafters, and not as ties. Nothing but the form of the joint and the weight on the rafters holds these pseudo-collars in place. There are neither tenons nor pins in them. Several new rafters have been put in.

The chimneys, since they are near the second summer, or girt between parlor and kitchen, and hence are back of the central axis of the building, come through the attic floor at some distance from the center of the house and consequently have to be corbelled over, or "carried," as the section shows, that they may rise in the usual way through the ridge. This we have never seen in old work. It is a proof that the chimneys are additions.

There are many houses of this period in the old jurisdiction of New Haven. Guilford is full of them, and they occur along the shore of the Sound, at least as far as Saybrook, though in steadily decreasing numbers. So numerous are they that even had we examined them all it would still have been necessary to select examples. Those we have discussed are typical of the time we have tried to explain.

The two-chimney house came shortly after this Caldwell house. There is one, now deserted, with its central hall and with an inch overhang all round and in the gables, facing the Sound on the north side of the post-road between Madison and Clinton.

BENJAMIN HOUSE.
MILFORD.

III.   THE BENJAMIN HOUSE.

This house, the latest of those whereof we shall have to treat, stands in Milford, scarce half a mile north of the main street, on the road which runs by the railroad station.

It was built, tradition says, by Michael Peck, which would place it as late as 1762. It may be of that date. At any rate it is down at the end of the limit to which the word "early" can by any means be applied.

It is an original lean-to house, with no overhangs. It betrays its late date partly by the height of its stories, and especially by the fact which we have already noted, that the summer is wanting, or at least is concealed by the plastering in the ceiling, in the first story rooms.

A beam there is in each room, but it is now no deeper than the joists which span the distance between it and the old front girt. The progress of improvement has driven out the old deep summer projecting into the room. With it much of the picturesqueness of the earlier scheme has also vanished. The level

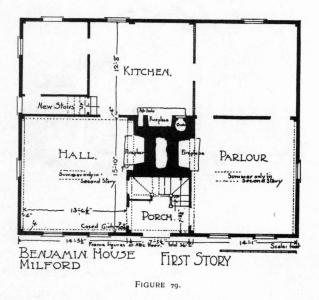

BENJAMIN HOUSE
MILFORD

FIRST STORY

FIGURE 79.

plaster surface is, to the artistic eye, a poor substitute for the ancient planed and chamfered summer, with its well-wrought, small-sized joists.

The section will show the interesting method of constructing the lean-to roof, a method precisely similar to that used in the Rhode Island houses with the original lean-to. It is an irrefutable proof that this lean-to was built as part of the house.

On the first floor the lean-to is said to have been originally one large kitchen. We are inclined to think, however, that the "buttery" existed even at the beginning.

The chimney is of stone to a point just under the roof-boards. Above this it is of brick.

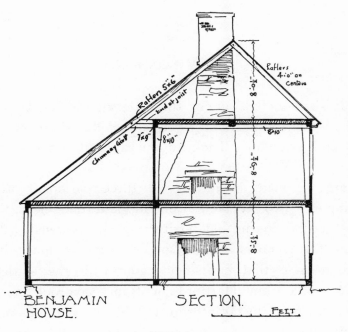

FIGURE 80.

CHAPTER VIII.

NEW LONDON.

E shall include under this title all the territory lying east of the Connecticut river, along the shore of the Sound, and stretching back to the ancient northern confine of Norwich.[1]

We are fortunate in having all three periods represented by fine examples—two at New London, and one near the present Versailles station, in the old territory of the Norwich settlement.

As the settlement of New London was not made in haste, it is fair to assume that craftsmen came with the settlers. They may have come from Hartford, or from Saybrook, as temporary residents, employed by Winthrop and his companions to build for them their dwellings; or, what is more likely, they may have been of the number of the actual planters.

There must have been houses, as in all the settlements, from the beginning, and the building of these required skilled labor. There may have been some specimens of the "cellar," as in the other colonies, but we hear nothing of them; and from the facts that this plantation was made later than the two others, and that, as it was on the coast, communication with the older settlements

---

[1] See the map of early Connecticut, on p. 3.

was easy, it may be assumed that the primitive "dug-out" did not have any great vogue.

A mason must have been in the town early, for Winthrop caused a stone house to be built for himself, probably with stone from the quarry near what is now Quaker Hill, a quarry which we know from the records was worked in 1659, and which must have been opened as soon as the settlement was fairly begun. From the records we infer the presence of a mason in 1661, for such was undoubtedly the trade of Nathaniel Pryce, who, in that year, was ordered to dig a cellar under the minister's house " of the size of one room and seven feet deep," with a " stack of stone chimneys in the midst." It is curious to note the use of the word chimneys where we should speak of " flues," an instance of which occurred, it will be remembered, in Talcott's memorandum.[1]

The recorded evidence as to carpenters and their work begins with the advent of John Elderkin, of that craft, in 1651. He came to New England in 1637, and had lived at Lynn, at Dedham, and perhaps at Providence, though no record of him appears at this last settlement.[2] He took, in this same year, a contract to build a meeting-house and to clapboard it for £8. The fact that houses were built as soon as the place was settled is proved by another entry in the records which speaks of a lean-to addition. Happily we know something of what the dwellings were from the rough specification given in 1666 for the minister's house already mentioned   " The dimentions," says the old town record, " are to be 36 foote in length and 25 in breadth and thirteen foote

---

[1] See p. 13 of this book.

[2] Miss F. M. Caulkins *History of New London*, pp. 158–9.   Elderkin died at Norwich, June 23, 1687. *Ibid.* Compare also the same author's *History of Norwich*, p 117.

stud betwixt ye joynts with a stack of stone chimneys in the midst. The house to be a girt house.[1] "

This last expression means that the house was to have no studs and was to be boarded vertically, and the use of such words shows that this was an exception, while the use of studs was the rule. This was to have been apparently a two-story building. It is of extraordinary width for that early date, and it certainly looks as if the town fathers, who voted to spend £100 on the building beside paying for the mason work, meant to have a lean-to house.

The original type of house, however, seems to have been a one or two-room structure to which the lean-to was added later. Of course we have very few examples to which we can appeal, because of the burning of New London by Arnold; but the express mention of the lean-to as an addition, the late date of the enactment about the minister's house, and the lateness of all houses now standing with lean-to roofs, all go to strengthen the statement.

In the second period, and, indeed, at the end of the first, as the vote about the parsonage shows, the wider form of house is used with one or more narrow rooms, one of which is the kitchen, at the rear of the main apartments; and these rooms, at least at first, take the form of the lean-to.

In the third period, the wide house becomes the type for the plan, while in elevation the type is either a lean-to or two full stories, as in the other settlements. The whole dwelling, also, is larger.

Brick comes into use for parts of the chimney, and sometimes

---

[1] New London records, quoted by Miss Caulkins, *History*, pp. 139-40.

for the whole at some time after 1680.[1] The cheapness of stone in the old Norwich territory caused the material to be used till very recent times. In this Norwich is like the "South County" of Rhode Island, which, indeed, it strongly resembles in other ways, and like Guilford in the New Haven jurisdiction.

It is worthy of remark that, in the later development of the plan, we find in New London large houses with a chimney at each end, and, both in that city and in Norwich, hip-roofed houses with a chimney in the outer wall in each of the four rooms which they contain.

Let us now turn to the examples. Of these we shall consider but three:[2]

I. THE HEMPSTEAD HOUSE, NEW LONDON, WEST END, 1647, EAST END, 1678.

II. THE CADY HOUSE, PUTNAM, C. 1714.

III. THE KINSMAN HOUSE, LISBON, NEAR VERSAILLES, C. 1745.

---

[1] "Clay pits" on the Quinnebaug river are mentioned in 1687. Miss Caulkins' *History of Norwich*, p. 166.

[2] The Coit-Belden house, on Main street, at the foot of Federal, is said to be very old. We have not yet examined it.

HEMPSTEAD HOUSE
NEW LONDON

I. THE HEMPSTEAD HOUSE.

This dwelling, one of the most interesting in all New England, stands with its back to Hempstead court, perhaps half a mile from the waterside, and not far from State street, in the city of New London.   It is of unusual length, and consists of two parts, one on each side of the central chimney, which is of stone to a point above the third floor, though the top is of brick.   One of these parts, the western, is the older, and was built by Robert Hempstead, one of the original settlers, in 1647.   The eastern half was built by this man's son in 1678.   The lean-to, as it now stands, is partly a restoration.   It is certainly a late addition.

The evidence for these dates is very strong.   We know from the Hempstead diary that the house had already been standing 65 years in 1743.   That is decisive for the date 1678.   Now, on examining the house it is very easy to see that the two parts of it are not of the same date, and that the western half is by far the older of the two. No one who examines the building with any care can doubt this statement, which will appear more clearly as we describe the house in detail. The traditional date, then, of 1647 is, for the western end of the house, certainly correct.

The western part, shown in black on the plan, extended originally to the point A, which was just east of the original chimney or of the chimney in its original form. Beyond that point we find the second floor of the eastern end four inches higher than that of the older part, and the plate, too, at least on the

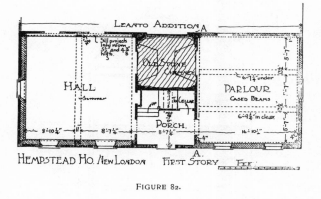

FIGURE 82.

frontage, at a higher level. The original building was, then, an end-chimney house, though the chimney was probably not on the outside of the wall.

The summer and two posts — the others are buried in the thick walls — are shown in the old hall in the western first story, and we meet once more that rare and ancient feature, the sill above the joists, projecting into the room. Another peculiarity is the running of the summer across the house, with a post under each end, as in the Roger Williams house in Salem, an arrangement repeated in the second story. The chamfer of this summer is a filleted quarter-round, and the stop is unique. The southern and western walls are thickened and are filled with brick and eel-grass. The north wall, once the outside wall of the house, was treated in the same manner. The post under the summer in that wall is pinned into the sill.

The roof of this house, over the western end, is original. When the eastern part was added the cornice was raised on the

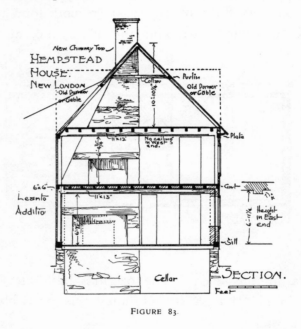

FIGURE 83.

front, as the perspective shows. The rafter in the western gable was left in its old place and a new rafter put in above it. The other rafters were treated differently. The collar beams were pulled out of their mortises in the front rafters and these were then spread, turning on the pins at their tops, till they reached the span required to make them align with the rafters of the newer roof. The collars were then brought against the rafters and fastened to them considerably below these old mortises which, though filled up, may still be seen. On each face of the older roof there still remains the framing for a dormer window. On the rear face the rafter over the middle of the dormer-space stops, as it originally did, on a header or cross-beam (see the section), while on the front face the space below the header was filled, by those who altered the roof, with a continuation of the rafter above.

The cellar is under the western end only. It is of good masonry, laid in lime mortar. The joists of the first floor, which are heavy and regular, are built into the wall, and the sill runs over them on the top of the masonry. The framing for a cellar window exists, and traces of the window-opening remain in the south wall. The entrance from out of doors is at the south of the west end. Under the porch or entry the framing is lighter. Perhaps a trap-door originally existed there. One of the most noteworthy characteristics of this cellar is the use of quarried stone in the walls of it. Several of the stones show drill-marks and roughly split surfaces. These are the only instances of quarry marks which we have seen.

Whether or not the staircase is as old as either part of the house it is hard to say. The cage in which it stands is no doubt contemporary, at least, with the later end, and probably with the earlier, for it strongly resembles that in the Whitman house.

The eastern or newer end of the house presents one peculiarity —two parallel summers in the parlor where we should expect one. Two summers exist in the Perkins or Warner house, Warwick, R. I., and in the Roger Williams house, Salem, but in these cases they ran across the building like that in the old part of this

Hempstead house, while these run as we should expect to find the one summer running, that is, parallel with the front of the building.

In one corner of the chamber of this eastern end a space is partitioned off, and here we can see, bare of plaster, one of the two second-story summers; the other is covered, like the posts and outside studding, with a later finish of lath and plaster. The brace in the corner goes from the post to the girt, as in the Gleason house, and not from the post to the plate.

CADY HOUSE RUINS.
PUTNAM HEIGHTS.

II.   THE CADY HOUSE.

This house stood near the city of Putnam till 1898.   It was built about 1714[1] by Justice Joseph Cady.   A half-tone of it, given in the *Connecticut Quarterly*, shows that it had a lean-to, though whether this was original or not we can not say, as we did not examine the building.   A gable overhang also appears in the picture, with the usual projecting plate.

We give a view of the ruins and a plan based upon measurements taken by Mr. E. W. Husband.   Such a ruin is always more

---

[1] Miss Ellen D. Larned, "Three Killingly Boys," in the *Connecticut Quarterly*, vol. III, No. 2, p. 221.

important than it at first might seem, for it gives an opportunity to study the construction of the chimney which in this case is

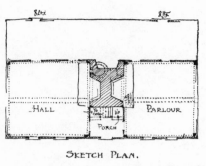

SKETCH PLAN.

FIGURE 85.—THE CADY HOUSE.

quite interesting. In our plan in Figure 86 it will be seen that the oven, in a house even as late as this, is an addition. In the section the method of turning all the flues into one is noteworthy, as well as the management of the first-story flue under the hearth in the second story, and the way in which that hearth is supported.

This turning of all the flues into one was probably the most common fashion of chimney building. It certainly was the cheapest. Whether it was always used or not, it is difficult to say. We think that separate flues may be found in stone work in Connecticut as in Rhode Island. In brick chimneys they certainly can be seen in houses as early as this or earlier, as in the Sheldon Woodbridge house.

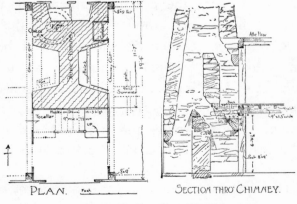

PLAN.   SECTION THRO' CHIMNEY.

FIGURE 86.—THE CADY HOUSE.

III. THE KINSMAN HOUSE.

This house, abandoned and fast going to ruin, stands north of the New England railroad track, near Versailles station, about six miles from Norwich on the road from Canterbury to Versailles. It was probably built about 1745–50. It is a house of the regular plan so familiar in the Connecticut colony in the third period, with lengthwise summers in the first story, a large porch and wide stairway, and a kitchen with pantry or chamber at the rear. In the second story the summer runs across the house to form a tie for the roof. The building is a specimen of the "girt house" referred to in the New London records. It is boarded vertically on the outside, with studs only at the windows.[1] These windows were probably double, or wide in proportion to their height, like those in the Whitman house, for the studs came right for the later colonial windows, though they may have been put in for these. Instead of wainscot carried horizontally around the walls, as in the Whitman house, the building has a late coat of plaster over a system of vertical inside boarding, which is two and a half inches, the thickness of the window studs, away from the outer boarding. This exists in part of the north wall of the house, showing that it was one of the form outlined in black on the plan in Figure 87.

In the first story some of the beams over the kitchen and the

---

[1] This vertical boarding, the rule in Rhode Island, and common east of that colony, in Plymouth, is rare in Connecticut, It occurs as far west as Saybrook, but, so far as we can find, no further, except in barns. Eastern Connecticut and Narragansett, in Rhode Island, are much alike architecturally.

room at the side thereof are framed into the girts at the side of the front rooms. The others are framed into the posts on the north line of the parlor and hall—the parlor is here the east room—to form a tie across the house. In the second story the beams are spliced to the ends of the summers and of the girts.

The roof is boarded vertically on purlins carried by the rafters. Though common in New Haven, as we saw, this is rather rare

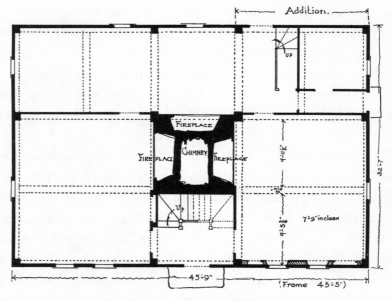

FIGURE 87.—KINSMAN HOUSE, FIRST STORY.

so far east as this. The chimney is stone throughout, but the top shows no panelling or pilasters.

At the rear of the house is an addition a story-and-a-half high, with small windows under the eaves, and a summer in the second floor. It has an end chimney of stone, which, like the rest of the addition, is in ruins. It was never on the outside at the upper part, as the mortise for the girt outside of it still exists

in one of the corner posts.   It may, like one stone chimney in
old Saybrook, and one brick example in Guilford, have shown on
the outside below that girt.

The way in which the ends of the summer in the garret floor
of the main house are cut over the plate and carry the cornice like
an overhang, as shown in Figure 106, is very interesting.

The parlor is now panelled on the fireplace end in much the
same manner as in the Dorus Barnard house.   On the front of the

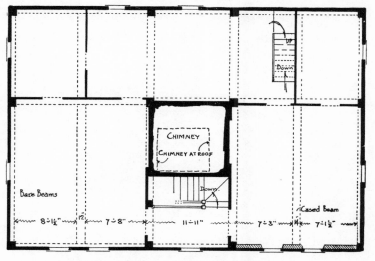

FIGURE 88.—KINSMAN HOUSE, SECOND STORY.

house the wall is lined with panelling set out from the old wall
so as to form cupboards, at the back of which, in grooves on the
chair rail and in a grooved piece fastened to the girt above, moved
sliding shutters of panelled wood.   This whole arrangement dates
probably from about 1780.   On this front wall, concealed by the
newer panelling, is the old vertical wainscot of the room, of
matched boards in sections, resembling those in the Whitman
house, and stopping against a wide oak " ground " or strip, above

which is plaster. This wainscot occurs in the passage behind the parlor. The ground occurs without the wainscot in the hall on the north side. This wainscot is later than the house, as the fact that the chimney is laid in clay mixed with hay instead of in lime mortar—for the lime in the stone-work is of later patching—is conclusive proof that there was no plaster in the original house.

CHAPTER IX.

CONSTRUCTION.

L ET us now consider in detail the construction of the various houses which we have discussed in the preceding chapters. To do this we must first study the materials of the buildings, then the details which we have till now looked at only in their relation to the whole structure of which they formed parts, and finally the methods of workmanship and the tools of the workmen. We shall not divide the chapter just in this way, for often all these subjects can be disposed of under one heading; but we shall, aside from the direct study of materials, endeavor to treat each part of the construction under the three-fold aspect of the material of which it is composed, its form and duty in the building, and the tools used in working it.

I. STONE-WORK AND BRICK-WORK.

STONE. There are two kinds of stone to be found in the early houses of Connecticut: field stone and quarried stone. The former is used mostly in the hilly country, the latter in the river valleys. The field stone are mainly bowlders or fragment of bowlders from the glacial drift. They are mostly of granite though other rocks, trap, greenstone, sandstone, gneiss, occur among them.

They occur also as a kind of flat stone, in some places, Wethersfield among them, along the shore of the Connecticut river, as they occur at some points along the Sound. The bowlders can be broken up in one way or another with the mason's hammer, but the settlers seem not to have done this, but to have used the field stones as they picked them up.

QUARRYING began early in Hartford. The red sandstone of the district crops out in the bed and on the banks of the Little River, and there we find a quarry in the "stone pits," in reference to which there are several town orders.

In September, 1639, it was "orderd that non shall dig ston on the falles by goodman lords."[1] If the location of Goodman Lord's lot on Porter's map is correct, this primitive quarry was on the north bank of the Little River, a short distance west of the Main street bridge. The digging for stone there, as the old recorder calls quarrying, had evidently been going on long enough to have become a nuisance, for there is, under the date of 1635, and perhaps copied from some older papers of that date, a fragment of an order which seems to be of the same purport as this.[2]

One order or two did not stop the trouble, and in January, 1639–40, we find that the quarrying had been carried so far that the highways were in danger. and an order was issued at the town-meeting requiring those whose digging had injured the road to fill up their pits within "three Mounthes after this tyme If they haue Ceassed digging or w^{th}in three mounthes after they haue Ceassed," under penalty of a fine.[3]

---

[1] Conn. Historical Society, *Collections*, vol. VI, p. 7.

[2] *Ibid*, p. 2.

[3] *Ibid*, p. 13.

Even this did not bring the practice into order. On May 16, 1642, it was recorded: " It is ordered that noone shall dige any stons at the riueret without order from the townsmen." [1] And yet again the persistent masons were met by three enactments passed on November 18, 1644. Says the record: " it is ordered that if any man shall haue liberty to dig stons by the riuer he shall haue noe liberty to dig any more stons six weeks after the grantt."

" it is ordered that the pitts that are alredy opend thos that haue mad them shall haue noe liberty to dig any longer then six weeks after the makin of this order: the former orders of filing of the pitts and of saufing the town from damag stand still in forse."

" if any man shall pase the time alowd him to dig stons aboue written he shall forfitt to the town for any such defallt 5^s: fiue shilings." [2]

Whether this last legislation was effectual we can not discover, but nothing more appears on the record about the stone pits till December 23, 1696, when permission was given to "set up a saw mill upon the mill Riuer about the Stone pits." [3]

In Windsor, William Hayden, who was apparently a mason, had a stone quarry as early as 1644. On February 16, 1651 – 2, it was "granted by the Town that William Hayden shall have leave to dig for a quarry of stone on the Common Hill and shall have it to his own property for seven years, and no man shall molest by digging within a rod of his pit. His limits are within 3 rods square." [4]

---

[1] *Ibid*, p. 63.

[2] *Ibid*, pp. 71–2.

[3] *Ibid*, p. 247.

[4] Stiles, *History of Ancient Windsor*, vol. I, p. 144.

In Middletown the stone now so well known was probably
worked from the first settlement, if, indeed, the ledge did not form
the principal attraction for the first inhabitants.

At a town-meeting at Middletown, in 1665, "it was resolved
that no man should dig or raise stones at the rocks on the east
side of the river but an inhabitant of Middletown, and that twelve
pence should be paid to the town for every tun (sic) of stones
taken."[1]   Field goes on to say, "as early as this they were trans-
ported in vessels to other places."

The truth of this statement is attested by the presence in the
burial ground of the Greene family in Old Warwick, Rhode Island,
of a stone evidently from this quarry, with the date 1668 cut
upon it, and an inscription in lettering undoubtedly of that date
or shortly after it.[2]   The monument to Lady Fenwick also is said
to be of this stone, cut by Matthew Griswold, of Lyme, who, no
doubt, carved the final word over the remains of many of the
colony's dead.[3]

Some of the stones in the Center Church yard in Hartford are
from Middletown, though many of the old ones, from their extremely red color, seem to belong to the deposit of the "stone
pits."

Beyond stone for monuments, however, there was little export-
ing from the quarries, except as the material could be carried up

---

[1] David D. Field, *Statistical Account of the County of Middlesex in Connecticut*, 1819, p. 58.

[2] Almost all 17th century lettering in Rhode Island and Connecticut is in capitals.

[3] Miss Caulkins, *History of New London*, pp. 173-4.

It seems strange that no one has as yet attempted a scientific study of the tombstones of
colonial times; yet in that humble subject will be found the beginnings of stone carving, if not of
sculpture, in America.   Enough has been said about the epitaphs; let some student seriously clas-
sify the motives of the decoration, the styles of lettering—many of them very beautiful—with the
dates of each, the methods of work, and the tools, and finally the men who did the conscientious,
if sometimes uncouth, carving of the time.

and down the river. Portland stone, as a building material, does not occur in Rhode Island, at least, till 1730.

The quarried sandstone, as we find it in the chimneys and cellar walls of the earliest buildings in the Connecticut colony, is of rubble or roughly split work. Squared work with fair quarry-face surface appears only in the topping-out of chimneys, and the only instances of this are the Whitman house, Farmington, and the quaint Root house in Plainville. The Clark house, Farmington, was another instance like the Whitman.

Later, or at any rate at the end of the third period, as in the Webb house, the stone was squared and well wrought, with smooth surfaces and rusticated joints.

We have met with no mention of quarries at New Haven proper. Quarrying, however, if we can trust tradition, must have begun very early in that colony. The stone of which the Whitfield house is built is said to have been a kind of granite, taken from a ledge east of the site.[1] The later chimneys in Guilford are, many of them, built of gneiss or stratified granite, well-squared and laid up like brick on edge, so that the wall of the flue is apparently very thin.

In New London quarrying began with the settlement, for Winthrop built a stone house in 1648. A little later, in 1652, we find a house lot granted to John Stoddard, at Foxen's Hill, with the reservation: "highwaies to be allowed to common land and to fetch stones."[2] "A highway to the Quarry," Miss Caulkins says, was reserved in other grants near this granite ledge, which she

---

[1] R. D. Smith, *History of Guilford.*

[2] Miss Caulkins, New London, p. 84. There were two stone houses at New London beside Winthrop's. *Ibid.*

places a mile from the town, a location which would bring it into the neighborhood of Quaker Hill.

A clear proof that the stone at "Foxen's hill" was quarried and not picked up from the surface is found in the tool-marks of which we have already spoken, which are found on the stone in the cellar of the Hempstead house. These date from at least 1647.[1]

Gneiss is a common material in the old territory of Norwich, or at least a part of it, and there we find, as in the Kinsman house and several others in that region, the same squared stone chimneys which we meet in Guilford, and in South County in Rhode Island. Some very large stones are used, also, especially over the fireplace openings, where earlier or less favored builders used beams of wood. Even the rough work of some of the chimneys is laid in roughly squared blocks of this stone, which splits with great ease and regularity. The whole of extreme eastern Connecticut, as far as we have seen it, is a stone-using country till very late, even after brick were manufactured there.

Quarrying, or "digging," for stone requires tools beside the axe or hammer, namely, the drill and the wedge. These we do not find in the inventories. The estate of Governor Eaton contained two stone-axes,[2] but even he had, at least when he died, no drills or wedges, though we might suppose he could have worked the ledges at his Stony River farm.

BRICK. One of the earliest entries in the town records of Hartford is an order "that Thomas Scott shall keep in good Repayre

---

[1] Mary Hempstead, eldest child of Robert, was born March 26, 1647. *Ibid*, pp. 72, 272.

[2] See Appendix I.

the bridg over the bri[ck kill] swam brooke. . . . . "[1] This is under the date of 1635, though the record was really made in 1638.

Again, in September, 1639, we find the record: "It is orderd that Jo Gening shall sweepe all the Chimnes & haue 6[d] for brick & 3[d] for Clay."[2]

For forty-six years after this entry the records are silent on the subject. Then, "at a town meeting desember 24 1685:"— "The Town Granted Even Davy liberty to make a Brick yarde In the comon Highway to improue it in makeing of Brick as he shall have occasion by or neer Steven Hopkins lot he mayntaining a Good High way up the Hill wher he makes brick . . . . to haue & to hold the same so long as he shall improue it in making of brick & no longer."[3]

Whether Davy gave up the grant, or whether it lapsed at his death, the town, December 29, 1702, "gave liberty to Wilterton Merrill, James Easton & Richard Seamor to make brick for this year in the highway at the place called y[e] brick yard"[4] . . . . This last expression makes it probable that, whatever the fate of Davy, the industry had lived, and that these men were to work on the same spot where their predecessors had labored.

It appears, then, that brick were made very early in Hartford, probably at the instance of the wealthier settlers. The working of the clay deposits may have gone on in an intermittent fashion through the first period, but the grant to Davy, in 1685, marks the serious introduction of the material. There is no brick-work

[1] Conn. Hist. Soc., *Collections*, VI, p. 2.
[2] The same, p. 7.
[3] The same, pp. 217-18.
[4] The same, p. 266.

older than that date now existing in the river towns around Hartford. In Hartford itself only the chimneys of the two Barnard houses might claim greater antiquity, or even as great, and these are almost certainly later additions.

In New Haven we find brick mentioned at the very outset, as in Hartford. In the court order of June 11, 1640, the New Haven Statute of Laborers, as we might call it, " bricklayers . . . . ma^r workemen" were directed not to take above 2s 6d. a day for twelve hours or at least ten, nor above 2s. in winter for at least eight hours.[1]

On January 2, 1644, an order was issued about " the brick kilns in the plains,"[2] and on June 16, 1645, it was noted that " John Benham now makes bricks w^hin the compass of Mr. Eaton's farme."[3]

Richard Beach, before the court, December 8, 1645, " engaged his house, barn, cellar, and well, valued at £40 with the seven acres of land on which it stands, the house and barn and cellar . . . . being built with brick and stone."[4]

On February 23, 1645, the court " Ordered that the clay-pits on the north side of the town . . . . be reserved and kept as a common."[5]

Again, the court, on March 16, 1646, granted that " Edward Shipfield might have liberty to make bricks in the plains under the west rock."[6]

With all this brick manufactured on the spot the fathers of

---

[1] *New Haven Colonial Records*, vol. I, p. 36.
[2] The same, p. 151.
[3] The same, p. 167.
[4] The same, p. 184.
[5] The same, p. 209.
[6] The same, p. 226.

New Haven did some importing — the only instance we know in New England, except the ten thousand brick recorded as to be shipped to Massachusetts Bay in 1628. Mr. Atwater records the finding of the word " London " stamped on the brick which were taken out while a very old house in New Haven, the Atwater mansion, was being torn down.[1] These brick may have come with the lime in the ships which brought the Guilford and Southold people.[2]

The sizes of some of these old brick may be of interest. Those in the chimney of the Dorus Barnard house, Hartford, are 4 by 8¼ inches, and 2⅝ inches thick. The older brick are the larger, as a rule. That is, they were made very large, then smaller, until in our own day they are large again. Two sizes did exist together in Providence in 1715. The brick in the Sheldon house are 2¼ to 2½ inches thick, 3⅞ to 4 inches wide, and 8 inches long. According to Nevill, a standard brick in England in 1685 was 4¼ by 8¾, and 2¼ thick.[3] This is a larger brick, it will be seen, than either of those we have given. It is older.

Early brick are apt to be badly moulded, and are often under-burnt. The clay was put into the moulds by hand, and, as no other pressure seems to have been applied, it never was as solid as in a modern specimen. The burn was purposely undertimed in many cases, for many of the brick, especially in the fillings of the walls of wooden houses, are little better than sun-dried. On the other hand many brick were burned until they were nearly vitrified, and were so composed that this burning brought out a splendid dull blue color, especially on the ends. The artistic use

---

[1] Atwater, *History*, pp. 46, 47, note.

[2] The same, p. 160, *et seq.*

[3] R. Nevill. *Old Cottage and Domestic Architecture in Southwest Surrey*, p. 27.

which the old workmen made of these blue brick we shall explain a little later.

In our day the trade of the mason includes work in both stone and brick. In early colonial days this was not the case. The mason worked in stone entirely, and his brother craftsman, who wrought well-bonded brickwork, went by the name of brick-layer. This distinction, which of course belonged to the England of our forefathers, exists in that country to-day. It is curious to observe that the court order in the Connecticut colony regulating wages speaks of the mason only, while that in New Haven, which we have so often quoted, mentions only the brick-layer. It is probable that from the presence in a town of only one of these craftsmen who thus had to do the work generally given to the other as well as that which by custom fell to him, the uniting of the two crafts in this country came about.

The mason used a trowel and an axe. The bricklayer used the trowel, but instead of the axe he employed a peculiar sort of hammer. Neither of these tools occurs in any inventory we have seen except that of Governor Eaton, where one item includes: "2 ston axes with brick, axes, & trowells."[1] We are tempted to reconstruct the text and to free the word brick from its curious association with the two stone-axes, so that the reading would become "brick axes," even though the comma stands where it does.

LIME. In the river towns, with the possible exception of Saybrook, this material appears, in the earliest days of the colony, to have been wholly wanting. The first mention of it in the town records of Hartford occurs under the date December 30, 1679,

---

[1] See Appendix I.

when: "The Towne gaue Liberty that Major Tallcott capt Nicho Olmsted Mr Jonathan gillbertt Engs Nathaniell Stanly and Caleb Stanley should Looke out sum Conveniant place Neere the Landing place ffor Thomas Viger to Burne Lyme and to sett a small Howse to secure his Lyme. . . . ."

"uppon which the said Vigers did promice the people of the Towne should not giue aboue eighteene pence a Bushel for the Lyme they bought of him."[1]

This entry marks the introduction of lime into Hartford and the surrounding country,[2] but at first the use of the new material must have been confined to the houses of the ministers and of the wealthier people. The employment of it gradually spread till, in the better houses of the third period, we find it universal in the older towns. Clay was still used, however, for a very long time in the outlying settlements, and, for inside work, in the more ancient towns also.

It would be very interesting to know where Vigers obtained his raw material. Did he import oyster-shells from Saybrook or from the New Haven colony? We do not remember an instance of shell lime in Hartford. Or did he receive the limestone from Lime Rock, near Providence, as the people of Massachusetts did even in 1763?

In a letter dated August 19, 1669,[3] and addressed "To my honored friend, Mr. John Winthrop, Governor of Connecticut, &c," Roger Williams says:

"Sir, I have encouraged Mr. Dexter to send you a limestone,

---

[1] Conn. Hist. Soc., *Collections*, VI, p. 189.

[2] Imported lime may possibly have been used as early as 1675.

[3] *Narragansett Club Publications*, vol. VI, pp. 321–2. (*Letters of Roger Williams.*) The Mr. Dexter was Gregory Dexter, one of the most prominent of the early settlers of Providence.

and to salute you with this enclosed. He is an intelligent man, a master-printer of London. . . . . Sir, if there be any occasion of yourself (or others) to use any of this stone, Mr. Dexter hath a lusty team and lusty sons, and very willing heart, (being a sanguine, cheerful man) to do yourself or any (at your word especially) service upon my honest and cheap considerations; . . . ."

It is very possible that we have here the source of Vigers' supply of limestone.

Lime was used in New London from the beginning of the settlement. Shell lime was probably used at the outset, though perhaps a supply was imported from Newport, where an island in the harbor is composed entirely of limestone. It is probable that, if Winthrop took advantage of Roger Williams' introduction to him of Gregory Dexter, owner of a limestone quarry near Providence, some good result therefrom would have come to his own settlement of New London.

In New Haven one of the first entries on the records of the colony speaks of the use of lime. Permission was given November 3, 1639, or, as the record has it, it was "ordered thatt Mr. Hopkins shall have two hogsheads of lime for his present vse, and as much more as will finnish his house as he now intends itt, he thinking that two hogsheads more will serve." [1]

Again, in the order regulating prices, passed June 11, 1640, we find the following:

" Lime well burnt vnslaked, and brought by water to the landing place of the towne, by the bushell heaped, not above 9^d, a bushell, by the hogshead, full gage and so putt in that when

---

[1] *New Haven Colonial Records*, I, p. 24.

carted from the water side to the place where it shall be vsed the hogshead may yet remaine full, not above 5ˢ, ℔ hogshead."[1]

Here we again encounter the question, whence the lime was to be brought to the landing-place of the town. The presence of lime is certain, from the permission given to Hopkins, and it seems almost equally sure that the supply was not very great. It does not seem possible that any lime could have been brought from England by Davenport's company, for they did not come directly to New Haven. The truth probably is that several hogsheads came in the ships which, in the summer of 1639,[2] brought the settlers of Guilford and of Southold to the harbor of Quinnipiac, and that the fathers of New Haven expected more, which may or may not have come, for the commerce of the new colony never attained the limit set by the hopes of good Governor Eaton.

A little later, July 1, 1640, we find that Arthur Halbidz was "charged wᵗh falce measure in lime."[3]

We know, from the Baldwin house, Branford, and from the Painter house, West Haven, that shell lime was used in the New Haven jurisdiction. The amount of imported lime, if there was any, was probably small, and the price of it high. The records, so far as we know them, do not speak directly of shell lime. They do, however, speak of the oyster-shell field[4] and of those accustomed to use it.

Oyster shells can be burnt and thus made to yield a carbonate

---

[1] *New Haven Colonial Records*, I, p. 24.

[2] Atwater, *History*, p. 160, *et seq*. It is possible that the deposit of limestone which, Lambert says, exists in the northern part of the Milford settlement furnished the lime which the New Haven builders would have to be measured with such care.

Limestone was imported into Virginia from Bermuda.

[3] *New Haven Col. Rec.*, I, p. 38.

[4] "Feb. 25, 1641. It is ordered that the common field called the oyster shell field shall be let to such persons whose present need requires it." *N. H. Col. Rec.* I, p. 62.

of lime which will slake, exhibiting in so doing the heat characteristic of stone lime, though not to so great a degree, and producing a hydrate of lime in the same way. Only from sixty to sixty-five per cent. of the bushel of burnt shells was carbonate of lime, however, so that the product did not compare favorably, except in cheapness, with the lime made by burning the natural stone. It was, at times, all that could be obtained, and, such as it was, the settlers used it, and in Virginia[1] found it superior to some kinds to which they had been accustomed in Old England.

The fact that, away from the Sound and the large rivers, we find no lime till very late, is proof that, whether made from shell or from stone, the material was scarce and dear.

MORTAR. In Hartford the early mortar, as we should expect from the records, contains no lime. It is merely clay mixed with hay in a very ancient fashion, found even at Mycenæ and Tiryns, where chopped straw binds the clay mortar, which still exists in the gigantic masonry. All the old chimneys in Hartford and the neighboring towns are laid in this primitive mortar, a fact which accounts for the persistent habit of electing chimney-viewers.

This clay mortar is pretty closely confined to the river towns and to the settlements descended from them. It disappeared slowly after lime was introduced, that is after 1679, as after that date we begin to find lime mortar in the walls of the Connecticut houses.

In New London and its dependencies we have only once found the clay, but in its stead the lime mortar to which we are accustomed in Rhode Island work.

---

[1] Bullock's *Virginia*, p. 3, quoted by Bruce. *Economic History of Virginia*, II, p. 158.

In New Haven, as we might expect from the records already quoted, lime mortar was the rule. An analysis of the mortar from the cellar wall in the Baldwin house at Branford gave the following results:

"Silica (sand)............................. 30.14
Lime Carbonate........................... 51.44
Clay 3.70
Iron Oxide 4.10
Organic................................. 10.10
                                         ————
                                         99.48

Sample also contains traces of calcium hydroxide and of magnesium carbonates." [1]

FOUNDATIONS.   The foundation, or the underpinning as it was called, was built of the stone in common use in each settlement. Sometimes, that is to say, it was of field stone; sometimes of roughly quarried material.

In early times, and in all periods to a certain extent, where lime was scarce, the walls of the cellars were laid up dry. At a later date lime mortar appears, as in the Hollister house; and it is probable that many old walls were pointed over, that is, had their joints filled with mortar, after the new material became common.

But, while around Hartford scarcely any old walls with lime mortar occur before 1680, there were, in the New Haven and New London settlements, some walls, at least, which were laid in that material even at the beginning of those plantations.

[1] Report of analysis made by Prof. E. E. Calder of Brown University.

These remarks generally hold true of the foundations under the chimneys, though here there may be instances of the use of clay mortar.

Where there was no cellar the foundations were laid in trenches which may not always have been carried deep enough to avoid frost — as under the back wall of the lean-to in the John Barnard house, Hartford, built 1767, where the stones seem thrown about by the process of freezing and thawing. Generally, from what we have seen in Rhode Island, the pertinacity with which these old pieces of wall will stay in place, especially at a corner, makes us think that the trenches were fairly deep.

Brick underpinning, now so common, does not appear till quite late, as in the Meggatt house, Wethersfield, 1730, where it is laid in lime mortar. We have already spoken of the elaborately wrought brown stone underpinning of the Webb house, in the same town.

CHIMNEYS. The word chimney, in the mouth of the early craftsmen, meant generally what we call a flue, while our chimney was to them a stack. Thus, in the records of New London, occurs an order, which we have already quoted, about the minister's house which was to have "a stack of stone chimneys in the midst."

The chimney appears very early in the records of Hartford, in a vote which introduces us to that time-honored officer of the river towns, the "chimney-viewer," and informs us that, in September, 1639, certain chimneys in the place were of brick and others of clay. The brick chimneys must have belonged to Pastor Hooker, Governor Haynes, Mr. Wyllys, and a few others. It is very strange that stone stacks should not be mentioned, when the very next order on the same page is the prohibition of digging stone at "Goodman Lord's." Perhaps, because they had much thicker walls than the brick chimneys, they were considered to be secure. It is quite likely, on the other hand, that we must take the record to mean literally that, outside of the wealthy houses, all the chimneys at that early time were of clay.

A clay chimney was either of small logs laid cob-fashion and plastered inside and out with the material from which it took its name, or it was made of four upright posts, between which laths or "wattle"—small interwoven branches—were secured and plastered heavily on both inner and outer faces with clay which had been well mixed with hay. Nor is this form of chimney so much a makeshift of the frontier as many imagine. It was a very ancient type in England, and one which was in good standing, or at least in use, in many places in the mother country at the time our fathers migrated. Mr. Nevill[1] cites the vote of the "chief inhabitants and headboroughs of Clare," a Suffolk town, ordering certain "clay" chimneys of this class to be torn down and the places of them to be supplied with stacks of brick. Stone chimneys may have been new to the earlier settlers of Hartford, who very likely came, as we know some of them did, from brick or timber districts.

Clay chimneys had need, of course, of careful watching on the part of the viewers. But it must not be supposed that, because the office endured for a long time, that form of chimney lasted as long. The stone chimney drove it out of use in a short time; but even the stone chimney, secure as it seemed at first, did not do away with the services of the "looker." These stacks were built of the material which prevailed in the district: field stone, rough-

---

[1] R. Nevill, *Ancient Cottage and Domestic Architecture, etc.*, pp. v–vi (2d edition).

hewn stone from the quarries, or both; and in the Connecticut colony this material was laid in mortar composed of wet clay mixed with hay. As long as the clay was moist it filled the joints very well; but, since the heat of the fire gradually dried it, and since the masonry was generally of inferior workmanship, the clay, in spite of the binding influence of the hay, tended constantly to drop out, leaving passages for sparks and flames. Hence, the habit of electing chimney-viewers persisted so long in the river towns, or at least in Hartford. If this persistence had been due to the continued building of clay chimneys these must have been used as late as 1706, the date of the election of the last chimney-viewer who figures in the Hartford book of town votes.

The tops of the stone chimneys in Connecticut were generally of squared stone laid with considerable care, and capped with one or more thin courses, which project like moulded bands and cast excellent shadows. In the Whitman house, Farmington, there are three courses, forming three successive projections. In the Clark house, in the same town, there were two sharply defined projecting courses, one at very top, the other a little way below it.

There is, just above the point where the slope of the roof meets the face of the stack, a water-table or narrow projecting strip of stone which prevented the rain-water from following down the stone-work into the house. It is curious, however, that the ledge which, in Rhode Island, performs the same office on each side of the chimney above the ridge, is not common in Connecticut in any colony.

The pilastered chimney, too, which, in stone, is characteristic of Rhode Island, and which, in brick, is common to that colony and to Massachusetts, we have never found in the limits of Connecticut.

We have already said that the chimneys of the New Haven and New London jurisdictions are, as a rule, laid in mortar of lime. The tops are generally very plain, and the later ones of stone—stone chimneys lingered long in Guilford—are of squared gneiss, with projecting courses as a cap. Brick tops are very common for stone chimneys in these colonies, as indeed they are in Connecticut, and it is often impossible, in the later examples espe-

WHITFIELD HOUSE

FIGURE 89.—CHIMNEY OF WHITFIELD HOUSE.

cially, to say whether these are original or whether they simply replace older tops which have succumbed to the weather.

The most interesting chimney in Connecticut, and the oldest, is that at the north end of the Whitfield house at Guilford. This is built of roughly quarried stone laid in lime mortar, and now covered with cement stucco. It is very wide at the base, where it projects some three feet from the end of the house; and as it

rises it narrows on each side—but not on the back which main-
tains the same projection—a narrowing accomplished by the same
off-sets and sloped weatherings which we find in church but-

FIGURE 90.—CHIMNEY OF THOROUGHGOOD HOUSE.

tresses, and which we usually associate with "Gothic" architecture. This off-setting of chimneys was common enough in England, and here, too, in brick and stone houses, though all other
examples in New England have disappeared. It still exists in the

brick house of Adam Thoroughgood, 2d, built 1640–50,[1] in Princess Anne County, Virginia. There are traces of it also still remaining, though obscured by alterations, in the Malvern house, near Malvern Hill, in the same State. This also is of brick.[2]

The brick chimneys are of the same general form as those of stone. We have already remarked on the number of instances in which a brick topping-out of a stone stack occurs. In one example, the Dorus Barnard house, Hartford, the chimney is of stone up to the second floor, and of brick above that point, as in the Field house and the Waterman house in Providence. The brick stack no doubt replaced a ruinous construction of stone. It is worthy of remark that the stone part of this chimney appears on the outside of the house at the back, and was not originally covered. This is unique. There is a chimney at Saybrook which appears on the outside for one story at the end of a house, but this coming to the outside at the back, where there was, as a rule, a foot or more between chimney and studs, is very peculiar.[3]

The brick tops, whether they crown chimneys which are wholly of brick or chimneys which are of stone to the roof or to some point below it, are of a very plain type. That of the Sheldon Woodbridge house, Hartford, has two string courses, each consisting of one projecting course, drawn around it at different heights. The most picturesque decoration occurs in the Talcott house, a late example, at Glastonbury. In this stack there are two strings

---

[1] We know this house by photographs kindly loaned to us by the Virginia Historical Society through its former Corresponding Secretary, Mr. Philip A. Bruce, author of *The Economic History of Virginia in the XVIIth Century.*

[2] See drawing in *Battles and Leaders of the Civil War*, vol. II, p. 422. Note the pattern on the chimney.

[3] There is a brick — end one — story house — or story-and-a-half — in Guilford, the gable of which, above the brick, is of wood.

at different levels, but they consist of courses which are not of
simple projecting brick, but, as the drawing in Figure 91 shows,
of brick set with their angles outward, so as to make a horizontal
saw-tooth or zig-zag. This is not uncommon between two plain
projecting courses, but, used alone and with as bold projection and
strong coloring as this, for many of the brick are blue, it is a
rare and striking combination. The same effect is repeated, not
quite so well, in a house in East Hartford. Beyond these two

FIGURE 91.—CHIMNEY OF TALCOTT HOUSE.

examples we have seen no other instance of this original treatment, which certainly deserves to be put into use again.

The chimneys of the Sheldon Woodbridge house are in the
end walls, and here, as we have already explained, the north wall
is practically only the back of the stack. In this north wall we
find the earliest remaining example of the use of the blue headers
to which we referred in the pages on brick. The work is laid
partly in Flemish, partly in running a bond—which, except lengthwise, is no bond at all. Five courses are laid all stretchers—bricks

set lengthwise in the wall—and then come two courses laid in Flemish bond, that is with the stretchers and headers—bricks with their length across the wall—in alternation. The bond is so arranged, too, that the headers in the upper course come over the centers of the stretchers of the lower course, and the reverse, as will be plain from the Figure. And, as the headers are burned

to a dark blue, it will be seen that a very effective, though simple, pattern is the result. In the gable of this same north end is a quite complicated piece of herring-bone work, as it is called, where the brick, laid zig-zag—the meaning of herring-bone— are combined into a rectangular panel.

This use of blue headers persisted long in the Connecticut valley, and produced some very artistic results. There is one house in South

FIGURE 92—BRICK DETAILS OF SHELDON WOODBRIDGE HOUSE.

Windsor, built as late as the first quarter of this century, which has worked out upon its walls in blue headers just such a diaper pattern of intersecting diagonal lines as we see in old French work, or in the old walls of Hampton Court Palace. The checker pattern of light and dark brick is characteristic of old work in Virginia, and the Connecticut fondness for Flemish bond is also a strong reminder of the Old Dominion. The same traditions of brick-laying must have come with the settlers of both colonies.[1]

The chimneys of the oldest type had but two fireplaces, which were never very large. The opening was spanned by a wooden lintel, which, in the Paterson house, Berlin, rested at each end on a wooden tie reaching from face to face of the stack, and supporting in the same manner the lintel of the opposite fireplace, while it served also to tie together the clumsily built stone-work of the chimney.

Fireplaces in the second story were rare in early times, and were confined to the houses of the richer sort. The stack above the roof, therefore, generally contained one large flue or two flues separated by a " withe " of thin stone on edge, and was oblong in plan. In the oldest houses it often went through the roof behind the ridge, or at any rate with its center behind the peak, though this must not be relied on as a mark of an old house, for the Benjamin house, Milford, which is very late, has this characteristic.

The hearths of the stone chimneys were of flat stone, as were sometimes those of the brick chimneys also. Brick hearths, on the other hand, occur not only with brick chimneys, but with stone where the old wide fireplace has been filled up, as many of our plans and sections will show, with a smaller brick fireplace which has an oven at one side of it.

This occurs in the old hall very often, but it also meets us in the new fireplace built at the back of the old chimney when the lean-to was added to the house. These new fireplaces are backed up against the old stack, which is sometimes cut into to accom-

---

[1] In Rhode Island, English bond is the rule. Flemish, though used, appears generally only in belt courses. The Israel Sayles house, Moshassuck, has a fine three-course belt in Flemish bond with blue headers. The date is c. 1730.

modate them, and the flue is run up along the back of the original chimney, generally in a clumsy way impossible to mistake, and is either taken through the roof behind the old top, as at the Whitman house, so that the joint is apparent, or is blended with the old flues into a new cap, so that it is only in the garret and the lean-to chamber that the addition can be detected. The L-shaped plan occurs above the roof, notably in the John Barnard and in the Sheldon Woodbridge house, Hartford. In the Fitz-Greene Halleck house, Guilford, and in the Shelley house, Madison, both late, the flues are combined to form a cross-shaped plan above the ridge.

PLASTER. This appears in Hartford, Windsor, and Wethersfield, in the last quarter of the seventeenth century, or about the time Thomas Viger set up his lime kiln in the year 1679.[1] Its introduction was doubtless gradual. The richer houses would, of course, be plastered first.

For the minister's house in Simsbury, in 1697, were required, among other materials, a "load of lath timber,"[2] which may have meant the laths themselves, or the oak boards from which they were to be riven, and "two days' plastering."

We do not know, even approximately, the date at which plaster came into use in New London, but we may assume that it was somewhere near the time at which it appeared in Hartford, though, from the prevalence of lime in the early work, we might be justified in claiming an earlier introduction.

In this, as in other material, the superior wealth of New Haven put it in advance of the other settlements.

---

[1] The *Windsor Records* contain an item of £5 for lath and nails for the meeting-house in 1661.
[2] A. C. Bates, *Rev. Dudley Woodbridge, his Church Record at Simsbury in Conn., 1697-1710.* H'f'd, 1894.

In an order concerning wages, passed in May, 1641, we find the following:

"Plastering, for drawing and carrying water, scaffolding, lathing, laying and finishing the plastering, provideing and paying his labo^rer, haveing the lime clay, sand, hayre, hay wth materialls for scaffolding layd neare the place.

By the yeard for seeling 4—ob, for the side walls, being whole or in great paines 4^d, betwixt the studs, the studs not measured, 5^d—ob. rendring between the studs 2^d."[1]

The lime, sand, and hair in this list of the ingredients of the plaster which existed or was to exist in New Haven, are familiar in our modern work. Not so the clay and the hay, however. The presence of these admits of two explanations. One is that the mixture was used for filling between the studs, in the fashion familiar to the carpenters in their old home, whether the filling was plastered on the outside with lime or was covered with clapboards. The other is that hay and clay were used, either on lath or on brick filling, as a first coat. Both these methods were no doubt in use. The former is the older, and disappeared so soon as brick became common. It still survives in the back wall, or a part of it, in the Roger Williams house at Salem, where it can be seen in the garret over the old hall chamber.

Lathing, laying, and finishing is the process used for "seeling" or plastering overhead. Rendering is the name given to the first coat on the side walls, because these were of clay and hay or of brick filled in between the studs. "Rendering" is to-day the English workman's expression for the first coat on a brick wall, while "laying" means to him the first coat on laths, just as it

---

[1] *New Haven Colonial Records*, vol. I, p. 55.

meant to the plasterer in early New Haven. These names for the processes have disappeared from our New England vocabulary.

The word "paine" or pane, means the same as panel, and is used for the wide space between the posts at the corners, or between these and the posts at the doors or at any intermediate point, in distinction from the little spaces between the studs which, because of the greater care required, took more time and hence cost more.

Plaster was in use at Stamford as early as 1644, for, according to the court record of that year, an Indian struck a woman of the town with a lathing hammer.[1]

II. Wood-Work and Framing.

BOARDS AND TIMBER. Our forefathers brought over with them certain ideas about the sizes of timber, the measurement of it, and the names by which the different varieties should be known. Although the sizes they used coincide in remarkable ways with those we have inherited from them, the mode of measuring and the names were often quite different. In the matter of names, we have discarded several terms which are still found in the vocabulary of the English architects and builders.

The saw mill was not an early institution in Connecticut. The pit appears first and holds its own for many years. In Hartford it was voted, January 7, 1639: "that whoesoever hath digged any Saw pitts or other pitts not now in vse—shall ffill vpe the same . . . . or whosoever hath digged Anny such pitt . . . . and is in vse he shall Cover the same when they are absent."[2]

---

[1] *New Haven Col. Rec.*, I, p. 135. The word lath may mean only clay-work, it must be noted.
[2] Conn. Hist. Soc., *Collections*, VI, p. 11.

In these pits. with their top-sawyers and pitmen, boards and slit work were sawn, as in the following order of February 10, 1639: "noe man shall take aboue iiij[s] vj[d] ffor saweing of Boards, and v[s] vj[d] a[c] for slit woork, the tymber beeing squard and layd at the pitt." [1]

Two years later, June 7, 1641, the price had fallen somewhat, perhaps because labor was cheaper: "Also sawyers shall not take abouve 4s. 2d. for slit work or three-inch plank, nor above 3s. 6d. for boards, by the hundred. Also boards shall not be sold for above 5s. vid. the hundred." [2]   Boards here are of any width, and an inch or an inch and a quarter thick. The English rule for the width of boards is between 4 and 9 inches, but the size of our trees soon threw that into disuse. Slit work was halved boarding, i. e. half an inch thick.

The court order in New Haven establishes the prices for working lumber, and gives a very clear picture of the process of getting out board, plank, and framing timber.

The price for felling comes first in the section which treats of heavy timber, for the old order, which bears the mark of Eaton's long acquaintance with mercantile affairs, is very methodical.

"Falling of timber, that w[ch] is full 2 foote ou[r] or above, one wth another not above 3[d] a foote; lesser timber, being yett full 18 inches ou[r] and under 2 foote, not above 2[d] a foote; all other trees of lesser size not 18 inches ou[r], either by dayes wages, or as shall be reasonably agreed." [3]   The order of May, 1641, re-enacts this of June, 1640, almost in the same words, with a reduction of prices. It speaks, however, of "fellers of timber," and

[1] Conn. Hist. Soc., *Collections*, vol. VI, p. 28.
[2] *Col. Rec. of Conn.*, p. 65.   See also Conn. Hist. Soc., *Collections*, VI, pp. 27-8.
[3] *New Haven Col. Records*, I, p. 37.

fixes their wages as: "in som^r nott above 18^d, in winter nott above 14^d." [1]   This difference between the winter and the summer wage was based on the legal day's work, which, it was enacted, should be ten or twelve hours in summer and only eight in winter.

There were a good many notions, some of them excellent, which were current in the England of our forefathers as to the time and method of cutting and seasoning timber.   These ideas came over with the old carpenters and woodmen, but we can trace them only in the quality of the timber these men put into the houses they built.   We can not tell whether the trees were ever "cut down after the full of the moone, that the sap rot not. *Prove not worm eaten.*" [2]   We do know that the old oak must have been pretty well seasoned in those houses which have survived, for, while the exposed parts of the stick might have done their seasoning in the building, it would not be so with the joints. These will stand, as far as we have observed, until water gets into them.   In unseasoned sticks dry rot attacks the end fibres of the tenons where they abut against the pins or treenails.

There are instances which go contrary to this general statement, notably the trouble which the New Haven men had over the rotting "pillars and groundsells" of the meeting-house; [3] and in this case we can prove that there was no seasoning of the frame, for an order of the court, of November 25, 1639, reads: " Itt is ordered that a meeting house shall be built forthw^{t}h, fifty

---

[1] *New Haven Col. Rec.*, I, p. 53.

[2] *The Gate of Languages Unlocked,* J. A. Comenio, trans. by Tho. Horn.   Sixth ed., London, 1643, in the Library of the Connecticut Historical Society.   The passage is in section 528.   The words in italics are in that type in the margin.

[3] *New Haven Col. Rec.*, I, p. 423-4.

foote square, and that the carpenters shall fall timber where they can finde it till allotm[ts] be laid out." [1]

The lack of ventilation in the cellars produced dry rot, so that few floors retain their original frames. The lowness of the underpinnings, and the old habit of banking up around the house in winter with turf, leaves, or sea-weed, caused an alternate wetness and dryness fatal not only to the base board and the lowest courses of shingles or clapboards, but also to the sill and the posts. Most failures in the frames of these houses are due to decay in the sill or at the feet of the posts.

When the tree was on the ground and the branches had been cut off, the next operation was that of "crosscutting" or sawing the trunk into the lengths desired, which was to be paid for "by the day, as other lab[rs], or as shall be agreed wth equity." [2] This work was done by two men with the large two-handed "crosscut" saw, also called a "frameing saw," which is used now as much as it was then on all heavy framing, and which every one has seen.

These two processes disposed of, the order goes on to give the proper wage for hewing. Mark that, while framing timber was sometimes sawn, as we shall see, there is no talk of sawing these heaviest sticks. The law says:

"Hewing and squaring timber of severall sizes, one w[t]h another, butt the least 15 inches square, well done that a karfe or planke of 2 inches thicke being taken off on 2 sides, the rest may be square for boards or for other vse, not above 18[d] a tun girt measure. And for timber sleightly hewen a price proportion-

---

[1] *New Haven Col. Rec.*, I, p. 25.

[2] The same, p. 37.

able, or by day wages.   As for sills, beames, plates or such like timber, square hewen to build w'h, not above a peny a foote running measure." [1]

This kerf was not a saw cut, but the slab, as we should call it, the side of the round stick necessarily hewn away to reduce it to a beam with two flat sides.   The hewing down was done, as Figure 93 explains, by cutting " scores " at intervals along the stick as deep as it was intended to hew, and then splitting away the wood between them.   These old score-marks are almost always plainly seen on all framing timber which was not planed.   If the log was to be sent to the saw-pit for conversion into boards the hewing evidently stopped here.   If not, the log was turned over and the work went on till the state was reached which is described as " square hewn to build with."

THE KERF - SCORING - SAWING

FIGURE 93.

The smaller sticks must have been held in a " clave-stock " while they were being hewn.   This was the same as the standing vise which stair builders, in the days of curved stairs, used in hewing out their rails.   It was awkward to hew the smaller timber, however, and much of it was sawed or split.   The rafters in the Hempstead house, which go back to 1647, are not only sawed but planed.   Those in the Joseph Whiting house are sawed.

Hewing was by no means the long and wearisome process it is sometimes thought to have been.   Any one who has seen work

---

[1] *New Haven Col. Rec.*, I. p, 37.
[2] *The Gate of Knowledge Unlocked*, § 527.

go on in a ship-yard knows that a skillful man with a sharp broad-axe (the tool these old woodmen used) can hew heavy timber with a deftness and certainty which others cannot attain, even in sharpening a lead pencil with a small knife.

The method was not that of a modern, or even of an ancient, saw-mill, but it was a natural one to the minds of those who used it, and it remained the chief method of getting out framing timber till long after the Revolution. In the remoter parts of the State there are carpenters now living who have wrought their timber in that way. The early craftsmen had attained in their hewing a wonderful degree of skill. They made no false strokes.

One reason for hewing may have been found in the curves usual in the posts and even the girts in England, traces of which, as explained under the word " post," can be found in the work here in New England.

Let us return to our New Haven law. The heaviest hewn timber is measured by quite a different standard from that which we now use. At present all lumber is measured by the board foot, a square foot one inch thick, and is reduced to terms of this standard no matter what the cross section may be. A beam twelve by sixteen inches contains sixteen board feet for every foot of its length. A board twelve inches by one inch contains one board foot for every foot of length. In old New Haven we have the " tun," a measure not unfamiliar in Great Britain to-day,[1] but utterly forgotten among ourselves. It meant forty cubic feet of round timber, or fifty-four of square.[2] The girt measure was one-

---

[1] " At Dublin, deals are sold by the London or Dublin standard of 120, 12 x 9 x 3 ; square timber by the ton of 40 feet, string measurement." Gwilt, *Encyclopædia of Architecture*, p. 504.

[2] *Imperial Dictionary.*

quarter of the circumference of the log, which was reckoned as the side of the square beam which could be cut from the trunk.[1]

We will now turn our attention to the log with a kerf hewn off on each of its two sides, and follow the process of converting it into boards. This was done by placing the stick over the saw-pit in which one man, the pitman, stood and moved one end of the "whipsaw," a two-handed affair exactly like that used for cross-cutting, except that, as it had to be a splitting or ripping saw, as carpenters call it, its teeth had more "hook," that is, were bent forward more than those of the cross-cut saw. This difference in the teeth can be readily seen in the smaller handsaws which now serve similar purposes.[2] Above the log stood the top-sawyer, whose name has passed into a by-word, and he managed the upper end of the heavy tool with which the two worked. The other tools needed were a wedge to put in the end of the cut so that it should not bind the saw, as, on account of its length, it was apt to do, and hooks to secure the log, with rollers and crow-bars wherewith to move it.

All this is quaintly set forth in the old law, which ordains the wages of the laborers and the price they may ask as follows:

"Sawing by the hundred not above 4ˢ 6ᵈ for boards. 5ˢ for planks. 5ˢ 6ᵈ for slitworke and to be payd for no more than they cutt full and true measure. If by the dayes worke, the top man or he that guides the worke and phaps findes the tooles, not above 2ˢ 6ᵈ a day in somʳ, and the pitt ma̅, and he whose skill and charge is lesse, not above 2ˢ, and a proportionable in winter

---

[1] Gwilt, *Encyclopædia of Architecture*, p. 1203.

[2] That is, splitting and cutting. A whipsaw belonged to Gov. Eaton. See Appendix I.

as before.   If they be equall in skill and charge, then to agree or divide the 4ˢ 6ᵈ betwixt them." [1]

Boards, we see here, are measured by the hundred; not the hundred of square or board feet, but of boards, and probably "six score" went to the hundred at that.   This was the same standard as that used in Hartford.

These boards were an inch or an inch and a quarter thick. Slit work meant boards half an inch thick, as at present in England. [2]   Plank were, as now in this country, two inches thick.

In New Haven slit work is more costly than plank, while in Hartford it was of the same expense.   We need not wonder, for the extra labor, at two-and-sixpence a day in the old saw-pit, which the thinner "slit" board required, with its three cuts of the heavy whipsaw to the one needed for the plank, fully offset the difference in thickness of wood.

It is evident that all kinds of timber were sold in the woods to be hauled to the building by the carpenter or the owner, according as either was bound to furnish the materials. [3]   The old order closes with a list of the prices of the various classes of sawn lumber in the woods and "in the towne."

"Inch bords to be sould in the woods nott above 5ˢ 9ᵈ ℔ hundred.

halfe inch boards in the woods not above 5—2 ℔ 100.

2 inch planke in the woods not above 7—0 ℔ 100.

---

[1] *New Haven Col. Rec.*, I, p. 36.

[2] Gwilt, *Encyclopædia*, p. 1159.   See the definition of *deal*, *board*, and *plank*, at this same reference.

[3] In New London we find the town contracting with John Elderkin, August 29, 1651, to build a meeting-house for which they were to "cary the tymber to the place and find nales."   Miss Caulkins, *History*, p. 108.   Sawing timber, boards, and planks, mentioned February 25, 1659-60. Miss Caulkins, *History*, p. 93.

inch boards sould in the towne not above 7—9 ℔ 100.

halfe inch boards in the towne, nott above 6—2 ℔ 100.

2 inch planke in the towne not above 11—0 ℔ 100.

Sawen timber 6 inches broad and three inches thicke ⎱ ¾ far^d
in the woods running measure not above   ⎰ ℔ foote

   in the towne not above 1^d ℔ foote.

Sawne timber 8 inches square running measure in ⎱ P^d ¼
the woods not above   ⎰ ℔ foote.

   in the towne not above 2^d ℔ foote."

The first saw-mill in the present limits of Connecticut was probably that of William Goodwin, which must have been set up some time before we hear of it, for the court, on October 3, 1654, gave him liberty "to use timber from waste land to keep the saw mill at work."[1]

Governor Winthrop, however, had received from the General Court, September 8, 1653, liberty to find a place for a saw-mill, provided it "do not prejudice plantations or farms already laid out."[2] It is probable that this surveillance exercised by the court over so private an enterprise as a saw-mill arose from the fear that all the good timber would be cut off and exported, a fear which finds expression more than once in the acts of the Hartford town councils, as well as in this of the General Court.[3] It may be, therefore, that his saw-mill was the earliest; and again, some nameless timber merchant may have been the pioneer in sawing by water power. A town vote in Hartford, December 27, 1686, speaks of "the Sawmills on the west Side of Connecticut

---

[1] *Conn Col. Rec.*, I, p. 262.

[2] Same, p. 246.

[3] Conn. Hist. Soc., *Collections*, VI, pp. 188, 221.

riuor within this Towne Ship,"[1] implying quite a number of them. Liberty was given to establish such a mill in Hartford in 1696.[2]

The method of sawing boards, whether by hand or by mill, which we have been describing, consists, as *A* in Figure 94 will show, in a series of parallel cuts from the top to the bottom of the log, as the latter is moved sidewise upon its supports. This does well enough for common boards, and in oak or soft pine would be respectable for flooring. It was, no doubt, the common way of sawing, as it is to-day. But it produces mainly what are called "slashway" boards, and can not be relied on where first-

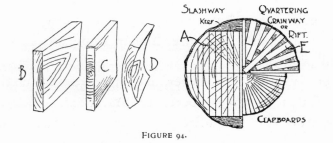

FIGURE 94.

class flooring or fine boards for cabinet or joiner work are required. The reason of this will be apparent on a little study of Figure 94. At *A* we see that the cut of the saw crosses the annual rings at a constantly varying angle. It is at right angles to them only at the middle of the log. At the side, in a large stick, it would be nearly parallel with them. The result of this, familiar to every one who has endured that curse of housekeepers,

[1] Conn. Hist. Soc., *Collections*, VI, p. 221.

[2] The same, p. 247.

"Laid out to Sec. Allyn, Mar. 19th, 1672-3, a neck of land abutting on the Saw-Mill River, commonly called Hoccanum River, towards the south and towards the east" &c. *Conn. Col. Rec.*, II, p. 178.

This was granted for a saw-mill May 11, 1671. *Ibid*, p. 147.

a slashway hard pine floor, is shown at B in the same figure. Here we have the curving layers plainly marked, while in C, supposed to be the board from the center of the log, we have the even grain. Now the even grain makes the better board by far. The curved-grain board will splinter with wear, like the aforesaid floor; and further, since this splintering is of no account in oak, it will curl and warp in the direction of the rings, that is, it will tend to become more and more curved, as in D. For this reason all first-class flooring, and all wood for fine work, is sawn as nearly as possible on the radii of the log, as in E, so that each board shall be like the center one, B, of the other method. Wood thus sawn is called "quartered" in oak, and "grainway" or "rift" in hard pine or other woods. The structure of oak, in which there are medullary rays running out like radii of the circle from the heart of the tree to its bark, lends a peculiar beauty to this method of sawing, for the saw runs parallel to these rays, or cuts them at a low angle, and thereby produces the beautiful "silver grain," as it is called, of quartered oak.

All this was well known to the mediæval joiners,[1] and had been handed down to our forefathers. Once in a while we meet a piece of framing timber, always small, which is beautifully quartered, and which makes us suspect that we have found a specimen of that sort of cutting. It may be that we have only run across the center-piece of the slashway process, which, of course, was cut on the radius. Still, from the size, it may be that it was of the other kind. The quartering was more difficult to saw, as will be evident from the figure, so that, among the mediæval men, and no doubt among our old craftsmen, the log, after two saw cuts on

---

[1] Viollet-le-duc, *Dictionnaire raisonné du mobilier français*, Tome, VI, pp. 346, 347, note. Gwilt, *Encyclopædia of Architecture*, p. 505.

the diameters at right angles, was split up on the radial lines,[1] or was "rived," to use their old word which still survives in our "rift" as a name for the kind of board which is sawed in that radial fashion. Old Evelyn, in his *Sylva*, says: "Timber which is cleft is nothing so obnoxious to reft and cleave as what is hewn; nor that which is squared as what is round."[2] It is probable that most of the oak from which our old joiners wrought chests, livery cupboards, and the various kinds of tables was, at least in the smaller sizes, of this split manner of working. The heavy top, in several boards two inches thick, which covers the mighty draw table now owned by the Connecticut Historical Society, a table which Dr. Lyon saw strong grounds for assigning to the household furnishing of Governor Winthrop,[3] is of this quartered oak.

THE FRAME.

SILLS. The sill or groundsill as it was often called—"grundsell" it was sometimes spelt—was the heavy timber which lay immediately upon the underpinning and into which were framed the posts and studs of the wall. In the oldest examples, as in the Baldwin house, Branford, and the Hempstead house, New London, it projects into the room. Later on it is below the floor as it is now-a-days. In the latter case the joists of the first floor are framed into it; in the former these joists are built into

---

[1] Viollet-le-duc, *Dictionnaire raisonné du mobilier français*, Tome, VI, pp. 346, 347, note. Gwilt, *Encyclopædia of Architecture*, p. 634.

[2] Gwilt, *Encyclopædia of Architecture*, p. 505. Evelyn's *Silva, with notes by Jno. Hunter*, London, 1825, vol. II, p. 233.

[3] Dr. I. W. Lyon, *Colonial Furniture in New England*, pp. 195, 196, 218. Dr. Lyon thinks this table was made in England.

the stone wall, and the sill runs along the top of the wall independently of them, as in Figure 83.

In size the sill is eight or nine inches square. Those in the Painter house and the Hollister house, both of the second period, are nine by nine. That in the Gleason, c. 1650-60, is eight by eight. That in the older part of the Hempstead house, 1647, is very nearly seven by seven. Its exact size can only be estimated, as it is partly covered, though it does appear in the room.

POSTS. In the house of the first period, or of any period where there were but two rooms and no lean-to, there were eight posts, one at each corner, one at each side of the entry on the front, and one at each side of the chimney on the rear. When the lean-to was added four more posts, corresponding in position to the four in the back wall, were added to the number. After the "upright" or two-story houses on the lean-to plan came into vogue in the third period there was, in some instances, notably the Meggatt house, and one side of the Webb house, Wethersfield, as also the Sheldon house, Hartford, a doing away with the intermediate posts on the end and in the middle of the house, the line of posts, that is, which represented the back wall in the original houses. The majority of the wide two-story dwellings, however, are like the Kinsman house, Versailles, and the Belden-Butler house, Wethersfield, in that they retain the full number of twelve posts.

The posts are tenoned and pinned, or simply tenoned into the sills. They support the second floor by means of the girts which are mortised into them. The corner posts take two girts each, the intermediates take three. Again the posts carry the third floor and the roof by means of the plates and the end girts which are framed upon their heads. All this, as well as the number and disposition of the posts, will be plainer to the reader if he will refer to the framing drawings in Figures 96, 97, 98, and Plates I to VII.

Let us now proceed to analyse the joints we have enumerated, beginning with those at the second-story level. We shall consider only the unbroken posts under this heading. Those which are complicated with the overhang we will consider under that division. A plain corner post, then, with its end girt and back girt, would be what is shown at *A* in Figure 95. The relation of end and front girt would be the same. In the upper part of Plate I is seen the east side of the intermediate post at the rear of the Gleason house at the rear of the chimney, post "*D*" on the plan of that house. It will be noted that each of these posts in each story is about three inches deeper at the top than at the bottom. This does not occur in Rhode Island work, and not always in Connecticut, but it is very common, almost common enough to be called the rule. It will be interesting to compare this gradual increase with the sharp bracket form in the Roger Williams house in Salem. The bracket is sometimes used in the first story in Connecticut, where the post is only one story high, as in lean-tos. It is generally a mark, where used, of the top of the post.

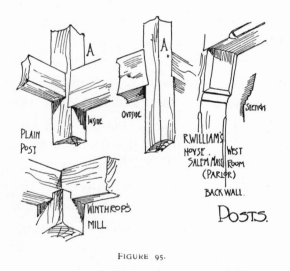

FIGURE 95.

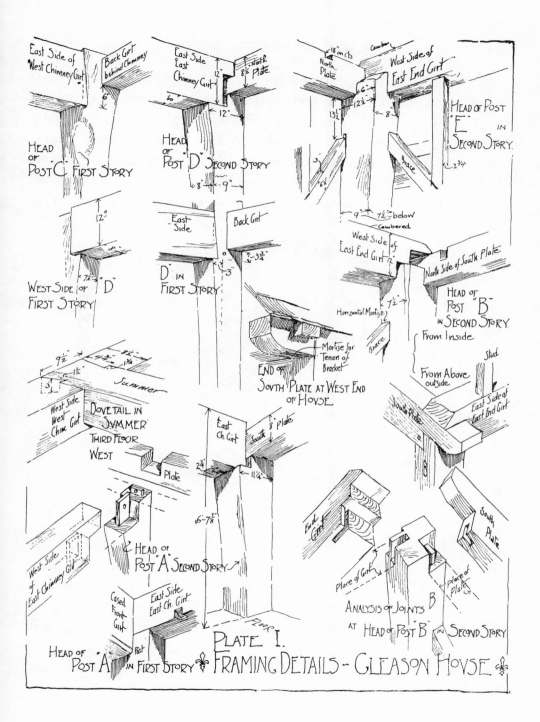

East Side of West Chimney Girt

Back Girt behind Chimney

6

HEAD OF POST "C" FIRST STORY

East Side East Chimney Girt

12"

8½" North Plate

30

12"

HEAD OF POST "D" SECOND STORY

8" — 9"

18" on cts.

Camber

North Plate

West Side of East End Girt

6"

13½"

12½"

8

HEAD OF POST "E" IN SECOND STORY

3

6½

Brace

2¾

12"

7½" D

WEST SIDE of D FIRST STORY

East Side

Back Girt

D IN FIRST STORY

3½"

3

9" 7½" below Cambered

West Side of East End Girt 12

North Side of South Plate

7½"

HEAD OF POST "B" IN SECOND STORY

From Inside

Horizontal Mortise

Mortise for Tenon of Bracket

END OF SOUTH PLATE AT WEST END OF HOUSE

Brace

From Above outside

Stud

South Plate

East Side of East End Girt

9½"

8½

1¾

3½

1½

Summer

West Side West Chim Girt

DOVETAIL IN SUMMER THIRD FLOOR WEST

Plate

East Ch. Girt

South

8" Plate

2¼

11¼

16-7⅞

HEAD OF POST "A" SECOND STORY

West Side of East Chimney Girt

Cased Front Girt

East Side East Ch. Girt

Post

Floor

HEAD OF POST "A" IN FIRST STORY

End Girt

Place of Girt

South Plate

place of Plate Girt

ANALYSIS OF JOINTS B AT HEAD OF POST "B" IN SECOND STORY

PLATE. I. FRAMING DETAILS — GLEASON HOUSE

The skill of the old carpenter is most apparent where it was tested most severely, and this, outside the overhangs, occurred at the top of the post, where the third-story girts met the plate. The strange-looking and complicated but really brilliant joints[1] are better explained in the plates, which give the framing details of the several different houses, than by many pages of printed description. The corner post is apt to be the most complicated, as

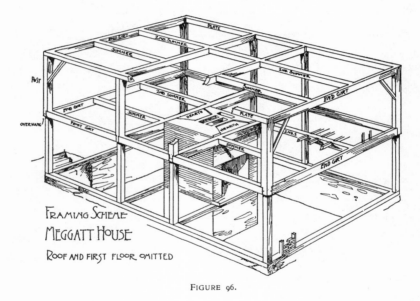

FRAMING SCHEME
MEGGATT HOUSE
ROOF AND FIRST FLOOR OMITTED

FIGURE 96.

post E in the Gleason house. A peculiarity here is the cutting down of the head of the post to form a seat for each beam, leaving thereby a square projection in the angle. This occurs in Rhode Island and in some Massachusetts work, but it is not common in Connecticut. We find it in the posts of Winthrop's mill

---

[1] Our sketches of these joints are more numerous than of any others, for not only are they more interesting but nearly always more accessible.

at New London, which are the only parts of that structure dating back to the original settlement.

The BRACES which secure the angles between the posts and the sills, girts, or plates, are shown in the detailed sketches or in the perspectives of the frames. The object of them is to keep the corner square. This they do not always succeed in doing, to judge by the present condition of the houses. Sometimes many of them are used, sometimes few. The Benjamin house has a great number. Where few are used they are sometimes long, and are run from the post down to the girt in the second-story wall, as in the Gleason and the Patterson house, instead of from the post up to the plate in the usual manner. This method may be of Kentish origin, for it occurs in old half-timber work in that county. A brace under a girt inside the house, that is, not in the outer wall, occurs in the Sheldon house, Hartford.

The second-story GIRTS are the heavy timbers framed between the posts at the level of the second floor. The END GIRT, as its name implies, runs from one corner post to the other—or from corner post to intermediate where the house is two rooms deep—at one end or the other of the building. The CHIMNEY GIRT spans the hall or the parlor and continues its way across the kitchen at the back also where that room exists, whether in a lean-to or in a full two-story house, as the plans and the perspectives of the framing in Figures 96, 97, 98, will explain. In some cases, as in the Meggatt, the Sheldon, and in one side of the Webb house, the end girt and the chimney girt run from corner to corner, or from intermediate post on the front to intermediate on the back, with no post at the line of the rear wall of hall or parlor.

The FRONT GIRT, in three sections, spans the intervals between the four posts on the front. Where there is a framed overhang there are two of these front girts side by side, as will be explained more in detail when we consider the overhangs.

The BACK GIRT traverses the back wall of the house in the

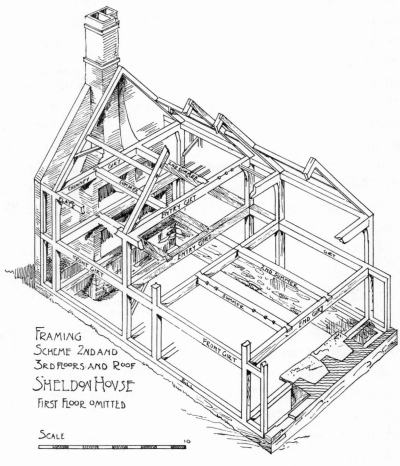

FIGURE 97.

same three sections which we noted in the case of the front girt. In lean-to houses there is really no back girt, for a plate is put into the rear wall to carry the rafters and joists, and the former back girt, which still retains its place in the framing, see Figure 65, becomes a sort of second summer. This is actually the case in those houses already mentioned, where the end girt and the chimney girt run across the house with no posts except at the ends of them. Then these girts support both the main summer and the second summer—the old back girt—just as if there were two summers in the width of the house. For this late and rare

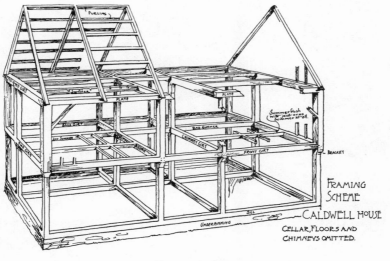

FIGURE 98.

manner we refer the reader to the framing of the Sheldon house in Figure 97, and to that of the Meggatt house in Figure 96. The usual fashion he will find illustrated in Figure 98, which sets forth the framing of the Caldwell house in Guilford. Many of the sections given with the descriptions of the houses will explain the relation between the lean-to plate and the original back girt, a relation the same whether the lean-to is original or an addition.

It is in order to receive these second-story girts that the posts

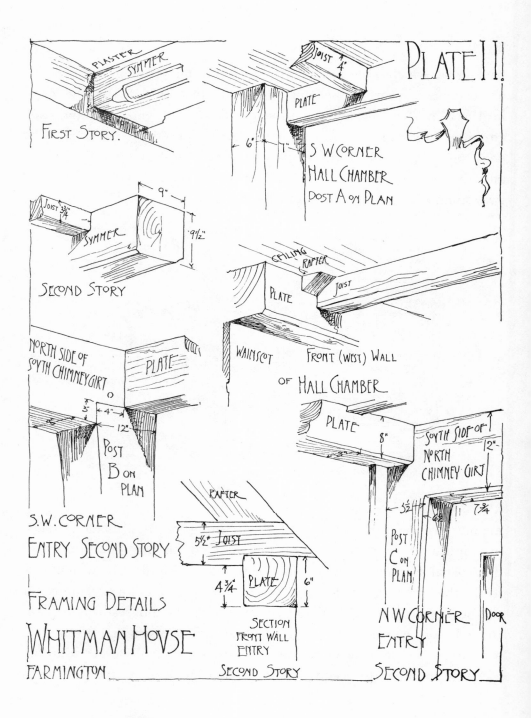

FIRST STORY.

PLASTER
SYMMER

JOIST 4"
PLATE
6" 7"

S W CORNER
HALL CHAMBER
POST A ON PLAN

PLATE II!

JOIST 3¾"
9"
SYMMER
9½"

SECOND STORY

CEILING
RAFTER
PLATE
JOIST
WAINSCOT

FRONT (WEST) WALL
OF HALL CHAMBER

NORTH SIDE OF
SOUTH CHIMNEY GIRT
PLATE

O
5"
4"
12"

POST
B ON
PLAN

S.W. CORNER
ENTRY SECOND STORY

PLATE
8"
3"

SOUTH SIDE OF
NORTH
CHIMNEY GIRT
12"

5½"
6¾"
7¾"

POST
C ON
PLAN

RAFTER
5½" JOIST
4¾"
PLATE
6"

SECTION
FRONT WALL
ENTRY
SECOND STORY

N W CORNER
ENTRY
SECOND STORY

DOOR

FRAMING DETAILS
WHITMAN HOUSE
FARMINGTON

are made larger at the joint with the girt than they are at the sill line. The chimney girts and the end girts which, except in the Hempstead house, have to carry the summer, are, except in that instance, larger than the other. The average size of them is from 6 or 8 by 9 to 8 by 12 or even 14½, and 9 by 14; not quite so deep, it will be seen, as in Rhode Island, where 8 by 16 for an end girt is not unknown, but where 9 inches in width would be very strange. It is to provide a seat for these heavier girts that the special flare of the post is hewn out, and, except in one case—the second story of the Baldwin house—this flare is always turned in the direction of the length of these girts. In this instance the front and back girts, which elsewhere, because of their small size—indeed they are only of ordinary size here —run square into the flat side of the post, have the flare under them instead of under the end and chimney girts.

All this somewhat lengthy explanation will be much clearer if the reader will consult the drawings of the different girts, given, with those of the posts to which they belong, in Plates I to VII.

The tops of all the girts are kept flush, that is, at the same level. Flush with them are the tops of the FLOOR JOISTS, which are framed into the front and back girts and into the summer. These, in the second story, of which we are speaking, and in the third, are almost always very small compared with those used now-a-days. They are of oak—except, perhaps, in the Moore house, where all the framing visible is of hard pine—and are about 2½ inches by 5. That is the exact size of them in the Patterson house, where they are spaced 21 inches on centers, and where their edges are beaded.

The joists in the first floor are often very rough, but this is where the floor has been renewed. In the Baldwin house they

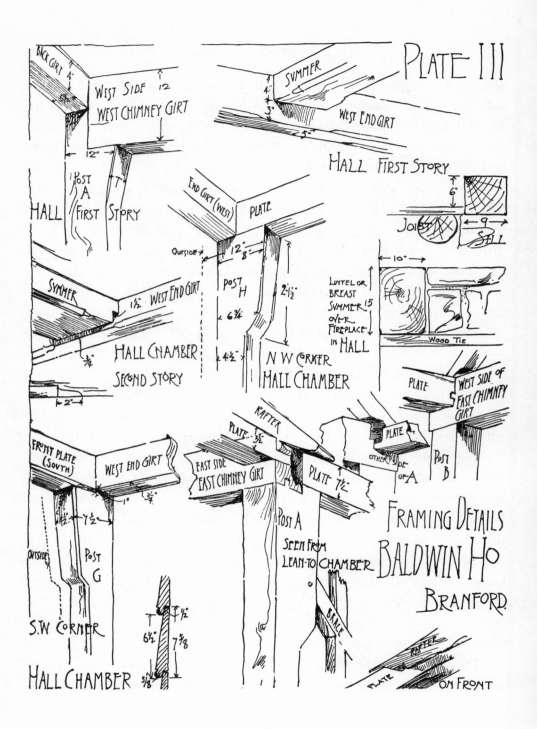

PLATE III

BACK GIRT 4"

WEST SIDE 12
WEST CHIMNEY GIRT

SUMMER
4"
3"
5"
WEST END GIRT

HALL FIRST STORY

12"

POST A FIRST STORY 7"

HALL FIRST STORY

END GIRT (WEST)   PLATE

JOIST   6"
9"
SILL

HALL

OUTSIDE   12"
8"

POST H

2-1½"

SUMMER   1½"   WEST END GIRT

6¾"

LINTEL OR BREAST SUMMER 15 OVER FIREPLACE IN HALL

10"

HALL CHAMBER   ¾"

SECOND STORY

4½"

N W CORNER HALL CHAMBER

WOOD TIE

PLATE   WEST SIDE OF EAST CHIMNEY GIRT

2"

FRONT PLATE (SOUTH)   WEST END GIRT

RAFTER
PLATE 5½"
PLATE
OTHER SIDE OF A
PLATE
POST B

EAST SIDE EAST CHIMNEY GIRT

PLATE 7½"

1"   ¾"

4½"   7½"

OUTSIDE

POST A

SEEN FROM LEAN-TO CHAMBER

FRAMING DETAILS

BALDWIN HO

BRANFORD.

POST G

½"

S.W. CORNER   6½"   7⅝"

BRACE

HALL CHAMBER   ⅝"

RAFTER

PLATE   ON FRONT

are logs square only on the upper sides. They are not framed into the sills, but are built into the wall, as we have already explained. They span the whole width of the cellar, as is the case also where, as in the Painter house and the Hollister house, the joists are square hewn. In these houses the common custom of laying the joists of the first floor flatwise is followed. In one house only which we have examined, the Gleason at Farmington, is the first floor framed exactly as were the upper floors. This is no doubt the oldest way in those houses where the sill was used to carry the joists. The single-span system was descended from the older arrangement seen in the Baldwin house, the sill over the joists, that is to say, and independent of them, just as this old scheme is, in its turn, descended from the still more ancient disposition where there was no cellar and no floor but the pounded earth, or beaten clay and lime, or perhaps wooden blocks, and where, consequently, no floor joists were needed.

The end girt appears in the third story. It calls for no special remark except that, in some cases where there was a gable overhang, it was "cambered," that is, made deeper in the center than at the ends. The Gleason furnishes an example of this, where the end girt at the center is 9 by 14½ inches. The form comes down from the half-timber construction of the old country where the cambering showed on the outside, and where it still adds to the picturesqueness of many a plastered gable.

The chimney girt also re-appears in the third floor, and, in the Benjamin house, Milford, Figure 80, it runs across the head of the post at the back of the chimney till it meets the rafter of the main and the lean-to roof, which is one timber, and thus forms itself into a tie-beam. This framing we have met in the present territory of Connecticut only in this house. It does not

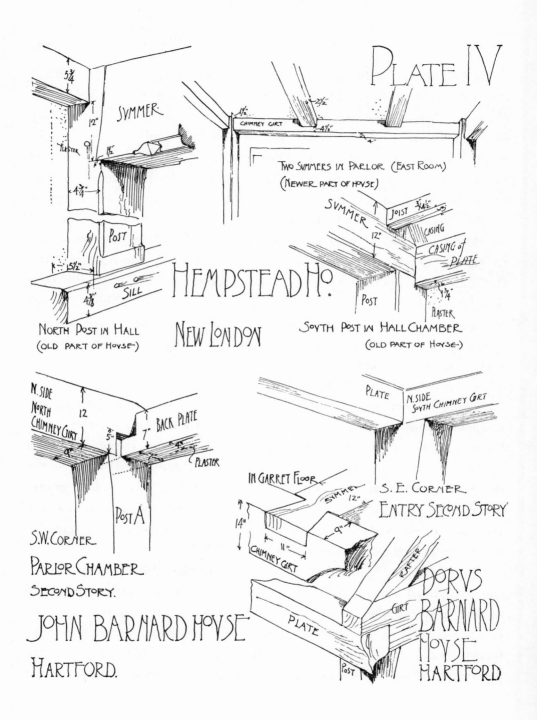

PLATE IV

5¾"
12"
SVMMER
1½"
PLASTER
4¾"
POST
15½"
4⅛" SILL

NORTH POST IN HALL
(OLD PART OF HOVSE)

HEMPSTEAD H?.

NEW LONDON

2½"
1½"
CHIMNEY GIRT
4½"
4"

TWO SVMMERS IN PARLOR (EAST ROOM)
(NEWER PART OF HOVSE)

SVMMER
JOIST
¾"
4½"
CASING
CASING OF PLATE
12"
POST
1¾"
PLASTER

SOVTH POST IN HALL CHAMBER
(OLD PART OF HOVSE)

N. SIDE
NORTH
CHIMNEY GIRT
12
¾"
5"
7" BACK PLATE
4"
PLASTER
POST A

S.W. CORNER

PARLOR CHAMBER

SECOND STORY.

JOHN BARNARD HOVSE

HARTFORD.

PLATE
N. SIDE
SOVTH CHIMNEY GIRT

IN GARRET FLOOR
SVMMEL
12"
14"
9"
11"
CHIMNEY GIRT
PLATE
POST

S. E. CORNER

ENTRY SECOND STORY

RAFTER
DORVS
GIRT
BARNARD
HOVSE
HARTFORD

occur in Hartford, but, as the only three examples of the original lean-to house now known in the old Providence Plantations are built in that way, it was once, no doubt, more common.

The places of the front girt and the back girt at the third floor level were taken by the front and back PLATES. These are the beams which rest on the tops of the posts and carry the rafters and the joists of the third floor. In a story-and-a-half house they have only to carry the rafters. The plates meet the end girts on the corner posts and the chimney girts on the intermediates—see the sections and the perspectives of framing in Figures 96, 97, and 98, and it is to accommodate both sticks without weakening the joints that the heads of the posts are flared and bracketed, even when they are not so at the second floor, and that such wonderful feats of mortise-and-tenon work are accomplished as are set forth in the details of plates I to VI.

In the two-story house two rooms deep the back plate, that is, the plate which would be over the back wall of the house if it were only one room deep, becomes a sort of second summer like the back girt in the second floor of a house of the same kind.

In a lean-to house, where the lean-to is part of the original construction, the back plate—or what would be the back plate if the house were one room deep—is still used as a plate which carries the feet of the upper rafters and the heads of the rafters of the lean-to, for these are not in one stick. The feet of the lean-to rafters rest on the plate in the back wall of the lean-to at the level of the second floor. The Benjamin house is an exception to this. Here the rafters are in one piece of timber, and the old back plate does act like a second summer in the garret floor, for it carries the ends of the joists which run over it to meet the rafters, as the section of the house in Figure 80 will explain.

The cuts for the rafters, which will be explained with those timbers, and the notches for the third-story floor joists are ranged, the former on the front, the latter on the back, or inside, of the plate. It is not uncommon for the joists, as in the Dorus Barnard and the Patterson house, to rest on the plate instead of being framed into it with their tops flush with its top.

The SUMMER is the great beam which traverses the rooms in both stories from chimney girt to end girt, and thus parallel with the front wall of the house. The word, as we explained in " Early Rhode Island Houses," comes down from the Latin "sagmarius," a pack-horse, through the Norman French "sommier." It is still in use in Connecticut, as elsewhere in New England, and appears often in the combination "summer tree," in which tree, in the sense of beam, has as right Saxon a flavor as the other word has Norman.

Judge Sewall, in his diary, uses the word when he records the raising of his brother's house.[1]

The most interesting literary evidence for the word, however, occurs in Increase Mather's *Illustrious Providences*. The author is recounting a miraculous escape from a powder explosion at Windsor. He says:

" John Bissell, on a morning, about break of day, taking nails out of a great barrel, wherein was a considerable quantity of gunpowder and bullets, having a candle in his hand, the powder took fire, Thomas Bissell was then putting on his clothes, standing by a window, which though well-fastened, was by the force of the powder carried away at least four rods; the partition-wall from another room was broken in pieces; the roof of the house opened

---

[1] Samuel Sewall's *Diary*. Mass. Hist. Soc., *Collections, Fifth Series*, vol. V, p. 9.

and slipt off the plates about five feet down; also the great girt of the house at one end [the end girt] broke out so far that it drew from the summer to the end most of its tenant." [1]

To the rule that the summer should run parallel to the front there is one exception and, so far as we are aware, only one. In the older half of the Hempstead house at New London the summer runs from back girt to front girt, parallel to the end of the house, and there is a post under it in the back wall,[2] and probably in the front wall as well, though it is covered. This crosswise direction. so to speak, of the summer is very common in Massachusetts Bay. Something like it does occur in the north end of the Webb house, and of the Grant house, but even in these instances, though the summer runs parallel to the end of the house, it nevertheless runs into the chimney girt. The summer in the south end of each of these houses, while it runs parallel to the front, has really far more of the look of Massachusetts work, as it runs parallel to the front of the fireplace also.

Of other peculiar ways of placing the summer only two appear. In the newer half of the Hempstead house there are two summers in the narrow space where we should expect only one; and neither of these was ever a back girt. In the Moore house at Windsor we find that rare disposition, the crossed summers, the only instance of it in Connecticut. The diagonal summer was used in Surrey, but we have never seen it in New England.

---

[1] Rev. Increase Mather, *An Essay for the Recording of Illustrious Providences*, Boston, 1684 Reprinted with introduction by George Offor, London, 1856. Page 27 of this reprint. The passage is quoted by Stiles, *Ancient Windsor*, I, p. 187.

[2] For a post with the summer framed into it in the Plymouth colony in 1658, see Mather's work, p. 52.

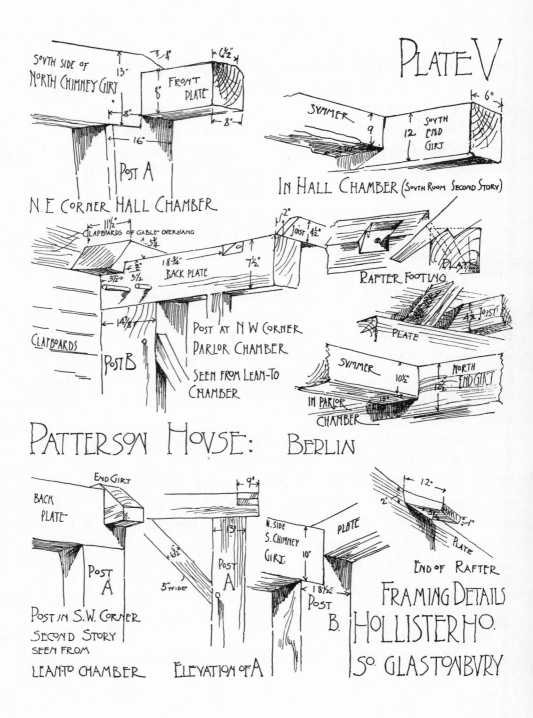

PLATE V

SOUTH SIDE OF NORTH CHIMNEY GIRT

13"

¾" 4"

6½"

FRONT PLATE

6"

8"

16"

8"

POST A

N.E. CORNER HALL CHAMBER

SYMMER

9

SOUTH END GIRT

12

6"

IN HALL CHAMBER (SOUTH ROOM SECOND STORY)

11½"

CLAPBOARDS OF GABLE OVERHANG

3¾

½"

18¾"

7½"

BACK PLATE

3½

3½

14⅞"

CLAPBOARDS

POST B

POST AT N.W. CORNER PARLOR CHAMBER

SEEN FROM LEAN-TO CHAMBER

2"

JOIST 4½"

RAFTER FOOTING

PLATE

4½ JOIST

PLATE

SYMMER

10½"

NORTH END GIRT

12½

IN PARLOR CHAMBER

PATTERSON HOUSE: BERLIN

END GIRT

BACK PLATE

9"

POST A

6½"

5" WIDE

POST A

3"

N. SIDE S. CHIMNEY GIRT

10"

PLATE

18½"

POST B.

POST IN S.W. CORNER SECOND STORY SEEN FROM LEAN-TO CHAMBER

ELEVATION OF A

12"

2"

1"

PLATE

END OF RAFTER

FRAMING DETAILS HOLLISTER HO. S° GLASTONBURY

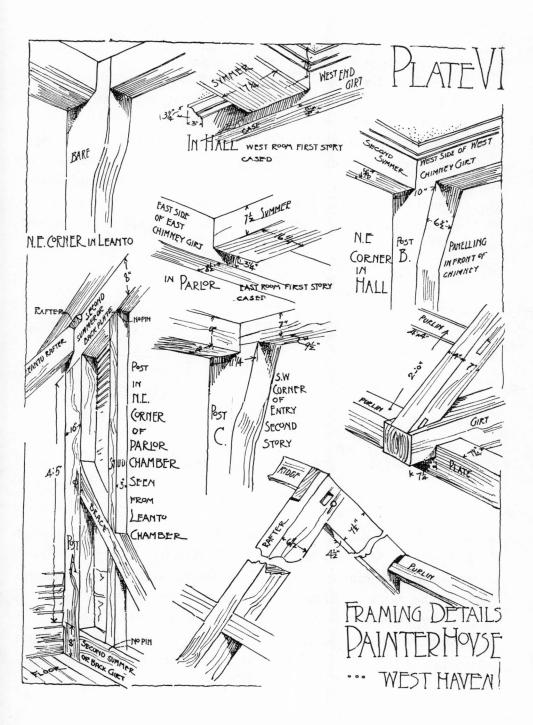

PLATE VI

In Hall WEST ROOM FIRST STORY CASED

SUMMER 7¼

WEST END GIRT

CASE 3½ 3"

BARE

N.E. CORNER in LEANTO

SECOND SUMMER

WEST SIDE OF WEST CHIMNEY GIRT

10"

6½

N.E. CORNER B. IN HALL

POST B.

PANELLING IN FRONT OF CHIMNEY

EAST SIDE OF EAST CHIMNEY GIRT

SUMMER 7½

6"

8½ 3¼

In Parlor   EAST ROOM FIRST STORY CASED

8"

RAFTER

SECOND SUMMER OR BACK PLATE

PANTU RAFTER

NO PIN

POST IN N.E. CORNER OF PARLOR CHAMBER SEEN FROM LEANTO CHAMBER

16"

4:5

STUD 3"

BRACE

POST

NO PIN

FLOOR

SECOND SUMMER OR BACK GIRT

9"

2"

9½"

11¼

POST C.

S.W. CORNER OF ENTRY SECOND STORY

PURLIN 2½x4½

2:0"

7

PURLIN

GIRT

7½

7¼

PLATE

RIDGE

RAFTER

7½"

4½

PURLIN

FRAMING DETAILS
PAINTER HOUSE
··· WEST HAVEN

The size of the beam varies. It was often laid flatwise. In the third floor of the Dorus Barnard house it is 12 by 12. That in the second floor of the Whiting, which is not cased, is 12¾ wide. The main summer in the Moore house is 13½ inches wide, while the cross summer is only 10. Both these timbers are of hard pine. In the parlor chamber of the John Barnard house the original summer carrying the third floor had been taken out and replaced by a new stick which was 11 by 12 and yet was

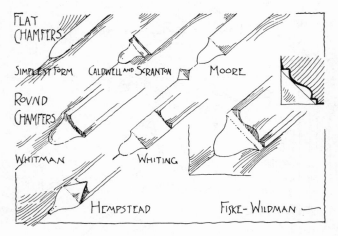

FIGURE 99.—CHAMFERS.

smaller than the other. The beam left in the girt traces of what looked like a tusk mortise under the dovetail, though we have never seen this joint in Connecticut except in the cambered end girt in the Gleason house. The dovetail, as shown in Plate I, seems the universal mode of framing the two sticks together. It is a very fair joint and forms a good tie, for the dovetail is not easily pulled out, but it weakens the girt more than the tusk-and-tenon.

The edges of the summer, as of all the heavy timber, were chamfered, sometimes with a plain bevel, sometimes with a filleted quarter-round, and these CHAMFERS were finished with stops which, many of them very quaint and full of mediæval spirit, exhibit the variety shown in Figure 99.

The STUDS are the small vertical timbers which are tenoned at the bottom into the sill and at the top into a girt, or at the bottom into a girt, and at the top into a girt or a plate, or are used to fill a gable, according to the position they occupy. The space between them is generally filled with brick or, in the earlier examples, with the clay and hay which, in England, it was their original office to carry, and they support on the outside the clapboards, on the inside the wainscoting or the plastering when that comes into use. They are set flatwise and vary somewhat in size, but are generally from 2 by 3 to 3 by 5. They were framed into the other beams on the ground, and the whole side wall raised at one time. On the ends they had to be put in afterward.

The RAFTERS are of two kinds, principal and common. In many roofs, especially in the Connecticut colony, there are four pairs of quite large principal rafters, one pair over each girt. Each pair forms, with that girt, a triangular truss in which there may or may not be a COLLAR-BEAM or tie between the rafters just above a man's head. Between one pair of principals and the next pair PURLINS, as they were called, were framed — see the perspective of framing in Figure 97; and these purlins, which were practically girders, carried the smaller common rafters.

In other cases, especially in the New Haven colony, there was a large number of principal rafters and a large number also of purlins spanning the short spaces between them. Here the boarding was vertical on the purlins and there were no common rafters.

This scheme appears, curiously enough, in the Kinsman house in the old Norwich settlement—this house has also the great width of entry characteristic of New Haven—and occurs as far east as an interesting old one-story, single-room house in Foster, Rhode Island. Beside these two examples we have seen it only in the New Haven jurisdiction, though the influence of it is felt in the habit, which appeared in the second period in Hartford, of leaving out the collar-beams. The arrangement is illustrated in Figure 98, the framing of the Caldwell house, and in Plate VI. There can be no doubt that it originated in thatching, which prevailed in New Haven[1] as well as in the other colonies,[2] and which may have lingered a long time in that somewhat conservative settlement.

The bundles of straw or coarse salt hay of which the thatch consisted were tied with rope or birch withes to the horizontal purlins which were spaced closer than they were after boarding came into use. Another reason for the close spacing of the rafters so common in New Haven might be found in the habit, to be noticed later, of using clapboards for roofing.

The feet of the rafters were fastened to the plate with pins, but a notch, shown in Plate V, was skillfully used to relieve the treenail. The end of the rafter projected about twelve inches beyond the frame, as the drawing shows in Plates III and V. The roof boarding and the shingles followed the projection of the rafter, and this was all the cornice the oldest houses, and some of the

---

[1] The court order in New Haven, June 11, 1640, regulated the wages of "A skilfull thatcher, working dilligently." *New Haven Colonial Records*, I, p 37.

[2] Increase Mather, in recounting an escape from lightning in Northampton in 1664, mentions thatch. *Illustrious Providences*, edit. cited, p. 53. For a reference by him to "principal rafter," see the same, p. 52, and for a reference to a rafter as a "spar," an old English name, see the same, p. 56, where the gable is in question.

later ones, possessed. The effect, however, was very good, as any one can see who visits the Patterson house before it goes to pieces, for that house still has its original cornice or "jet."

The problem of supporting the new cornice, built up of thin boards in imitation of one of the "orders," was met, when that cornice came into fashion, in much the same way as in Rhode Island. This is shown in Figure 106 and in Plate VI. The appearance of this framing in the Painter house in 1685, and possibly in the Hollister some years earlier, shows that the box cornice, in a rudimentary form, is very old. It is almost the first sign of Jones and Wren that we find.

RIDGES or ridge-poles occur only where the roof is of horizontal purlins. Then the purlin at the peak might be called the ridge, but it is never part of the framing; that is, the rafters are never framed into it,[1] they are always halved together and pinned, as in Hartford.

The OVERHANG. We do not by this word generally mean the gable overhang. That we shall treat under GABLE in its separate place. We shall speak here of the projection of the second story over the face of the wall in the first story.

This occurs principally in the Connecticut and New Haven settlements. We have not yet seen an example in New London, though some exist in Norwich. It was once common, therefore, to many of the older towns of the present State, though, no doubt, more in vogue in the two original colonies.

There are among overhangs two types which we have already named the *framed* and the *hewn*. They seem to have sprung

---

[1] This occurs in very late work, c. 1820, in southern New Hampshire, in Francestown, among or near the Scotch-Irish settlements.

from the different traditions of the two older jurisdictions. The first is characteristic of Connecticut, the second appears to have originated in New Haven and to have spread northward into the river colony. A third form, a late and slight modification of the hewn type, prevails in both settlements and in some of the later towns.

In Farmington, as the reader is aware, there are still to be seen four examples of the heavy framed projection on the front of the house, and two other instances formerly existed there. Those which remain are probably the survivors of a once numerous class.

FIGURE 100.—OVERHANG DETAILS.

In Windsor one example is still standing, while another was pulled down some years ago. In Hartford itself there are now no framed overhangs, and however numerous they may have been in the other river towns—and the overhang of the Sheldon house, Deerfield, goes to show that they were the rule and not the exception—there are now none of them left, so far as we can discover, beside the few we have named. The six which, only a few years ago, stood in Farmington, are an extraordinary number for one place. We know of no other town in New England which retains so many.

These overhangs on the front of the houses are sometimes accompanied by another at each end which varies from six or perhaps eight inches, as in the Clark house, to four inches, as in the Lewis house, now a part of the Elm Tree Inn. No others of the houses under discussion have this end overhang.

The details of these overhangs are shown in Figure 100, which gives that of the Clark house, Farmington, drawn from a photograph of the house taken several years ago, before the building was destroyed. The same figure gives that of the Gleason house, and Figure 101 contains that of the Whitman. The overhang of the Cowles house, which resembles that of the Gleason, will be found clearly enough explained in Figure 13. The drops under the second-story posts — hewn out of the posts themselves — vary through the forms which the drawings show. The number of these curious old ornaments preserved in the neighborhood of Hartford, though it is only three, is very remarkable:

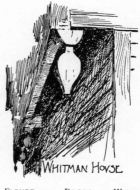

FIGURE 101 —DROPS IN WHITMAN HOUSE.

everywhere else they have been sawn off. Indeed, it is a question whether any ever existed in the Gleason or the Cowles house. Turned drops were at the ends of the posts in the Sueton Grant house, Newport, now unfortunately destroyed, but they looked very much like restorations. All those we have shown have a strong flavor of the Elizabethan and Jacobean England to which they belong.

Geometrical drawings of certain of these overhangs, including that of the Moore house, Windsor, are given in Figure 102. The framing is carefully explained in Plate VII.

The framed overhang did not survive into the second period. In its stead we find the hewn overhang, where the projection, which is thus necessarily small, is cut out of the solid post. This method is clearly illustrated in Plate VII. In the earlier examples in the Connecticut jurisdiction the transition between the upper and the lower part of the post is managed by a bracket, as in the Patterson house, and in a more elaborate form in the Hollister.

Later on the bracket was left out, though in some cases it may have been cut away since for the convenience of carpenters in renewing the clapboards, as so nearly happened in the Hollister house.

The framed overhang was not used on the backs of the houses, and at first the hewn overhang was not; but as time went on it became customary to carry the projection around the entire building, as in the Meggatt house. The final step was to reduce the width of it, so that the second story was only an inch or so beyond the first. This third form, which we said was a slight modification of the hewn type, was very tenacious of life. It lingered well on toward the Revolution. The coming in of the newer details, those generally called "colonial," the advent of houses like the Webb and the Grant, finally drove it out of existence.

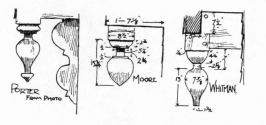

FIGURE 102.—SCALE DRAWINGS OF OVERHANGS.

In the New Haven jurisdiction the framed overhang does not appear, and all the projections we meet are of the hewn type. The house in Norwalk, which seems to be an exception to this statement, is really not an exception, for that settlement was a part of the Connecticut colony.

Early examples of the overhang do not meet us in the New Haven towns. Yet it must have been in use, for the Fiske house and the Caldwell show bracketed forms of it which must be descended from a very old type. There is an instance of it in Branford, and one in West Haven, neither of which has the brackets, though, as we have shown, these might easily have been removed. The overhang in the Fiske house we have given in

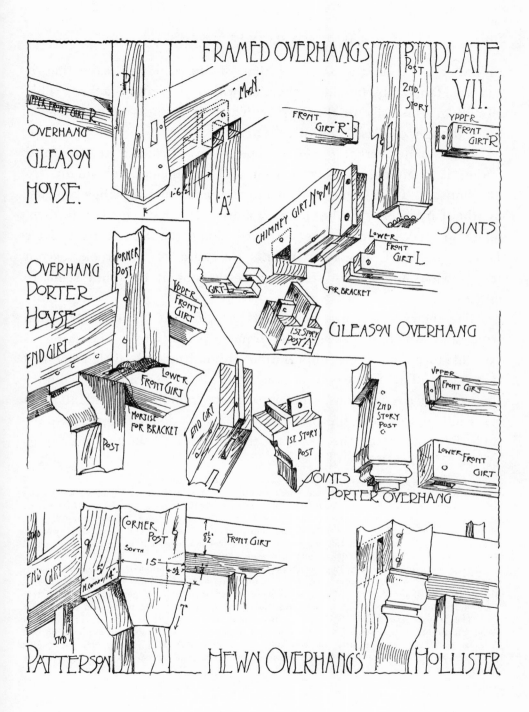

FRAMED OVERHANGS

PLATE VII.

JOINTS

"P"   "M&N"

UPPER FRONT GIRT R.

OVERHANG GLEASON HOUSE.

1·6½   "A"

POST 2ND STORY

FRONT GIRT "R"

UPPER FRONT GIRT "R"

CHIMNEY GIRT N&M

LOWER FRONT GIRT L

FOR BRACKET

GIRT F

1ST STORY POST "A"

GLEASON OVERHANG

OVERHANG PORTER HOUSE

CORNER POST

UPPER FRONT GIRT

END GIRT

LOWER FRONT GIRT

MORTISE FOR BRACKET

POST

END GIRT

1ST STORY POST

JOINTS

2ND STORY POST C.

UPPER FRONT GIRT

LOWER FRONT GIRT

PORTER OVERHANG

STUD

END GIRT

CORNER POST

SOUTH

15"

N.CORNER 14"

8½"   FRONT GIRT

15"   5½"   5½"

7"

STUD

PATTERSON

HEWN OVERHANGS

HOLLISTER

Figure 74.   It is the same as that of the Caldwell save that it has an elaborately moulded chamfer which the latter. lacks.   This moulding, especially in the stop in which it ends, is of a mediæval type, though of classic profile.

The small overhang which appears in Hartford in the third period is common, in New Haven and its ancient dependents, in late houses   It was the descendant of the hewn overhangs affected by the carpenters of the latter colony.   It exists in Guilford in many instances, and in the territory along the Sound from New Haven to the Connecticut river.   Eastward of Saybrook, except in Norwich, an offshoot from that settlement, it does not seem to occur.

The hewn overhang represents a different English tradition from that which we see in the framed projection.   The latter is an old form, a direct importation from England, little modified if at all.   The former is a late type, developed in this country for constructive reasons, and is a more remote descendant from its English forbears, the old Kentish[1] or Yorkshire corner "spur," and the bracket at the head of the lower post in the overhangs of the West of England.

---

[1] In reply to questions which we addressed to him, Mr. Reginald Blomfield, to whose *History of Renaissance Architecture in England* we have often referred, writes as follows : "In reference to the overhang of timber construction in England, the 'framed overhang,' to use your term, is a common form of English 17th century timber construction.   Of the second form, what you call 'hewn overhang,' I can not at this moment recall any instance here, but if I came across one I should certainly incline to consider it quite late work.

As to local differences in England, there are certain distinct variations between W. country work (Cheshire, Lancashire, Shropshire, and Herefordshire) and half-timber work in Kent, Sussex, the E. and S. E. of England.   The latter is more refined in detail, and generally less florid than W. country work, some of which is cut out of huge timbers and is almost barbaric in its rudeness.

The shaped 'spur' to which I have called attention, vol. II, p. 324, is more or less peculiar to Kent and Sussex.   By means of this excellent form the carpenter was enabled to overhang on both sides as by sketch herewith, and this was about the most skilful thing in carpentry our English carpenters arrived at.   The angle bracket shown in your photograph appears to me to be a reminiscence of this old Kentish construction."

In the houses with no overhangs, the posts, it will be remembered, were larger under the plate than they were at the bottom, whether they were larger at the second-story girts or not. The same is true of the posts in the houses with the framed overhang. This enlargement was gained by a flare or a bracket. The posts in the houses with the hewn overhangs have this same enlargement, but they never possess either flare or bracket on the inside. The post is square for its whole height in the second story as well as in the first. That is to say, the bracket of the overhang,

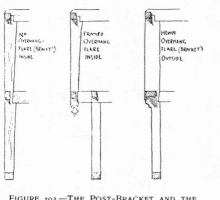

FIGURE 103.—THE POST-BRACKET AND THE OVERHANG.

Figure 103, takes the place of the inside flare or of the inside bracket, and is used for the same purpose. The only difference is that it is on the outside of the house, and is thus made to contribute to the adornment of the building.

Where did the hewn overhang first come into use? It is impossible to say. We believe that, as far as Connecticut is concerned, this single-post projection first appeared in New Haven. The reasons for this supposition lie in the ancestry of the form; for though, as we see it, it is late, it had forerunners in the colony. It is a combination of two lines of influence which converged at New Haven and its allied towns. One of these influences came with the Herefordshire men from the West of England and shows itself in the shape of the bracket under the projection. The double curve is to be seen in the half-timber gate-house at Stokesay Castle, in Shropshire, one of the western counties, Lancashire, Cheshire,

Shropshire, and Herefordshire, which made use of half timber construction.

The other line of influence came from the great timber district in the south-east of England, the ancient counties of Sussex and Kent. It is, as Mr. Blomfield suggests, the spur which the Kentish carpenters put under the corner of their overhang, as is explained

FIGURE 104.—DEVELOPMENT OF THE HEWN OVERHANG.

in Figure 104, which will also show how near some of the ancient forms of this spur come to the bracket in the Patterson house. This same spur was used in Yorkshire, as the reader may see in Orlando Jewitt's drawing of the old house in the Newgate at York,[1]

---

[1] J. H. Parker, *Concise Glossary of Architecture*, p. 285. Note the flare at the top of the second_ story post in this house.

and in the eastern counties also, as at Bury St. Edmund's,[1] in a house of the fifteenth century, and again in the west, as in the Double Butcher Row at Shrewsbury.[2]

It was through the men of Kent[3] or of Yorkshire at Quinni-piac, or the settlers from Kent, Surrey, and Sussex, who founded Guilford, that the spur form of overhang came into the New Haven jurisdiction where, in course of time, it was modified into the hewn overhang with which we are familiar. For the overhang in Europe, so far as we can see, was always framed, no matter how small its projection.

The form was carried northward by Sergeant Richard Beckley. It perhaps appears, indeed, in the end overhang of the Lewis house, now part of the Elm Tree Inn, at Farmington, a few years before he came, but he is to be credited, we think, with the general introduction of it. He was a carpenter from New Haven,[4] and he settled in Wethersfield about 1668. The Patterson house stands at no great distance from his homestead, and almost on the edge of the land granted him by the town of Wethersfield. The Hollister house, also, is within the ancient limits of that town. There is another house of this type with curved brackets, somewhere near Farmington, which we know by photograph, but we have not been able to ascertain its location, if, indeed, it is still standing.

One more fact bears upon the New Haven origin of the hewn overhang in Connecticut. The Rev. Ezekiel Rogers came to New Haven with a party of settlers from Yorkshire, among whom was the ill-fated Lamberton. The pastor afterwards concluded to settle

---

[1] Turner and Parker, *Domestic Architecture*, vol. III, p. 30.

[2] The same, vol. III, p. 36.

[3] Jarvis Boykin, carpenter, of New Haven, came from Charing in Kent.

[4] Richard Beckley's inventory, of August, 1690, on record at Hartford, includes tools valued at £1. His house consisted of an old part and a new.

in Massachusetts, and he founded the town of Rowley, near Ipswich. Not all his former parishioners would leave New Haven at his summons, but some of them did; so that we find a group of Yorkshire men not only in the quarter which bore their name at Quinnipiac, but on the shore of the Bay. Now the hewn overhang is very common in Ipswich, and there is an instance of the later small form of it in the Williams house at Rowley; while, so far as we know, it is not used in any other part of the Massachusetts colony. Precisely the same form of bracket and of chamfer occurs in the Fiske house in Guilford and in the so-called Saltonstall house in Ipswich, and the bracket without the chamfer appears in the Noyes house. The line of descent is the same in both cases whether we think that the Yorkshiremen brought the spur form with them or whether we surmise that it came from Norfolk with the settlers of the Bay colony, great numbers of whom were from the eastern counties. The fact that the peculiar form does not occur elsewhere in Massachusetts is strong evidence that it came with the Yorkshire carpenters from New Haven.

Much remains to be done to settle absolutely the questions which arise about the overhang. To answer them we must know the names of all our old carpenters and must know the towns in England from which they came. We must then learn what type of timber construction and what form of overhang prevailed in the English home of each of these old craftsmen.

GABLES. In Massachusetts, and occasionally in Rhode Island, gables were used on the fronts of the houses as well as on the ends.

We know of no houses now standing in Connecticut with these front gables, nor have we found traces of them in any roof we have examined.

They probably existed, however, for the Allyn house in Windsor had them, if we may trust the drawing in Stiles's history,[1] and we see one over the porch in the drawing of the old parsonage at Woodbury,[2] and in the woodcut which Barber gives of Pastor Hooker's house in Hartford.[3]

Of the end gables there are two classes, those which overhang and those which do not.

Those which do not overhang are framed with studs from the end girt in the floor up to the under sides of the rafters. They are covered, during the first two periods, and for a part, at least, of the third, with clapboards nailed directly to the studs without any outside boarding. The studs are set flatwise as they are in the main walls of the house. Somewhere in the third period the practice of using boarding, to which the clapboards were nailed, came in. It is very likely that the difficulty of obtaining sawn boards retarded the introduction of the fashion.

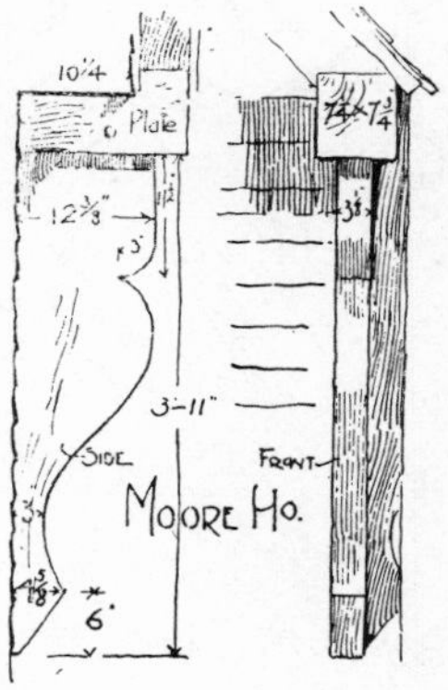

FIGURE 105.—GABLE BRACKET.

Of the class of gables which overhang there are two subdivisions:—that in which the overhang is formed by the projection of the end girt itself, as in the Gleason house at Farmington, and that in which there is a second girt carried out beyond the wall on the end of the plates, as in the Stowe house, Milford.

The former subdivision includes the vast array of overhanging

---

[1] Stiles, *Ancient Windsor*, vol. I, p. 420.

[2] Cothren, *History of Ancient Woodbury*, vol. I, p. 136.

[3] Barber, *Conn. Hist. Coll.*, p. 43. The openings which have left traces in the roof of the Hempstead house may, from the height of them, have been made for gables.

gables, small and great, in Connecticut. A glance at the detail of the Gleason house in Plate I will explain it.

The heavy cambered girt is, on the inside, flush with the studs of the end of the house, while on the outside it projects four inches beyond them and has its outer face flush with the studs of the gable above. Brackets at the end help to prevent the stick from rotating. The slight gable overhangs so common on the Sound and in the Connecticut valley northward are of this kind.

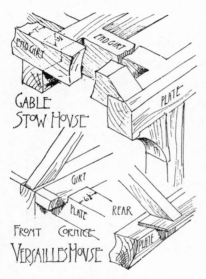

FIGURE 106.—FRAMING OF GABLE OVERHANG AND OF CORNICE.

The second subdivision contained, doubtless, its numerous examples, though we have but two of them left, the Moore house in Windsor, and the Stowe house in Milford.

In the Moore house the framing is not now to be seen. The amount of the projection, however, renders us certain as to the construction employed. The huge brackets here are mere ornaments, as indeed they were in the Gleason house. Their size and shape are, however, very interesting and noteworthy, especially as that size and shape are very closely repeated in the Sheldon house at Deerfield, the gable brackets of which are now preserved in the museum of that town.

At the Stowe house the two plates and the summer are all visible from below, as they come through the end wall of the house to carry the projecting girt which forms the tie-beam of the gable. The construction, which we show in Figure 106, can also be verified in the attic of the house.

Gable overhangs of six inches or thereabouts are used in eastern Connecticut until quite late. There is one, near Plainfield, as far down as 1806. They much resemble the later specimens in Rhode Island, and there is not much doubt, from the close trade relations between Windham county and Providence since 1725, that there was copying on one side or the other.

THE COVERING.

CLAPBOARDS. These were of oak until very late. The process of getting them out seems to have been as follows: The preliminary work was done in the woods. A tree was selected, felled, and cut up into lengths, which varied of course with the length of clapboards required. At New Haven three lengths, at least, were in use, for, in the laws, clapboards are mentioned four feet, five feet, and six feet long.[1] In Hartford two lengths appear, three feet and six feet.[2] These lengths were riven into "bolts," which were probably quarters of the log. The bolts in their turn were hauled into the town, into the shops, perhaps, of the carpenters, or into the immediate neighborhood of the job for which they were intended. For the clapboards for the meeting-house at Windsor, or rather the bolts for them, were to "be brought home by the latter end of the week following —— and Samuel Grant is to cleave them when brought home; and so fit them and nail them about the meeting house."[3] This work was called "clab-

---

[1] *New Haven Col. Rec.*, I, p. 38.
[2] Conn. Hist. Soc., *Collections*, VI, p. 28.
[3] Stiles, *Ancient Windsor*, I, p. 42. Quoting records.

bing." The bolts then were still further split to form the clapboards, and this was done "quartering," or with the grain of the
tree and perpendicular to the circumference. The clapboard under
this process was split into its proper tapering feather-edged section by the single process, with perhaps a little shaving.

In the law of New Haven regulating building prices we read
of "hewing" clapboards, which seems to mean the same splitting
process, though it may indicate a way of getting out a flat board
of even thickness and of greater or less width and then hewing
down the edge with a hatchet before putting it on the building.
It is noteworthy that the law goes on to say, "and nailing them
on roofs and sides of houses."[1] We have never seen an instance
of this use of them in roofs, which, indeed, we do not meet again
in the documents, and it probably fell out of use very soon. It
left its mark in such roofs as that of the Baldwin house, where
the rafters are quite close together, and all equal; that is, there
are no principal pairs.

In width the clapboard was about the same as that now in
use. The boards a foot wide or so which we find in the oldest
houses, especially on the back or the ends, laid the upper lapping
over the lower, were not clapboards. They were what Increase
Mather calls "weather boards."[2]

The word clapboard was familiar to our forefathers in England,
more so than it is to their present descendants in that country.
It has a German equivalent "klappholz" from which it is probably derived,[3] as the original article was imported from north

---

[1] *N. H. Col. Rec.*, I, p. 38.

[2] Mather, *Illustrious Providences*, p. 101.

[3] By a substitution of *board* for "holz," which means *wood*, we get clapboard. The word
appears in the Paston letters in 1477 as "clappalde."

See Murray, *A New English Dictionary on Historical Principles*, commonly called the Oxford
Dictionary.

Germany a century or more before the settlement at Plymouth. The meaning of the word in the seventeenth century in England differed from that now current among us. It was, to quote Murray, "a smaller size of split oak, imported from north Germany, and used by coopers to make barrel staves; in later times also for wainscoting. App. now obsolete except as a traditional term in the Customs schedules; quot. 1833 gives an interpretation of it for fiscal purposes." The quotation under date of 1833 referred to is Act 3 and 4, William IV, c. 56, and reads: "Wood Staves above 3 inches in thickness or above 7 inches in breadth, and not exceeding 63 Inches in length, shall be deemed Clapboards, and be charged with Duty accordingly."[1]

The seventeenth century clapboard in England, then, was a piece of oak, generally obtained from abroad, about 3 inches by 7 or more in section, and about 5 feet long. This was split up by coopers, by means of tool called in the old inventories the "froe," into barrel staves.

FIGURE 107.—THE FROE.

Bailey, in his Dictionary, editions from 1721–1800, defines clapboard as a "board cut ready to make casks, etc."

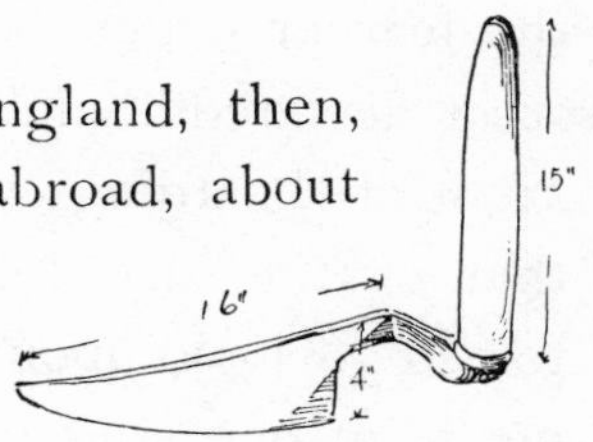

Clapboards appear in New England very early. Winthrop records in his journal, under August, 1632: "Mr. Oldham had a small house near the wear at Watertown, made all of clap-

---

[1] See Murray, *The Oxford Dictionary*, under clapboard and clapholt, for an interesting account of the derivation, meaning, and early use of the word.

It must be remembered that clapboard was originally the name of a kind of oak, as was wainscot also. This meaning the words still retained a few years ago in English building parlance. "There is a species of oak imported from Norway, which has received the name of *clapboard*, and another imported from Holland, known under the name of *Dutch wainscot*, though grown in Germany, whence it is floated down the Rhine for exportation." Gwilt, *Encyclopædia of Architecture*, p. 496. Wainscot means quartered oak to this day in England. *Builder*, Jan. 4, 1896, p. 20.

boards, burnt down by making a fire in it when it had no chimney." [1]

At first the colonists exported clapboards for coopers' use in old England, or in the West Indies, but they soon began to need them so much for building purposes as to pass laws restricting exportations. [2]

The question now is: how did clapboards come to be used on the outside of houses? We have already answered this question by a theory put forth in Early Rhode Island Houses, [3] namely, that after trying the half-timber construction of studs with plastered brick or clay between them, the carpenters were driven to the feather-edged boarding as a protection against the leaks which soon declared themselves between the studs and their filling. The kind of boarding which suited this new outside sheathing was that of the size known as "clapboards," those they were accustomed to look upon as cooper's material. These were short, reaching from one stud to the second beyond it, light and easily handled at a height upon a ladder or a staging, and easily shaved down on one edge to allow the upper course to lap over the lower.

Later research has strengthened in our minds this theory of the use of clapboards to protect the plastered walls. The process may have been going on in England at the time when our fathers left their old homes. It certainly has been going on in parts of England since, perhaps as a result of the custom in New England.

---

[1] Savage's *Winthrop.* vol. I, p. 88 (p. 73 of the original).

[2] They are mentioned in the Rhode Island (Portsmouth) records in 1639 in such a prohibitory order, thus: "clapboards and paile at twelve pence a foot by the Stubb —" where the "stubb" seems to be the equivalent of the bolt. *R. I. Col. Rec.*, I, p. 97.

On April 3, 1640, at New Haven, Arthur Halbidge was fined for selling clapboards. *New Haven Colonial Records*, I, p. 32.

[3] Pp. 86, 87.

Nevill[1] shows that tiles have been used for the same purpose, and Blomfield[2] illustrates some of the plastered buildings in which the whole of the outside walls was covered, as in the Old Feather Store in Boston, which was a New England example of the same treatment.

An instance of the covering of half-timber work with wood appears in fifteenth century French domestic work. There is a house in Rouen with its brick-filled stud walls covered with panelling so that it is like a huge piece of joiner-work, as Viollet-le-duc expresses it.[3]

The idea, then, of covering the filling of the timber frame with overlapping boards may not have been a new thing to our ancestors. The application of "clapboards" to that purpose was at any rate a novelty. Indeed many of our old houses still exhibit weather-boards a foot wide instead of common clapboarding.

Was any of the half-timber work which existed in the earliest years of the New England colonies to be credited to the Connecticut settlements? We think there was. The statement is difficult to prove, but there are certain facts in its favor. Not all the houses in England were covered with weather-boards, for the number of "black and white," or pure half-timber houses, and those too of late date, is quite large. So that we do not need to

---

[1] "It is in consequence of the decay of the timbers . . . . that the walls have been covered with hanging or, as they are called, weather tiles. As far as I know, this plan obtains more universally in this part of Surrey than anywhere else.* . . . . I doubt if any of it be older than 150 years, and most of it has certainly been done during the last century. . . . . the framing, etc., is always to be found complete under it." . . . . (Foot note.)* "In Kent the old cottages have, for the same reason, been very much covered with weather-boards . . . . the elaborate plaster-work of Essex and Suffolk is also an addition on the original timbers." R. Nevill, *Old Cottage and Domestic Architecture*, etc., pp. 21–22.

[2] R. Blomfield, *History of Renaissance Architecture in England*, vol. II, pp. 367, 369, 370.

[3] Viollet-le-duc, *Dict. raisonné de l'Arch.* Tome, VI, pp. 268, 270, art. *Maison.*

assume that every house was clapboarded here in the first four or five years.

The provisions of the second New Haven court order or "Statute of Laborers," in that section of it which treats of plastering,[1] will, if read carefully, show traces of the clay filling and the coat of plaster. The inside was certainly so managed. The outside must have been in some cases, for there was little need, in the interior of those low-studded houses, for the "materialls for scaffolding layd neare the place."

The old Stoughton house, the so-called fort, at Windsor, as it is described by Oliver Ellsworth, Junior, sustains this theory of clapboarded half-timber work: "old frame still remaining is very large strong work, and the old walls of the house, in many places now remaining, were built of mud and stones filled in between the joists or timbers and then on the outside covered with boards. The north wall of the present house is built of stone."[2]

BOARDING. All the oldest houses in Connecticut and New Haven have the clapboards nailed directly to the studs. Even in late instances this is also true, and the boarding, in examples which belong as far down as 1715, is sometimes an addition due to some later repairs.

This boarding, when it appears, is sometimes of oak, and sometimes, in the later examples, of pine. It is always horizontal.

An exception to this is the early boarding, under shingles, in Southold.

Vertical boarding, so characteristic of Plymouth, and especially

---

[1] *N. H. Col. Rec.*, I, p. 55. The quotation is from the second enactment, with lower rates, passed in May, 1641.

[2] Quoted by Stiles, *Ancient Windsor*, I, p. 142. The house was pulled down in 1809. Ellsworth wrote in 1802.

of Providence, while it is common enough in barns all over the present State of Connecticut, is met in houses only in a few in. stances and those in the eastern half of the State. That it occurred very early in New London we have already explained in commenting on the "girt house" to be built there; and a good example of it was still standing in the fall of 1898 in the Kinsman house near the railroad station at Versailles. The present hotel in Saybrook, the date of which can not be very remote, is also boarded vertically. This apparently foreign manner may have been due to the influence of John Elderkin, who had been a resident of Providence,[1] and perhaps of Plymouth. The vertical boarding is of oak in both the examples mentioned.

In Hartford and the other river towns the roofs are boarded horizontally with oak or with hard pine. In New Haven they are often boarded vertically, as we have explained, and this treatment we find in the Kinsman house in the ancient territory of Norwich.

SHINGLES. These were sometimes of the sizes common to-day, and sometimes very much longer, like those still to be seen in New Hampshire. A long form of shingle, also, is still to be found in Southold, where it is very common as a covering for walls, which, of course, had first to be boarded. This size goes back to the early settlement, as the following extract from the New Haven court order, which we have so often quoted, will help to show:

"Shingle, good stuff ¾ of an inch, and 6 or 7 or 8 inches broad, sorted in the woods, being 3 foote 2^s 6^d ℔ hundred. 2 foote 2^s. 14 inches 1^s ℔ hundred, butt if defective, price accord-

---

[1] Miss Caulkins, *History of New London*, p. 159.

ingly."[1] In the second order, passed in May, 1641, there are a few more particulars: "Hewing and shooting shingle, well done 3 foote nott above ʌ —, 2 foote nott above 9 ℔ 100, 14, 15 or 16 inches nott above 7ᵈ ℔ hundred. Lathing and laying shingle, squar worke wᵗʰ sawen laths 3 foote ʌ 2 foote 14, 15 or 16 inches long, 10ᵈ ℔ hundred — If hewed shingle 11ᵈ ℔ hundred. If there be diuʳˢ gutters to be laid, then together 13ᵈ ℔ hundred."[2]

The hewing means splitting out the shingle, shooting was planing the edges with a "shooter," a plane which we now should call a long "jointer." The lathing was laying on the rafters square or rectangular sticks of small size somewhat like the purlins so common in the New Haven territory. On these the shingle were nailed, as the thatch was tied to them, without boarding. This is an old English way of laying slate and no doubt shingle also,[3] and the inveterate habit which modern carpenters have of boarding roofs with wide joints is a survival of it. The gutter was what we should call a "valley," the trough at the junction of two roofs at right angles to each other. There were no gutters in our sense, and if there had been they would not have been shingled. This clause points to the presence of gables, but it is doubtful if these were common except on the meeting-houses.

In the votes about the meeting-house at Windsor we meet the gutter again. In December, 1659, the townsmen had voted "that the town barn shall be repaired and thatched." On January 7, 1660, they "met and agreed that the meeting house should be

---

[1] *New Haven Col. Rec.*, I, p, 38.

[2] The same, p. 55.

[3] Shingles occur, with the Latin name "cendulum," in the time of Henry III. See Turner and Parker, *Domestic Architecture*, I, p. 60. note. We can see, from the court order, that the occurrence of the word lath does not necessarily imply plastering.

shingled, all the gutters on both sides of the lanthorn, and not alter the form of the roof." [1] They contracted with Samuel Grant for the shingling of one side of the roof "with 18 inch shingle. He is to get the shingle in the woods, and but them and hew them, and lay them on one inch and a quarter thick, generally, and seven inches in breadth, one with another, and he is to have 4s per 100 for all plain work, and for the gutters, because of the more difficulty of laying these, he is to have what he shall in equity judge to be worth more than 4s. . . . ." [2]

As we might expect from these records, shingled side walls did not exist in Connecticut, outside of Southold, in the first two periods.

The WINDOWS were very small in the first two periods, and even well into the third. One still exists on the rear of the Meggatt house, which is 1'–7½" wide, and 1'–9¼" high. Earlier examples are wanting.

Of SASH there are several specimens preserved in the various museums of antiquities in New England. They betray the small size of the early windows. One of the most interesting of them is now in the collection of the Connecticut Historical Society at Hartford. It is unique in possessing a transom, as our drawing of it shows, though the same disposition appears in the old painting of the Roger Williams house at Salem. The stiles are ⅞ of an inch thick and 1⅜ inches wide, [3] with a rebate ¼ of an inch deep for the glass. The transom is half an inch wider than either top or bottom rail, which are equal and of the same width as the

---

[1] Stiles; *Ancient Windsor*, I, p. 890.

[2] The same, p. 890.

[3] The sizes we give are on the outside where the rebate is. A large quarter of an inch must be added to the stiles and rails, and a large half to the transom, to obtain the exact sections.

stiles or upright pieces. The marks of the strap hinges are plainly to be seen on the wood, which has weathered less where they protected it.

This sash once formed part of a double casement window. The weather-strip, which protected the vertical joint between the two casements, is still partly in place. This shows that such windows were not unknown, while the fact that the weather-strip is nailed on and that there is no rebate cut in the stile to receive the other sash proves that the casement was once single and that it closed a window of only its own width.

The old word for these sash was CASEMENT, and we still think, when we speak of casement windows, of sash hung at the side as these were, though these were always swung out instead of in to keep them tight. The word occurs in the Windsor records in 1669, where we read that " William Buell [who was a carpenter] came and brought two new casements for the corner windows of the meeting house." [1]

The word sash, which means the double-hung window, comes from the French " chasse." The " shas frames and shas lights," mentioned in Moxon's " Mechanick Exercises," in 1700, show an early form of the word. The date of the first double-hung window in the Connecticut colonies we have no means of determining. They were in use in Windsor as early as 1763, for, on June 23 of that year, there is a record of springs or weights for the windows of the meeting-house. [2] We do not believe that any hung sash were used before 1725, for they were hardly domesticated in England till the time of William III, though an example with cord and weight is said to occur in Wickham court, Kent,

---

[1] Stiles, *Ancient Windsor*, vol. I, p. 129.

[2] Same, p. 586.

as early as the reign of James I. Lambert's drawing of the Eaton house gives a line across the windows as though he meant to indicate double-hung sash. If such sash really existed in the house they must have been among the earliest instances, for the building was pulled down very early in the last century.

Perhaps the poorer settlers, if they were not content with mere wooden SHUTTERS wherewith to close their windows, used cloth or oiled paper instead of glass. The common idea is that oiled paper was used, but where the supply of paper came from, when that article must have been far too precious to divert from its ordinary use, nobody pretends to know. The very advice which some one gave to intending settlers, that they should bring oiled paper for windows, shows that little could be obtained here. It was probably glass or nothing in the earliest windows. The poor had a simple opening, closed when necessary with a wooden shutter; the richer householders had glass.

The wealthier of the settlers probably imported GLASS from the old country. Wyllys, Davenport, Eaton, and men of their standing, accustomed in England to glass as a necessity, and even as a decoration, would not go without it here. As a matter of fact, however, the commodity does not appear very soon in the records. On February 25, 1659, the town officers of New London were instructed that one of their duties was to provide glass windows for the meeting-house "with all convenient speed." [1]

In Hartford glass is not mentioned directly, but on "August last 1667, The towne by thair vote ordered and impowered the the townsmen to gett . . . . nessessary Lights for the Gallery." [2] This was in the meeting-house.

---

[1] Miss Caulkins, *New London*, p. 92.
[2] Conn. Hist. Soc., *Collections*, VI, p. 152.

In Windsor, in 1668, the town sent for John Gibbard "to get him to come and mend the glass of the meeting house windows," which would get broken, even in Puritan times.

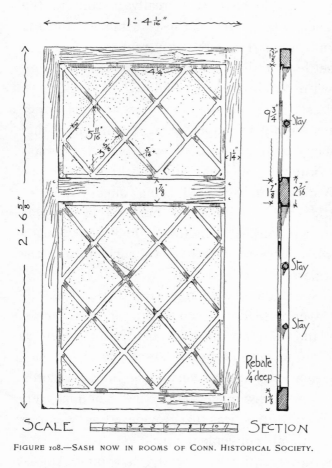

FIGURE 108.—SASH NOW IN ROOMS OF CONN. HISTORICAL SOCIETY.

Later on, in New London, in 1679, the town, contracting for a new meeting-house, agreed to furnish the glass.[1] Again, at Simsbury, in 1697, the Rev. Dudley Woodbridge's record gives: "journey to Windfor for glaffe," and "putting up Glaffe,"[2] as items in the account of the minister's house.

All the old glass, which was very green in color, though this quality has increased with age, consisted of diamond-shaped "quarrels," set, with their long axis vertical, in lead "calmes" or bars. Square panes, set in the same calmes, appear, but they must have

---

[1] Miss Caulkins, *New London*, p. 191.

[2] A. C. Bates, *The Rev. Dudley Woodbridge, his Church Record at Simsbury in Connecticut*, 1697–1710.

been quite rare. We have known of only two examples, one of which, that once in William Coddington's house, Newport, we have illustrated in *Early Rhode Island Houses*. Nevill says that the square form is later than the diamond, but, at the time our ancestors came over, the forms were contemporary, so that no such test can be applied here.

Glass was, in the periods of which we treat, sold by the square foot, as it is now. It was probably imported from England, and that very early, in boxes, perhaps sometimes already leaded, for some of the leaded work had to be curiously cut, as in the Arthur Fenner house, near Providence, to make it fit the casement.

The calmes were of the same *H* shape, so familiar in modern stained-glass work. A guess at the relative date of examples can be made from their weight. Early ones are heavier. They were made, in the third period, by machinery, for a miniature rolling-mill, now in the possession of the Connecticut Historical Society, was imported from London for the manufacture of them. The date on this quaint machine, 1718, shows how late the leaded casement must have persisted.[1] Indeed, the first hung sash were filled with leaded glass, just as were the old hinged windows.

The BARGE-BOARD or VERGE-BOARD was the false rafter which appeared to carry the projecting eaves of the roof on the slope of the gable, or the "rake," as it is technically called. The plate generally projected far enough in front of the gable wall to carry the foot of the board. The barge-board, which is essentially a mediæval device, and a very beautiful one, was once very common in New England, and very likely retained the cusping, which was

---

[1] Mr. A. C. Bates, Secretary of the Connecticut Historical Society, writes: "Rev. Mather Byles writing from New London in 1762 tells of an accident whereby 'ten Quarrels of Glass in the kitchen window' were broken."

not yet out of fashion in old England in the time of James I.
Old drawings show instances of the plain board in Massachusetts, and Lambert has indicated one, apparently with some sort
of cusping, in his drawing of Governor Eaton's house.[1]   The
board along the rake of the gable, which still in many instances
stands clear of the wall a little way, is the direct descendant of this
verge.   The Viall-Mowry house, in old Rehoboth, now East Providence, still has a barge-board, a narrow strip of wood distant
about six inches from the gable wall, with its foot resting on the
end of the heavy, projecting plate.   The marks of the barge-boards
are very plain in the Walker house, also in East Providence.

The PYRAMIDS were the finials which adorned the peaks of the
gables.   There are none of them left, but drawings of them exist
in Massachusetts, in the picture of the Roger Williams house, and
in that of the Bradstreet house; and the fact that John Elderkin and Samuel Lothrop, in their contract for the meeting-house
at New London, agreed to "set up on all the four gables of the
house pyramids comely and fit for the work"[2] shows that they
were used in the settlements of Connecticut.

DORMERS.   These were used very seldom, if at all, in early
work.   We know of only one house in which traces of them are
to be found — the Hempstead house in New London.[3]

The name they are often known by in the seventeenth century
was that of "lutheran" windows.   This may be a corruption of
"lanthorn," through the form "luthorn," in which the word for the

---

[1] This cusping may be only the brackets of a classic raking cornice. Such brackets are indicated in the level cornices.   They show, if they are authentic, that the house was revamped at
some time in the early 18th century.

[2] April 19, 1679. Miss Caulkins, *New London*, p. 191.

[3] "The older roofs rarely, if ever, have dormers."   R. Nevill, *Old Cottage and Domestic Architecture in Surrey*, p. 33.

dormer sometimes appears, or it may—and this is perhaps more likely—come from the French *lucarne*, possibly through some Norman French variation. The word lucan occurs in a letter of an Elizabethan craftsman quoted by Blomfield.[1]

THE INTERIOR.

Whether the upper FLOOR of the two which always exist in the first story of the early houses is original it is difficult to determine. In the second story and in the garret one floor is the rule. Oak and hard pine were the favorite materials. The floors in the Painter house are of oak, which is the prevailing material for garrets. In the second story, the hall chamber, of the Patterson house, the floor is of hard pine. The boards in this floor are sixteen inches wide and fourteen feet long, and, it need hardly be said, very heavy.

The boards were not put together with tongue and groove, as they are now, but were halved together, as in the example just mentioned in the Patterson house.

Till about 1735–40, in Hartford and the other Connecticut towns, the insides of the walls were covered with wide horizontal pine boards, grooved together, and adorned with mouldings at the joints, as in the Gleason and Whitman houses and several others.

This WAINSCOT is one of the most artistic touches which the old craftsmen gave their work. It would not answer on the outside, for the joints could not be kept tight as they could with the overlapping clapboards. Where, as in the Fairbanks house, at Dedham, Massachusetts, the feather-edged board is used on

---

[1] R. Blomfield, *A History of Renaissance Architecture in England*, I, p. 31.

the inside—a practice no instance of which occurs in Connecticut
—the lower edge of it is moulded. It is curious to note, also,
that in Plymouth, which, like Providence, abandoned the stud
system and used vertical boarding—as the Connecticut settlers did
for barns—we find similar mouldings applied to the vertical joints
in the boarding of the outer walls, because these showed inside the
rooms.[1] We give, in Figure 109, several sections of the joints
with the mouldings which belong to them.

In the third period this form of wainscoting was still used for
kitchens, but a more elaborate kind began to take the place of it
in the parlor. This is the panelling with stile and rail, a system
which in its mediæval garb of "pillar and pane" is as old as the
other, but which for some reason did not, so far as we can now
ascertain, find favor with the early Connecticut carpenters. Indeed,
though they were familiar with it in chests, they seem reluctant,
perhaps from the labor and consequent expense involved, to use
it in houses, for in the entry of the Sheldon house the panelling,
which forms a dado along the wall to a height of nearly three
feet, while it has its base, its cap moulding or chair rail, its top
and bottom stile, and its raised and bevelled panel, has no stiles
or upright divisions in its length, but forms a clear instance of
transition between the old wainscot and the new.

Some of the new panelling is very elegant, and, when it becomes fashionable it is excellently wrought, far better than the
old chests, though the difference between the oak of the chests
and the pine of the panelling must count for something.

The end of the hall, and of the parlor as well, and even of
the parlor chamber, was, in the latter part of the third period,

---

[1] In the Doten house, Plymouth, 1662.

often covered with panelling. But here we are beyond the limits to which we mean to confine ourselves, and are trenching on the Georgian work, the so-called "colonial" style.

Plastering was the rule on the side walls of the houses in New Haven, and we do not find the earlier wainscot. The habit of using the plaster on the lower part of the walls either existed or was expected to exist at the time of the wage order in 1641. The same things may be said about the later forms of panelling here as of those in Hartford, though we have seen no such form as that in the Sheldon house. The same is true of New London. Here, however, as we might expect from the vertical boarding, we find the wainscot set vertically in one example.

The origin of the word wainscot is obscure. It may be wand schot—wall protection—or, as is also given, wain (wagon) and schot (partition), the thin boards used for the sides of wagons. At all events it meant in England at the time our fathers left, and for three hundred years before that time, a certain kind of oak imported from the Netherlands, quartered oak, in fact, as we call it. From this use the word was transferred to the casing of walls, for which this wainscot oak was employed. In this sense it generally means panelling, and that is the generally accepted meaning of the word in our day.

Among our colonial forefathers in the earlier times the word had, however, another meaning. To them the horizontal and some-times vertical boarding which we have described, put together with tongue and groove, like our "matched and beaded" sheathing or siding, was also wainscot.

This is proved by the "Wenscutt plough" (wainscot) which appears in the inventory of "old Mr. William Carpenter," of the

Providence Plantations, at his death in 1685.[1]   There is no panel-
work in Rhode Island houses of this date, and no panelled chests
are certainly known to have been built there—except, perhaps, the
Field chest—but there is a good deal of upright partition work
put together with tongue and groove.

We know also from Governor Winthrop, of Massachusetts, that
the horizontal sheathing was called wainscot.   In his journal, in
1632, he records, as part of an interview with Mr. Ludlow: "The

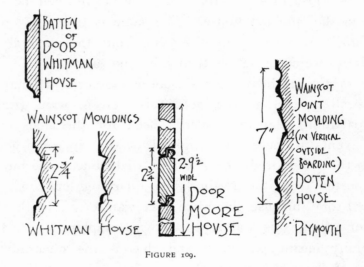

FIGURE 109.

Governor having formerly told him that he did not well to bestow
such cost about wainscoting and adorning his house, in the beginning of a plantation, both in regard of the necessity of public
changes, and for example etc., his answer now was, that it was
for the warmth of his house, and the charge was little, being but
clapboards nailed to the wall in the form of wainscot."[2]

[1] *Early Records of the Town of Providence*, VI, p. 150.
[2] Savage's *Winthrop*, I, p. 104 (p. 87 of original).   Mather speaks of boards before the chimney
as " deals."

The only PARTITIONS used in the houses of the earliest period, those houses which were but one room deep, will appear on any of the plans. They are those, namely, which separate the hall on one side and the parlor on the other from the chimney and from the porch or entry which contained the stairs, and that as well which shuts in the staircase itself. These partitions are made of inch boards of pine grooved and tongued together and adorned at the joints with the same mouldings which we find in the wainscot of the outer wall. Indeed the partition against the chimney, as can be seen in the section of the Whitman house, in Figure 16, is only a continuation of the wainscot. Around the staircase, however, and sometimes on the chimney end of the room, the boards are set vertically.

When the lean-to was added the wainscot on both sides of the studs of the original back wall formed the partition between the front rooms and the kitchen, and when the lean-to was built as part of the house this stud partition was still used. The partitions which separate the rooms in the lean-to are often of vertical boarding.

Stud partitions with plaster are not original till very late. Perhaps the earliest are in the Sheldon house, Hartford. They were common much earlier in New Haven. They are, like the wainscoted kitchen partitions, of studs set flatwise, and not of boards set an inch apart in the row, and plastered both sides on lath nailed directly to them, as was the Rhode Island custom.

Late in the third period, at about the time when plaster partitions came into vogue, the chimney partition is made of panelling, as we have explained above.

The earliest inside DOORS were of vertical wainscot, secured by battens on one side. The joints were exactly like those in the wall wainscot and in the partitions. It was no 'wonderful matter, then, for Mrs. Allerton to hide the regicides in a closet,[1] for it took no great skill to make a door of vertical boards look like an immovable part of a vertical partition, especially if the wall was hung with brass pans, and thus partly covered.

The oldest outside doors were of plain vertical boards on the outside, crossed, for strength, by horizontal boards within. A door in the back of the lean-to in the John Barnard house, which was very likely the original front door, was of this kind, a type in use in Old England.[2] We have never seen a pattern formed by nail heads on the outside. The Dutch door, as it is called, in which the top half can be opened separately from the bottom half—a most excellent device—may have been used very early. Lambert shows one in Gov. Eaton's house. The examples which now exist, however, are all very late.

The inside doors in the Whitman house, of which we give details in Figure 109, are original, and will repay study as they show how naturally the craftsmen added an artistic touch even to what we should call a common "batten" door. The successor of this earliest door is that with two large panels, each the width of the door, and with a rail between them about the middle of the height. After these came an increasing number of panels.

The outside doors become double in the third period, and are quite elaborately panelled in late examples, as the Grant house.

A mediæval fashion of building STAIRS was to make the steps of solid timber, triangular in section, formed by cutting beams

---

[1] Stiles, following tradition, says that Mrs. Eyers, Isaac Allerton's granddaughter, concealed the regicides. See, however, Atwater's comment in his *History*, pp. 434–5, note.

[2] R. Nevill, *Old Cottage, etc.*, p. 41.

along their diagonals. No example of this exists in New England in the first story, but both the Baldwin and the Patterson house

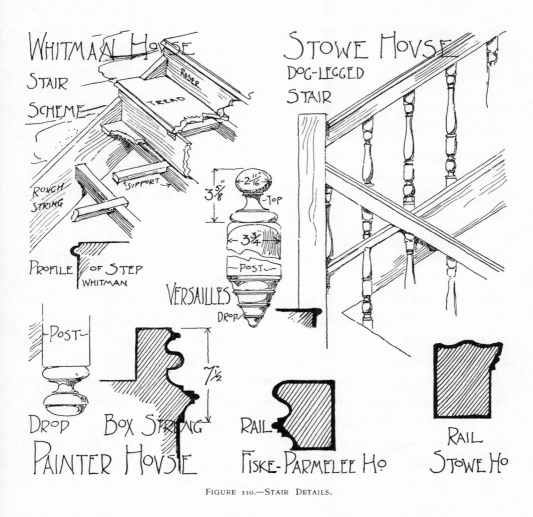

FIGURE 110.—STAIR DETAILS.

have flights of solid steps leading down into the cellar. Whether these steps are triangular or not we can not say. Our impression is that they are all full rectangles in section. In the Amos Wyman house, Billerica, Massachusetts, there is a cellar stair of triangular steps pinned to rough strings.[1]

While the stairs in the upper stories of the earlier houses are not of solid steps, and while the steps of them are built up of thin risers and treads like those of our own day, these risers and treads are put together and supported in a way very different from ours, and one which can hardly fail to be interesting even to those who are not fond of framing for its own sake.

There are three examples in the Connecticut jurisdiction: the Whitman house, Farmington; the John Barnard house, Hartford; and the Patterson house, Berlin. There is another in the New Haven settlement in the Baldwin house, at Branford; and, curiously, these four are very nearly the same.

In Figure 110 we give some details of the second-story staircase in the Whitman house. The front string was supported by the posts or studs of the partition, or sort of cage which enclosed the stair. The back string was carried at its foot by a stud in the wall of the parlor, and at its head by the chimney girt. The treads are not housed into either string but are supported partly by the risers, which are housed in, partly by the pieces under the risers, while they are stiffened in the center by the cross-piece framed into the riser top in front, and into the supporting piece already mentioned behind, under the next riser. The treads on the straight run are cut out in the way shown by the drawing to avoid housing them into the string and to let the string run by without cutting it into the saw teeth, to be seen in a modern rough string.

In Figure 111 we give the lower flight of stairs in the Patter-

---

[1] J. W. Freese, *Historic Houses and Spots in Cambridge and Nearby Towns*, p. 65.

son house. The drawing is a perspective taken from an imaginary point considerably below the floor. The partition or cage

FIGURE III.

of which we spoke in the Whitman house is here shown as if cut away. There is no wall string in the first flight, but the sticks carrying the treads are built into the masonry of the chimney.   In the second flight there is a wall string which is below the steps and serves to carry the strips from the risers which support the treads.

To these old flights of stairs, some of them all winders, succeeded the open flights with winders framed into posts, or with square platforms at the turns.   These, which are shown in most of the plans we have given, have what are called box strings, that is, the ends of the steps are housed into a closed string on the front and do not appear.   These strings are often elaborately moulded.   The posts are square, with moulded tops, and drops begin to appear.   The BALUSTERS, which are not always present, are turned and never sawed, as is often the case in Rhode Island. A judgment as to the age of the stair can be made by noting the turning of these balusters.   The stumpy forms, with short curves, are the older.   Balusters can be of very early date, though no examples remain back of the third period, when the new form of stairs began to come in.   They are mentioned in the Hartford records in March, 1639, when a committee was appointed to "build a strong sufficient Cart Bridg to bee xij ffoote wyde between the Rayles wth Turned Ballasters on the Tope."[1]

We give, in Figure 110, some details of the stairs of this class, notably that of the Stowe house, Milford, which is a " dog-legged " stair, one in which one post at the turn does the duty of two.   It is the only example we have seen.   Gotch gives one very much like it, at St. John's, Warwick.[2]   The gradual change of the shape of the rail is interesting.

After these box-string stairs came, later in the third period

---

[1] Conn. Hist. Soc., *Collections*, VI, p. 31.

[2] J. A. Gotch, *Architecture of the Renaissance in England*, Part I, p. 7.

—the two classes may have overlapped—the open-string stairs, with the ends plainly visible and adorned with brackets of fanciful shape under the returned nosing. Here belong the elaborate staircases of the Webb house, the Belden-Butler, the Grant, and others, with their carved and twisted balusters and moulded nosings relieved by a cove below them. These belong really to a time which it is not our province to discuss.

Sometimes the stairs are carried up between two walls outside of the main entry. The stairs in the Sheldon house and in the Marsh house are examples of this, as was the Ward house in Hartford, recently destroyed.

About the back stairs there is little to be said. They came in with the lean-to in the second and third periods. They seldom rise more than one story in the place usually given them. The stair to the garret very often goes up over the back of the chimney.

PAINTING. That this was not unknown in New Haven is proved by the court record of February 14, 1647:

"The Gouerner acquainted the courte that the Kinges Armes are cutt by Mr. Mullyner for the towne, wᶜh are to be primed and after sett vp in a publique convenient place." [1]

Just how much use of paint in the domestic work this old record implies we can not say. It certainly shows that the material could be obtained in the colony of New Haven.

Paint was not used in houses to any extent till late in the third period in Connecticut, for there are many fine specimens of pine panelling with no finish upon them. They do not need any. The wood is still sound, with perfectly sharp edges, and

---

[1] *New Haven Col. Rec.*, I, p. 369.

the coloring, partly from age and sun, partly from wood smoke, has become something very beautiful, unapproachable by any painted or varnished surface.

ALTERATIONS AND ADDITIONS. These were far more common than we generally have been accustomed to think them, and they are very skillfully handled.

The principal early addition was the lean-to. This was added generally without removing the clapboards at the back of the main house, except behind the chimney. Here the old covering

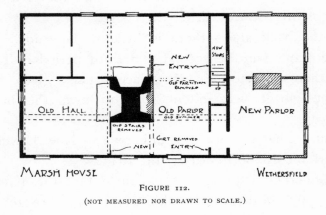

MARSH HOVSE   WETHERSFIELD

FIGURE 112.
(NOT MEASURED NOR DRAWN TO SCALE.)

had to come off to accommodate the workmen who built into the old stack the new flue coming from the added fireplace for the new kitchen. The Whitman house is an excellent example of this.

The addition of another room at the end of one of the houses of the old type, an addition which was itself of the third period, may be seen in the old Burnham-Marsh house in Wethersfield. The sketch in Figure 112 will make the new arrangement, which sought a passage through the house, much plainer than any words

can. The old stair is gone and the new one is pushed off to
one side, since evidently the idea of an artistic stair did not weigh
against the cost of the room it would take. This side arrangement of the stairs appears in the Sheldon house in Hartford.
The change in the Marsh house was made about 1750 or possibly later.

A very skillful addition, or rather series of additions, is in the
Elm Tree Inn at Farmington, which we have already mentioned.
The later long passage is very finely used to lead up to the
ancient staircase without disturbing the position of the latter, and
without breaking the effect of the wide hall, as the side-wall staircase often undeniably does.

Moving houses is not, as some may think, a modern accom-
plishment only. We have a case mentioned in the New Haven
records:

"Allen Ball . . . . said the house was vncomfortable to
live in because of the chimney and the sellar is falling downe,
that workemen saye it will cost 20ˡ to sett it in repaire, therefore
he thinkes it is the best way to take downe the ptitions wᵗhin &
make a barne of it, & if ther be cause, it maye be removed of
the sellar."[1]

No one can remember when the Gleason house was on the
street, but tradition claims that it was there, and the loss of its
chimney makes it look probable that it has been moved.

The fact that the framing of a house was changed at times
is shown by the new summer in the parlor chamber of the John
Barnard house. A change in the timbering of a stone house, or a
renewal, such as has taken place in the Whitfield as the result of a

---

[1] March 6, 1648. *New Haven Colonial Records*, I, p. 444.

fire, is much easier to execute than such an alteration in a wooden dwelling.

Tools. We do not mean to inflict upon our readers a complete list of the tools mentioned in the old inventories. The craftsmen of that day had all the tools we possess except, of course, such modern devices as the ratchet brace or the extension bit. The work these men left behind them shows that they were not lacking in tools any more than in technical knowledge.

The value of a carpenter's set of tools varied somewhat. Richard Beckly, who died in 1690, and who was an old man, had tools worth £1.[1] Henry Wells, of Wethersfield, who died in 1678, had a set rated at £3.[1] In the estate of James Hayward, of New Haven, were "carpenter's tools and lumber" valued at £57 18s 07d.[2] It would be interesting to know whether lumber here is used in its English sense of trash, or whether we have in it an instance of an older English usage, which, transplanted hither, has become a so-called Americanism. That is, may the word mean timber and boards? It seems hardly possible that any tools would foot up to £57, equivalent to a large sum of our money. Yet that must have been the case, if lumber meant trash, unless Munson and Andrews, themselves carpenters, set a high value on that trash.

Richard Lyman,[3] in 1641, left two saws, 16s, a broad-axe, two narrow axes, a "wimbell & chessells." These are tools any householder would be apt to have. The wimble, sometimes called a wimble-stock, was what we call a "brace" or bit-stock. It held

---

[1] *Probate Records* at Hartford.
[2] *New Haven Col. Rec.*, I, pp. 479-80.
[3] *Conn. Col. Rec.*, vol. I, p. 445.

a bit—called in a Providence inventory a "wimble bitt,"[1]—with which the hole was bored.

James Olmstead's inventory,[2] September 28, 1640, contains: two handsaws. one framing-saw, one hack-saw, the four valued at £1; also wimbles, chisels, hammers, and pincers, valued at 13s. The framing-saw we already know. The hack saw is not easily explained, except in its modern meaning as a tool for sawing metal.

In the estate of Edward Veir, Wethersfield,[3] July 19, 1645, were Two small saws, one long plane, two old small planes, one pricker, one chisel, two small augers. The long plane was either a jointer or a "shooter," as it is still called in England, which is still longer than a jointer.[4] The short planes may have been "jack" planes or smoothing planes. The pricker was a scratch-awl. The augers differed from the wimble in being of long shank, with a cross-bar at the end, and were worked with both hands as they are now. They were used in making mortises, and in boring holes for tree-nails or pins.

John Purkas, Hartford, 1645, and Timothy Standly, probably of Farmington, 1648, each possessed a cross-cut saw. These large saws were used for lumbering, or for cutting up wood on the farm as well as for framing.

Richard Pyper had a tennant or tenon saw, which either was what we call a back saw or was our panel saw, for cutting

---

[1] "A wimble stock, 3 wimble bitts," inventory of Epenetus Olney, 1698, *Prov. Rec.*, VI, p. 214. See inv. of Sam. Winsor, 1705. *Ibid*, p. 246.

[2] *Conn. Col. Rec*, vol. I, p. 448.

[3] The same, p. 464.

[4] The "joynter" occurs in Sam. Winsor's inv., cited above. These men had the plough, too, for a "joynter Plow" is in the same inv., p. 248. See the same vol. of *Prov. Rec.*, p. 150. A "halveing plane" occurs in some inventory, the reference to which has escaped us.

tenons. He had also a froe, which was a sort of inverted reaping hook, Figure 107, for cleaving barrel-staves and clapboards.

Governor Eaton left quite an assortment of carpenter's tools in his large estate.[1] The nails alone are appraised at £4 15s 08d. Of tools he had a whetstone, two iron squares, two hand-saws, a framing-saw, three axes, six hatchets, an adze, a pair of pincers, a drawing-shave, two whipsaws, a block-saw, two prisers, a set for a saw, a chisel, an iron crow weighing thirteen pounds, a grindstone—"grindlestone" the text has it—and a timber-chain.

The drawing-shave was the same as our drawing-knife. The whipsaw was a two-handed ripping saw. The block-saw had a piece on the upper edge like what we call a back saw.

An examination of the inventories of all the men known to have been carpenters would extend this list to a great length. Francis Stiles, of Windsor, who came from London; Jarvis Boykin from Charing in Kent—his inventory at New Haven tells nothing—William Andrews, of New Haven; George Clark, of Milford; William Pantry, of Hartford; John Elderkin, of New London and Norwich; and a host of others might be made to tell us more or less of their lives through what they left behind them. It were much to be desired that they could tell us from what part of England they each came, and who were their apprentices here.

III. Iron-Work.

The manufacture of iron did not begin at New Haven till about sixteen years after the beginning of the settlement. In

---

[1] See Appendix.

1655 John Winthrop the younger, and Stephen Goodyear, one of the London merchants who were of the first settlers of Quinnipiac, established iron-works at the southern end of what is now Lake Saltonstall.[1] Bog-ore furnished the raw material, and the fuel was charcoal.[2] Governor Eaton was interested in the enterprise, for in his inventory is recorded: "Itm for disbursments to the iron worke 7£ 10s 00d."

A few years afterward the works were let to Captain Clark and a Mr. Payne of Boston.[3] In behalf of this Thomas Clark "master of the Iron Workes of N: Haven," William Andrews, the carpenter, petitioned the General Court of Connecticut in 1669, and that court, on May 13, voted that the "persons & estates constantly and onely employed in the sayd worke . . . shall be and are hereby exempted from payeing country rates for seuen years next ensuing."[4] Lambert says that the business was abandoned in 1679, on the death of the principal workmen.[5]

Thomas Nash, who came with Whitfield, in July, 1639, left the Guilford planters, and settled in New Haven. He was a smith; so that, at least, one of the trade was present in early Quinnipiac.[6] John Potter appears as a smith at Branford in 1660.[7]

At Hartford, Thomas Hurlbut and Peter Bassaker, whose name has rather a French sound, appear to have been of this trade as early as 1643. Joseph Nash, also, was probably a smith. The town of Hartford gave him, in 1671, liberty to set up a shop, it

---

[1] Atwater, *History of the Colony of New Haven*, p. 224.
[2] Lambert, *History of New Haven*, p. 84. Atwater, as above.
[3] Atwater, as above, p. 225.
[4] *Conn. Col. Records*, II, p. 108.
[5] Lambert, as above, p. 84.
[6] Atwater, as above, pp. 125, 162-3.
[7] Rev. E. C. Baldwin, N. H. Hist. Soc., *Papers*, vol. III, p. 259.

is not said what for, on the town land.[1] We can find no trace of iron-works in the River towns till 1710.

In New London we find William Cheseborough, who had settled at Wequetequock, and whom the General Court compelled to live in New London on account of their fear that he would mend guns for the Indians.[2] Griswell and Parkes also appear as contractors for the iron-work of the house to be built "for the ministry," in 1662.[3]

When we turn from the material to the finished product we find no little artistic ability as well as unusual skill. Of course all the traditions of the work were English except, perhaps, in the case of Bassaker.

All NAILS were made by hand. They were probably made by special craftsmen as well as by the smiths, as in Rhode Island, where "Naylor Tom" was familiar in the Narragansett country. Peter Bassaker, and possibly Thomas Hurlbut, whom we named above, may perhaps have been such artisans. For, when Hurlbut was fined for overcharging, the court agreed to remit his fine if Bassaker, who intended to try the experiment, could not "make nayles wth less losse and at as cheape a rate." If Bassaker succeeded, the court would double the fine.[4]

HINGES were of iron and were of various forms. One of the oldest, as well as the most common, is the long strap form, with or without ornamentation at the end, fastened to the wood of the door by heavy-headed nails, and with its eye hung over a staple in the jamb. An example of this kind, from the Patterson house,

---

[1] Conn. Hist. Soc., *Collections*, VI, p. 164.

[2] Miss Caulkins, *History of New London*, pp. 99-100.

[3] The same, pp. 139-140.

[4] *Conn Col. Rec.*, I, pp. 81, 102.

is given in Figure 113. The shape and size varied, of course, with the weight of the door. We have never seen in Connecticut the fleur-de-lys which appears at the end of the hinge of the front door in the Arthur Fenner house, Cranston, in Rhode Island.

The HL hinge, as it is called, appears, but it is a late form. A fine example, which we give in Figure 113, is on the parlor door of the Sheldon Woodbridge house in Hartford. It is the exact counterpart of one from Oundle, Northamptonshire, shown by Gotch,[1] and of one given by Nevill.[2] The pattern, which goes

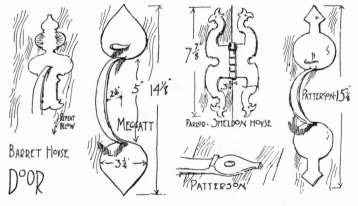

FIGURE 113.—HANDLES AND HINGES.

back to Roman times, is supposed to represent a cock's head. This particular specimen came, we are inclined to think, from the house of Governor Edward Hopkins, which stood where the Sheldon Woodbridge now is, or near the same site. Nevill says these old hinges were tinned over, and this one may be, under the paint which now covers it. We know one example in Massa-

---

[1] J. Alfred Gotch, *Architecture of the Renaissance in England*. Part I, p. 11.

[2] R. Nevill, *Old Cottage Arch., etc., in Surrey*, pp. 45–6.

chusetts which is tinned.   The existence of such a plating goes
to show that these specimens were imported.

LOCK-PLATES AND LATCHES show some very good forms, most
of them quite late, for many of the early latches were wooden
and had no locks.[1]   What the early ones could be may be seen
in Figure 114, where is given the elegant lock-plate from a trunk

FIGURE 114.

in the rooms of the New Haven Historical Society, with 1657
formed with brass nails on the top of it.   The inspiration is evidently English.   This plate should be compared with the hinge
in the Sheldon Woodbridge house.   In Figure 113 we give the
door-handle and plate of the Patterson house, that of the Meggatt, and that of the Barrett.   We should like to remind students,

---

[1] An iron door-bar is mentioned in Governor Eaton's inventory.   See Appendix III.

and, above all, collectors, that drawings of these details are very useful and will help a good many people, while the thing itself, if taken from its setting, unless that is ruinous, can help only a fad. These various forms of art among our forefathers are too little studied. The smiths who wrought these bits of iron-work put a good deal of honest skill into them.

ANDIRONS. Most of the early andirons were, no doubt, entirely of iron, as the name implies—possibly of cast-iron, too, for that material was used for andirons as far back as the 13th century. We have seen none in Connecticut, which even claimed to go so far back as the time of our own early settlements, though many are no doubt in existence.

The DOGS were of iron. These were a lower and rougher sort of andirons, which, in a large fireplace, held the back-log, while the more showy andirons carried the fore-log and its companions.

FIRE-BACK. This is another piece of mediæval iron-work which the wealthier of our ancestors used, though instances of it are very rare. One came to light during some repairs at the Pickering house, in Salem, with the date 1661 upon it; and one is mentioned in Governor Eaton's inventory as belonging in "Mrs. Eaton's chamber." They were of cast-iron, not always as large as the back of the fireplace, and stood behind the andirons or behind the dogs to protect the brick or stone.

CRANES. It would be interesting to know exactly when these came in. They probably were not used by the early settlers. Bars across the flues. with long TRAMMELS or HANGERS, which by the way occur very rarely in the inventories, held the pots and kettles over the fire. We occasionally meet with old cranes in the garrets, but they are impossible to date.

IV. BRASS-WORK.

Brass pots, pans, and kettles were common. Brass andirons also occur in Governor Eaton's inventory. Brass door-handles appear in the third period.

APPENDIX I.

THE JOSEPH WHITING HOUSE.[1]

It is possible that Andrew Bacon himself built this house. He owned two acres in a narrow strip extending along Main street from the present Sheldon street to what is now Charter Oak avenue, and upon this land stood his dwelling-house. Where did it stand? Porter, in his map of Hartford in 1642, places the building at the north end of the lot. It must, therefore, either have faced north on Sheldon street, as he has made several other houses to face, or it looked west on Main. The northern exposure was one which no seventeenth century builder, so far as we have seen, ever adopted. Is it possible that all the houses on these lots faced south upon Charter Oak avenue? In that case this Whiting house would be identical with that of Bacon and would date from 1639. Porter, indeed, was a careful worker, and probably had access to sources now lost to us. The fact that Bacon sold the south end of his lot as early as 1650, while he did not go to Hadley till 1659, and thus must have kept an abiding-place; and, further, the possibility that his house faced on Main street, are in favor of Porter's location. The reader may take his

---

[1] Through an error, the inventory of Governor Eaton is referred to by the text, as in Appendix I. It will be found in Appendix III.

own view. The fact that this house does not face Main street makes us incline to the earlier date.

The following extracts from the land records of Hartford bear upon this property:

1. In February, 1639.

"Severall parcells . . . . belonging to Andrew Bakon.

viz: One parcell on which his dwelling house now standith with other outhouses yards or gardens therein being, containeinge by estimation two acres mor or lesse, abutting upon the highway lying on the South side of the little river on the North and on the highway from Georg Steels to the South Meadow on the South, and on the highway leading from the Towne toward Wethersfield on the West, and on Nath Wards land on the east."

Hartford Land Records, Distributions, p. 251.

2. In January, 1650.

"Land in Hartford . . . . belonging to Ffrances Barnard. . . . .

viz: One psell on which his dwelling house now standeth with other out-houses, yerdes or gardins thare in being contan by estma. two roodes be it more or les, partt where of he bought of Andrew Backen, abutting on the hyway ledding from the bredg toward Wethersfield on the West, and on the hyway leding into the South Medow on the south and on Andrew Backens land on the north."

Hartford Land Records, Distributions, p. 483.

3. March 15, 1667.

"Land . . . . to Zachary Sandford. . . . .

more one parcell of land with a messuage or tenement standing there on which he bought of Francis Barnard contayning by estimation two roods be it more or less and abutteth on land sometime Andrew Bacon's on the North, and on the highway leading to Wethersfield on the West, and on the highway leading to the south meadow on the South, and on the pound East."

Hartford Land Records, Distributions, p. 399.

4. April 21, 1682.

"Land . . . . to Mr Joseph Whiting. . . . .

One parcell of land with a messuage or Tenement standing thereon which he bought of Zachary Sandford containing by estimation Two roods be it more or less, abutting on land sometime Andrew Bacons on the North on a high way leading to Wethersfield on the west, & on a high way leading into the South meadow on the south, & on the pownd on the East."

Hartford Land Records, vol. I, p. 69.

APPENDIX II.

THE WEBSTER HOUSES.

(BY DR. HENRY BARNARD OF HARTFORD.)

Robert Webster, son of Governor John Webster, died in Hartford in 1676, in possession of a large estate, leaving ten children, and making his wife, Susannah Treat Webster, his sole executrix. A portion of this estate is represented in the diagram below.

On this portion stand three houses, in none of which did

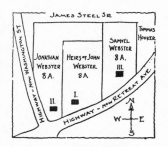

FIGURE 118.—THE WEBSTER ESTATE.

his father, Governor John Webster, ever live. Governor Webster's home lot was on the same plot with Governor Wyllys' (directly east of my residence), on the street now known as Governor street, and the house, which I recollect as far back as 1817, when I clambered over the fence to play with the Hinsdale boys, was always known to me as "the Webster house." His residence there, until his removal to Hadley in 1659-'60, as one of the four governors (Hopkins, Wyllys, Webster, and Seymour) living on it, has given the street its present name.

Susannah Treat Webster, by will made January 23, 1698, Hartford Probate Records, vol. 7, gave to the children of her son John

Webster, deceased (viz., John, Ebenezer, Jacob, Daniel, Sarah, Ann, and Abagail), in the right of their father, "all that capital messuage [1] (manor house or family home), tenement, barn, out-houses, and eight acres of land, being part of the home lot of my deceased husband."

Medad Webster, Hartford Land Records, January 7, 1786, as administrator of the estate of Ebenezer Webster, deceased (son of John), sells to Captain John Barnard "one parcel of land, being part of the home lot of said Ebenezer Webster deceased, with the dwelling house standing thereon, containing three and one-half acres, bounded south on the highway, west on that part of the lot sold to Stebbins Wilson, north on Barzilla Hudson's land, and east on the said John Barnard's land." This house (I) is still standing, and known as the Dorus Barnard house — so called because it was owned and occupied by Dorus Barnard, oldest son of Captain John Barnard, who deeded it to his son Dorus in 1804.

Susannah Treat Webster gave to her son Jonathan Webster "eight acres of my home lot, as he now hath it fenced in and improved, with his dwelling house, barn, out-houses" — and from her deed to him dated January 20, 1698, Hartford Land Records, this piece was bounded "northerly on land belonging to James Steele Sr., easterly on land belonging to Samuel Webster, southerly on land belonging to the heirs of her son John Webster deceased, and westerly on a highway." This house (II) is known

---

[1] The words *capital messuage* — "that occupied by the owner of a property containing several messuages" — (Murray, *New English Dict.*, called *Oxford Dict.*) identify, beyond question, this house as the dwelling of Robert Webster.

Messuage means: "In law, a dwelling-house, with the adjacent buildings and curtilage, appropriated to the use of the household; a manor-house." It is derived, like a host of other mediæval words for house, *mansio, mansus, mansura, masura, mansionaticum, mansuagium,* though more obscurely than they, from the classical Latin verb *manere,* to remain. The mediæval Latin form of it is *messuagium.*—AUTHORS' NOTE.

as the Grove Barnard house—so named because owned and occupied by Grove Barnard, second son of Captain John Barnard, by whom it was deeded in 1804. The house is no longer standing, but the property is still in the possession and occupancy of his descendants.

Susannah Treat Webster, by will made January 23, 1698, gave to her son Samuel Webster "eight acres of my home lot as he now hath it fenced in with his dwelling house, out-houses "—and from her deed to him, of same date as preceding, it was bounded "northerly on land belonging to James Steele, easterly on land belonging to Mr. Thomas Hooker, southerly on a highway, and westerly on lands (of the same lot) which she hath set out and given to her son Jonathan Webster and to the heirs of her son John Webster deceased." The house (III) on this property is known as the Captain John Barnard house, who came into its possession in 1765 in the following manner:

Samuel Webster, having no children, by will left his dwelling-house and homestead to Matthew and Medad, the two eldest sons of his nephew Ebenezer Webster, deceased (son of John)—after his wife's decease. Medad Webster, Hartford Land Records, April 6, 1747, for £60 paid by Matthew Webster, quitclaims a parcel of land containing one-half acre, "being part of the messuage or home lot lately belonging to Samuel Webster deceased, with the mansion house (III), barn, and other buildings thereon erected. The said one-half acre is bounded east and north on land owned in common by Matthew and Medad Webster, west on land of Ebenezer Webster, south on a highway, and extends in length from east to west ten rods, and in breadth from the highway south eight rods north."

Medad Webster, Hartford Land Records, December 17, 1750,

sells to Matthew Webster a parcel of land containing seven and one-half acres, the remainder of the eight-acre lot belonging to Samuel Webster.

Matthew Webster, Hartford Land Records, October 8, 1762, sells to Jonathan Bigelow "a piece of land containing by estimation one acre and three roods, with a mansion house (III) and barn thereon erected, bounded north on land of James Bunce, west partly on land of Jacob Webster and partly on land of Ebenezer Webster, south on a highway, and east on land of Moses Taylor."

Matthew Webster had previously sold, from the eight-acre lot that belonged to Samuel Webster, pieces as follows:

1. Thirty square rods from the south-east corner of the lot to Moses and Jemima Taylor, April 3, 1752 (afterwards land of James Barnard).

2. Three acres and one rood to James Steele, February 29, 1756.

3. One acre to James Steele, May 1, 1756.

4. One acre to James Bunce, July 5, 1757.

Jonathan Bigelow, of Hartford, Hartford Land Records, October 29, 1765, sells to John Barnard, Jr., of Hartford, "one certain messuage or lot of land containing two acres more or less, bounded south on the county road, east on Moses Taylor's land, north on James Bunce's land, and west partly on the widow Powel's land and partly on land of Ebenezer Webster, and is the same messuage in which the said John now lives, together with all the buildings and edifices thereon."

John Barnard, Jr. (Captain John Barnard of Indian and Revolutionary war service), from year to year purchased in various lots the property direct from the heirs of John Webster, or parties to whom they had sold their portions of the estate of Robert Webster; so that in 1804 he was in possession of the entire estate. In that year he conveys portions of the same as follows: To Dorus Barnard, April 19; Grove Barnard, April 19; Chauncey Barnard, October 10; James Barnard, May 15, 1805; continuing himself in occupancy of the messuage, which by his will of 1813 becomes in part the property of his son John Barnard. On his son John's death it continued in the occupancy of his daughters Cecelia and Lavinia Barnard; and on their death, by their joint will, it was conveyed to the children of their sister, Mrs. Delia Cone, namely: Mrs. Ella B. Pratt and John Barnard Cone, he holding the portion on which stands the house of Captain John Barnard.

APPENDIX III.

———

NOTE.—A single star means an omission in the original ; a double star means undecipherable. The sign | before and after a word or words means that those words are interlined in the original. The original MS was copied for us from the New Haven Probate Records by Miss Louise Tracy, of New Haven.

———

An Inventory of the estate of the Honourable Theophilus Eaton Esqr the late Governour of Newhaven Colony, deceased, taken, and apprized by Mathew Gilbert, Jo: Wakeman and Richard Miles in the twelveth moneth: 1657.

	£	s	d
Imprimis, all his weareing Apparell - - - - - -	050	00	00
Itm in plate - - - - - - - - - - -	107	11	00
Itm in a piece of gold 20ˢ & in silver 25ˢ - - - - -	002	05	00
Itm in 2 signet rings of gold - - - - - - -	02	12	00
Itm in provisions for the ffamily of wine, malt, butter, cheese, beife, porke, etc - - - - - - - - -	35.	00	00
Itm 3 barr of beife, & a barrell of porke - - - - -	10.	10.	00
Itm a " hides of tanned leather - - - - - -	11	00	00
Itm nailes of divers sorts - - - - - - - -	04,	15,	08
Itm Gun powder; shott mark & bullitts - - - - -	01,	02.	00
Itm candles, hopps, & sope - - - - - - - -	05	15,	00
Itm about 3 hundred weight of sugar - - - - - -	08,	00,	00
Itm, Ginger, Allom, gaules, gum, copperis & glew - - - -	01,	08,	05
Itm. 20 bush : of salt - - - - - - - - -	04	00	00
Itm. buttons silk, ribbing, thrid, tape, girtwebb, hookes & eyes small line, twine,. pins poynts & * - - - - - -	02,	09,	00
It, about 160ˡᵇ of cotton woole - - - - - - -	10.	00.	00

	£	s	d
It. 2 yards of broad cloth & 6 yards of kersy - - . -	02.	16.	00
It. 5 yards of w. cotton shagg, & 2 yards & half canvis - -	01.	06.	08.
It. 6 yards ½ of stuff & 2 yards ¾ |of| callicoe - - - -	01.	08.	00
It. a remnant of taffaty sarsnet, & 2 remnants of bolting cloath & a little remnant of stuff - - - - - - - -	00,	05	00
It 31 yards of bockrum - - - - - - - -	03.	05.	00
It. 2 pe woosted stockings, & 1 pe. |of| woolen stockens 6 pe Irish stockens, — 2 pe of leather stockin's - - - - -	01.	11.	08
Itm. 3^{lbs} of lead, & 12^{lb} of soder - - - - - -	00	13.	02
It a bridle, & a. pe of stirrups, leathers & 3 brushes - - -	00	06	06
	268	00	03
Itm, 3. pe of sheares, a. pe of sizers, & |a| rasor - - - -	00.	06,	04
Itm, 4 knives, a. pen knife, & whetston - - - - - -	00.	05.	00
Itm, a. pe of garden sheares, 3 sickles, & 5 hooks - - -	00.	08.	06
It, 2 iron squares, 2 hand sawes, a frameing saw, 3 axes, 3 hoes., 6 hachets, 3 bills, an adds, a. pe of pinchers & a drawing shave - - - - - - - - -	02.	16.	00
It. 2 sithes, 2 whip sawes, a block saw, 2 ston axes with brick, axes, & trowells - - - - - - - -	03	08	00
Itm. a surveying compass & chaine - - - - -	01	00	00
Itm. a napkin press, a cheese board & 2 boles - - -	00	05	00
Itm. 2 cart ropes, a stone Jugge. & 2 Jarrs - - - -	00	12	00
Itm. 2 dialls, & 2 pe of snuffers - - - - -	00	04	06
Itm 2 ** - - - - - - - - -	02	10	00
Itm a chaine 2 plow shares 38.^{lb} ¾ weight - - - -	01	01	10
Itm ā Iron barr of a door, serching iron, in 2. peeces[1] ^{30lb} -	00	10	00
Itm. an iron spoone, & an old mattock, an iron wedg, two prisers, a set for a saw & a chissell - - - - - -	00	08	00
Itm a hay hooke, & a marking iron - - - - -	00	02	04
Itm. 2. pe of brass scales, 4 brass weights, 15^{lb} & ¾ of lead & a vice of 31^{lb} iron, a case wth 13 bottles - - - -	02	07	00

[1] Blotted in original.

	£	s	d
Itm a standish 2 ink hornes, a paire of gold weights - - -	00	05	06
Itm a wire riddle, an iron Crow of 13ᵗᴸ - - - - - -	00	07	06
Itm. a woolen wheele, 4 Synes, & 5 old baggs - - - -	00	11	c6
Itm 228ᵗᴸ of old iron in the counting house - - - - -	03	16	00
Itm. 273ᵗᴸ of old yron in the ware house - - - - -	04	10	00
Itm. 2 iron beames, & 3 scales - - - - - - -	01	10	00
Itm a cast weight ᵒᶠ iron of half a hundred - - - - -	00	03	04
Itm of lead weights 245ᵗᴸ weight - - - - - -	03	01	03
It. for iron of cart wheeles about 144ᵗᴸ 2£ 8ˢ - - - -	02	08	00
It. 3 mattocks, 2 shovells, 2 pichforks & a spade ¹²ˢ ⁶ᵈ - - -	00	12	06
It. a beetle, with rings. & 8. iron wedges 15ˢ - - - -	00	15	00
Itm. a stubbing hoe, & a plow with irons - - - - -	00	16	00
Itm 36 quire of ** & 10 cask, tubbs, bucketts &c - - -	06	18	00
Itm. 2 pe of racks 3 spitts, a Jack, 4 gridirons, 3 dripping pans 5 panns, tongues, bellowes, smoothing irons, chaffing dishes fire- |irons| - - - - - - - - - - - -	04	18	00
It. a fish plate, an appleroaster, a pe snuffers, a lanthorne - -	00	06	00
Itm. a still - - - - - - - - - -	01	00	00
Itm. a chopping board, a little wheele, an old cupboard - -	00	06	00
Itm. a planke upon Tressills, & some sawed boards - - -	00	05	00
Itm. 7 earthen. potts, a platter, a salt, & a galley. pott - - -	00	04	00
Itm. a little brass kettle, a little brass pan - - - - -	00	07	06
Itm. a little trunke with a drawer - - - - - -	00	03	00
Itm. ā empty case & two earthen. potts - - - - -	00	02	00
Itm. 9 trayes, a platter, 3 little basketts & a voyder - - -	00	09	00
Itm a great brass kettle - - - - - - - -	01	12	00
Itm. a lesser kettle 29ᵗᴸ ½ weight - - - - - -	00	13	04
Itm. a litt iron pott 14ᵗᴸ half - - - - - - -	00	06	0
	52	10	11
It A little kettle, pott mettall 9 ᵗᴸ ½ —a little irō pott 10ᵗᴸ - -	00	08	06
Itm. a iron posnett, one great iron pott, 50 ᵗᴸ weight, a brasspot 31ᵗᴸ - - - - - - - - - - - -	01	03	04

	£	s	d
Itm. one frying pan 4ˢ 2 little brass posnetts. 4ˢ 6ᵈ 3 brass skimers |3ˢ 6ᵈ| - - - - - - - - - -	00	12	00
Itm 4 brass ladles 3ˢ 4 brass candlesticks 4ˢ fishooks, & aule blade, - - - - - - - - -	00	13	00
Itm in pewter 253ᵗᵇ weight - - - - - - - -	15	15	00
Itm. a clocke & a brass candlestick at Parloue door - - -	03	12	06
Itm. a cheny bason, & 5 earthen potts, 10 earthen dishes and a box with 10 trenchers - - - - - - - -	01	00	00
It. 2 warming pans. 10ˢ a ffowling peice 30ˢ - - - -	02	00	00
It. a barrell, & a locke for a fowling peice - - - - -	00	12	00
It. 3 carbines with firelocks. 36ˢ 4 machlock gunns 40ˢ - -	03	16	00
Itm. 4 swords, & a belt 27ˢ a fowling peece & a sword wᵗʰ Joh'n ** on 35ˢ - - - - - - - - - -	03	02	00
Itm a pe of pistolls with holsters - - - - - - -	01	06	08
Itm 5 pe of bandelears & a powder horne - - - - -	00	05	00
Itm 3 old holberds, & 5 * of ** - - - - -	00	08	00
Itm. in the greene chamber, a Cyprus chest - - - - -	01	10	00
Itm. a cubberd with drawers, 45ˢ a short table 6ˢ 8ᵈ - - -	02	11	08
Itm. a Bedsteed 10ˢ a Tapestry covering for a bed 4ᵗᵇ - -	04	10	00
Itm a Tapestry Carpet 4ᵗᵇ a bed coverlitt 13ˢ 4ᵈ - - - -	04	13	04
Itm a greene cubberd cloath 26ˢ 8ᵈ another cubberd cloth 15ˢ -	02	01	08
Itm. 6 cushions of Turky worke, a long window cushion - -	02	13	04
Itm 2 needleworke cushions, 16ˢ 6 gree|ne| cushions 20ˢ -	01	16	00
Itm a Couch with the appurtenances - - - - - -	01	10	00
It. a greene cubberd cloath. 6ˢ 8ᵈ a greene carpen fringed 30ˢ -	01	16	08
Itm. 2 white blanketts - - - - - - - - -	01	06	08
Itm. a red cubberd cloath laced - - - - - - -	00	05	06
Itm. a sett of currtens with vallens — fringed - - - -	01	10	00
Itm. a downe bed. 4 pillowes, & a feather bed bolster - - -	06	10	00
Itm. 3 white blankitts. 2ᵗᵇ 10ˢ arugg. 2ˡᵇ 10ˢ - - -	05	00	00
Itm a set of greene curtins & vallans fringed & laced - -	03	00	00
Itm. hangings about the chamber - - - - - - -	02	15	00
Itm. a. pe of brass Andirons doggs. firepanns & tongues of brass -	01	10	00

	£	s	d
Itm. a short greene Carpet 3^s 4^d a great chaire, & 2 little chaires 18^s - - - - - - - - - - -	01	01	04
Itm. 6 low stooles 24^s alooking glass 10^s - - - - -	01	14	00
Itm red vallens, cruell, & canvis - - - - - - -	00	10	00
Itm. In the Blew chamber, a cubberd wth drawers - - -	03	06	00
Itm. a bedsteed, & a short Table 15^s 6^d 2 trunks, & ā iron bound case |26^s 6^d | - - - - - . - - - -	02	02	00
Itm. 2 feather bedds, a bolster, & 2 pillows - - - - -	07	14	00
Itm a blew rugge, 24^s acubberd cloath & a carpet 10^s - -	01	10	00
Itm. hangings about the chamber - - - - - - - -	01	10	00
Itm. 3 pe of flaxen sheets 36^s 3 pe hollan sheets 3^{tb} 10^s - -	05	06	00
Itm. 9 pe of canvis sheets 3^{tb} 13^s 10 pe of pillow beares, 2^{tb} -	05	13	00
Itm 10 table clothes 2^{tb} 10^s 6 short towells 6^s - - - -	02	16	00
Itm 2 dossen of Table napkins of cotton - - - - - -	01	00	00
Itm. 1 dosen of table napkins of bockrum - - - - -	00	12	00
Itm 1 dosen of blew straked napkins 8^s - - - - -	00	08	00
Itm. 20. white sticht napkins - - - - - - - -	00	10	00
Itm. a long Table cloth, a short table cloth, a cubberd cloth, a towell. & 18 napkins all of Damask - - - - -	05	07	00
Itm. a long table cloth, a short tablecloth a cubberd cloth a towell. a doss. of napkins all of diaper - - - - -	03	12	00
Itm. a long tablecloth, a short tablecloth a cubberd cloth, a towell, a doss of napkins all of diap. - - - - -	02	12	00
Itm. a short tablecloth, a cubberd cloth a towell & a dosen of napkins of dyaper - - - - - - - - -	01	08	00
Itm. a short table cloth. a cubberd cloth & a dosen of napkins of flaxen - - - - - - - - - - -	01	02	00
Itm 2 dosen of dyaper napkins - - - - - - -	01	16	00
Itm. old broken linnen, a looking glass, & 3 brushes - - -	00	08	06
Itm. In the Hall, a drawing Table, & a round table - - -	01	18	00
Itm. a cubberd, & 2 long formes - - - - - - -	00	14	00
Itm a cubberd cloth, & cushions 13^s 4 setwork cushions 12^s -	01	05	00
Itm. 6 greene cushions 12^s a great chaire wth needleworke |13^s 4^d |	01	05	04
Itm. 2 high chaires setwork 20^s 4 high stooles setworke |26^s 8^d |	02	06	08

	£	s	d
Itm. 4 low chaires setworke 6.$ 8.^{d} - - - - - - -	01	06	08
Itm. 2 low stooles set worke - - - - - - - -	00	20	00
Itm. 2 Turky Carpetts. 2.^{lb} 6 highwyne stooles 6.$ - - -	02	06	00
Itm. a pewter cisterne, & candlestick - - - - - -	00	04	00
Itm. a pe of great brass Andirons - - - - - -	02	00	00
Itm. a pe of small Andirons - - - - - - -	00	06	08
Itm. a pe of doggs. - - - - - - - -	00	02	06
Itm. a pe of tongues, fire pan, & bellowes - - - - -	00	07	00
Itm in the Parlour a livery cubberd - - - - -	00	10	00
Itm a bedsteed, a trundle Bed, & a short table - - - -	01	02	06
Itm. a high chaire, 6 high stooles, w.th green & red covers - -	01	16	00
Itm a low chaire, & 2 low stooles - - - - - - -	00	08	00
Itm. a feather bed, & bolster & 2 pillowes - - - -	04	18	00
Itm. 3 blanketts, & an old green rugg - - - - - -	02	04	08
Itm. a pe of great brass Andirons a pe of doggs a fire pan &			
tongs of brass broken - - - - - - - -	02	00	00
Itm a set of curtins, & vallins - - - - - - -	01	05	00
Itm. in Mrs Eatons chamber, a little cubberd w.th drawers - -	00	14	00
Itm. 2 chests, a desk, & a Bedsteed - - - - - -	01	06	00
Itm. a little Table, a box, & a̅ empty case - - - - -	00	15	08
Itm. a case w.th 12 quart bottles, w.th a locke - - - -	00	05	0(
Itm a case with 12 pinte bottles W$_{th}$ a locke - - - -	00	03	06
Itm. 2 empty cases & 4 basketts - - - - - - -	00	07	06
Itm. 2 chaires, 2 high wyne stooles, & 3 low stooles - - -	00	14	00
Itm. 2 fether bedds, & 2 bolsters 5.^{lb} 8.$ - - - - -	05	08	00
Itm. a red coverlitt, a blew rugg, & 2 blanketts - - - -	01	06	08
Itm. a greene rugg - - - - - - - - -	01	04	00
Itm. curt |a| ins, & vallins of Canopy bed - - - - -	00	06	08
Itm. 2 ** curtaines, & a little coverlitt - - - - - -	00	14	08
Itm. hangings & window curtaines - - - - - - -	01	10	00
Itm. 3 blanketts, & a flock pillow - - - - - -	01	29	00
Itm. a sett of curtaines, & vallens - - - - - -	01	04	00
	63	00	02

	£	s	d
Itm. a paire of brass andirons, doggs, fire pan tongs, fire iron Back iron &c - - - - - - - - - -	01	04	00
Itm. in the chamber over the kitchen, a. bedsteed wth curtaines & vallins, & curtaine rods, & a presse - - - - -	00	18	04
Itm. a ffeather bed a bolster & 2 pillows - - - - -	04	07	00
Itm. a coverlitt, a rugg, & a Blankett - - - - - -	01	02	04
Itm. in the other Chamber, a half headed bedsteed, a trundle bed, & a closst stoole - - - - - - - - -	00	10	00
Itm a fflock bed, 2 bolsters, & a feather pillow - - - -	01	15	00
Itm. a red rugge & blanket, & a little rugg - - - - -	01	05	00
Itm in ye Garrett. a half headed Bedsteed & coard - - -	00	06	00
Itm. 3 flock bedds, & a bolster, & a feather bolster - - -	03	05	00
Itm. a blankit, a coverlit & a beare skin - - - - -	00	18	04
Itm. in the Counting house, a cubberd wth a chest & drawers -	04	00	00
Itm a square table & a chaire - - - - - - - -	00	10	00
Itm. 2 iron bound chests - - - - - - - - -	01	00	00
Itm. 2 half bushells. & 3 old boxes - - - - - -	00	09	00
Itm. a hatchell, a grindleston, & a wheelborrow - - - -	00	16	00
Itm. a copper in the brewhouse - - - - - - -	05	00	00
Itm 2 steele malt mills - - - - - - - - - -	01	10	00
Itm, bookes, & a Globe, & a mapp - - - - - - -	48	15	00
Itm one Cart with wheeles, & ye body of another Cart - -	02	10	00
Itm. a slide¹ wth an iron bolt - - - - - - - -	00	13	00
Itm 3 yoakes wth irons - - - - - - - - - -	00	07	06
Itm. 2 plow chaines, & a spanshakle 34^{lb} - - - - -	00	17	00
Itm. 2 oxen 12^{lb} 2 bulls 10^{lb} 2 kine 8^{lb} - - - - -	30	00	00
Itm 3 heiphers of 3 yeare old - - - - - - -	11	00	00
Itm. a heipher of 2 yeare old - - - - - - -	02	05	00
Itm 2 steares of 4 yeare old 9^{lb} 4 steares of 3 yeare old 13^{lb} -	22	00	00
Itm. 37 ewes 69^{lb} 7^s 6^d 2 rams & 4 weathers 4^{lb} 3^s 4^d - -	73	10	00
Itm. a sow, & a boare 22^s a mare 16^{lb} - - - - -	17	02	00
Itm. 5 acres of wheate, & one acre of rie sowne - - - -	07	00	00

¹ Our "sled." ?

	£	s	d
Itm. the house with all the accommodations there unto, wth the two ffarmes, & ye half. part of the Mill - - - - -	525	00	00
Itm for disbursments to the iron worke - - - -	07	10	00
Itm for hides, & skins at the Tanners - - - - - -	11	08	00
Itm at the Brickilne ffarme. 5 oxen 34ᵗᵇ 2 bulls 11ᵗᵇ - - -	45	00	00
Itm 7 kine 31ᵗᵇ 10ˢ a steare & a heipher of 2 yere old 7ᵗᵇ 10ˢ -	39	00	00
Itm. a cart, & a slide ¹ wth an iron bolt - - - - - -	02	12	00
Itm a spanshakle, 3 chaines, 3 yoakes wth irons - - - -	01	01	00
Itm. a plow with plow irons, & ā fforke 12ˢ a ffowling. peice |26ˢ 8ᵈ | - - - - - - - - - - - -	01	18	08
Itm. a sithe 2 ** hookes a axe. & 2 old hoes - - - -	00	05	06
Itm. 3 cneese fatts. & 4 trayes - - - - - -	00	06	08
Itm. an old fflock bed, a bolster. 20ᵗᵇ blankits, & 2 old sheets -	01	03	00
Itm. an old saw, & irons of ā. old churne - - - -	00	05	00
Itm upon the ground sowne, 5 acres of winter wheat, one acre of maslin. 2 acres of rie, half is prised at - - - - -	02	06	08
Itm at Stony River ffarme, 4 oxen 30ᵗᵇ 14 kine 66ᵗᵇ - - -	96	00	00
Itm a steare of 4 yeare old 4ᵗᵇ 6ˢ 8ᵈ a sow 1ᵗᵇ 10ˢ - - -	05	16	08
	989:	01	00
Itm. 4 heiphers, & a bull of a yeare old wch are to be divided, half is. prised at 4ᵗᵇ - - - - - - - -	04	00	00
3 steares of two yeare old half is prised - - - -	02	12	06
Itm. 2 hoggs, 6 shotes, & 4 piggs half. prised at - - - -	03	10	00
Itm. a Cart. 2 yoakes wth irons, a Timber chaine. 2 draft chaines, & a spanshakle - - - - - - - -	03	20	00
Itm an old plow wth irons a cock, & a hooke - - - -	00	12	00
Itm a slide,¹ a hay hooke, & yrons for a yoake - - - -	00	08.	00
Itm a stubbing how, & a fan to dress corne - - - -	00	07	06
Itm 6 racks, for cattell - - - - - - -	00	15.	00
Itm. a bras kettle, a brass pot & pot hooks - - - -	00	17	00
Itm a cheese presse 12 milk boles, & trayes - - - -	00	16	00

---

¹ Our "sled."   ?

	£	s	d
Itm a sword. - - - - - - - - - - - -	00	12	00
Itm a ffeather Bed. 2 bolsters, & a rugg. - - - - -	02	10	00
Itm 6 acres of winter wheat & 6 acres of rie sowne half is. prised at - - - - - - - - - - - -	07	00	00

	27	10	00
Totall Some	1515	12	06

In this Inventory is onely excepted Mrs Eatons Bed not vallued, & a Silver guilt bason & ewe by the approbation of the Court, vallued at o^℔ wch Mrs Eaton claims as her propy Estate

Mathew Gilbert
John: wakeman
Richard miles

New Haven Probate Records, vol. I, Part I, pp. 69–74.

From the inventory of Governor William Jones, who died in 1706:

" 1 great red chair 1£ 2 chairs and 2 stools
1 cabinet 3£ desk 6^s
hangings of middle chamber 30^s one great chest 25^s
one bed & the furniture. 15£ 6^s
one grett chair 30^s double chist of drawers.
Carpet 5^s Carpet 3^s 9^d Table 10^s 5 stools and five cushions.
one Chair table 10^s
one bed, bedstead & furniture. 8£ 16^s 6^d
Table 8^s morter 5^s iron pott hooks 1£
one chest 18^d
hangings of green chamber. 2 lbs. calleco carpet - - - 02. 11- 00
one lamp & other things
2. pr of sheets
1 bille
in plate 27£ "

From the inventory of his wife, Mrs. Hannah Jones, daughter of Governor Eaton, whose mansion descended to her; she died June 3, 1707:

" in plate 27$^£$

grt chist., bed bedstead cord and matt.

green curtains in the middle chamber 1£ 10s.

sheets & 2 diaper table cloths,

.   .   .   .   2 cannopy carpets 30ˢ

a brass kettle 4$^£$ 8ˢ a warming pan, a brass pan 25ˢ

Trammell, iron pott 5ˢ ½ a cart & impliments.

brass kettle, a smale Bed 8ˢ

needlework chaire 30ˢ

Tongs 2ˢ 6ᵈ, 2 chairs & cushions 14ˢ

cabinet with drawers 30ˢ

pair of handirons 8ˢ

curtain 5ˢ "

The house is mentioned, and, with five acres of "homelott," is valued at £190.

INDEX OF NAMES AND PLACES.

Allerton, Isaac, 95, 110, 111, 131, 262
    Mrs., 262
Allyn house, 241
    Secretary, 208
Andrews, William, 270, 272, 273
Arnold house, Benedict, 74
Atherton partners, 5
Atwater, 181.

Bacon, Andrew, 42, 279, 280, 281
Baldwin, 96, 125, 185, 187, 210, 219, 221,
    263, 264
Ball, Allen, 269
Barnard, Chauncey, 286
    Dorus, 44, 64, 75, 171, 181,
        193, 224, 228, 283, 286
    Francis, 42, 280
    Grove, 284, 286
    James, 285, 286
    Captain John, 44, 47, 59, 64,
        65, 188, 197, 228, 262, 283,
        284, 285
    John (son of Captain), 286
Barrett, 69, 70, 276
Bassaker, Peter, 273, 274
Bay Colony, 5, 149, 240
Beach, Richard, 180
Beckley, Richard, 59, 239, 270

Beckley Quarter, 59
Belden, 69, 86, 88, 211, 267
Benham, John, 180
Benjamin, 52, 144, 145, 155, 215, 221,
    223
Berkshire, 122
Berlin, 58, 196, 264
Bigelow, Jonathan, 64, 285
Billerica, 264
Bissell, John, 224
    Thomas, 224
Boston, 110, 146, 247
Boykin, Jarvis, 239, 272
Bradstreet, 256
Branford, 96, 125, 139, 185, 187, 210,
    219, 221, 263, 264
Britain, Great, 204
Bull, Governor Henry, 113
Bunce, James, 285
Burnham, 69, 79, 267, 268
Bury St. Edmund's, 239
Butler (Hartford), 69, 86
    (Wethersfield), see Belden
Byles, Rev. Mather, 255.

Cady, 161, 167
Caldwell, 144, 145, 150, 151, 217, 230,
    234, 236

Cambridge, 12
Canterbury, 169
Carpenter, William, 259
Charing, 272
Cheseborough, William, 274
Cheshire, 236, 237
Clare, 189
Clark, Captain, 273
    George, 272
    John, 18, 19, 21, 25, 26, 31, 32,
        36, 38, 39, 40, 177, 190, 232,
        233
    Nicholas, 7, 13, 14, 15
Cleveland, see Goldsmith
Clinton, 154
Cobbett, 149
Coddington, Governor William, 255
Connecticut, *passim*
Cowles, 19, 29, 39, 57, 233
Cranston, 149, 275
Crawford, John, 76

Davenport, Rev. John, 7, 93, 95, 98,
    109, 110, 111, 130, 131, 140, 185,
    253
Davy, Even, 179
Dedham, 6, 159, 257
Deerfield, 38, 232, 242
Dexter, Gregory, 183, 184
Dorchester, 12
Doten, 258
Dublin, 204

East Windsor Hill, 87
Easton, James, 179

Eaton, Hannah, 98
    Mrs., 99, 107, 108, 277
    Governor Theophilus, 95, 96,
        98, 101, 102, 104, 107, 109,
        110, 111, 114, 130, 131, 178,
        180, 182, 185, 200, 205, 253,
        256, 262, 272, 273, 277, 278,
        279, 287, 295
Egleston, James, 52
Elderkin, John, 159, 206, 249, 256, 272
Eliot, Wyllys, 119
Ellsworth, Oliver Jr., 248
Elm Tree Inn, 27, 28, 232, 239, 269
England, *passim*
Essex, 247
Evelyn, 210
Eyers, Mrs., 262

Fairbanks, 6, 257
Farmington, 18, 21, 27, 28, 31, 38, 57,
    62, 177, 190, 221, 232, 233, 239, 241,
    264, etc.
Fenner, Arthur, 149, 255, 275
Fenwick, 2
        Lady, 176
Field, 193
Fiske, 126, 144, 145, 146, 148, 149, 150,
    234, 240
Foxen's Hill, 177, 178

Gibbard, John, 254
Gibbons, William, 16
Gilbert, Matthew, 97, 287, 295
Gening, Jo, 179
Glastonbury, 193

Glastonbury, South, 54

Gleason, 19, 21, 29, 30, 31, 32, 34, 35, 38, 39, 47, 57, 211, 212, 214, 215, 221, 228, 233, 241, 242, 257, 269

Goldsmith, 132, 140

Goodwin, William, 207

Goodyear, Stephen, 273

Grant, Ebenezer, 9, 86, 87, 225, 234, 262, 267

　　　Matthew, 87

　　　Samuel, 2d, 87, 92, 243, 251

　　　Sueton (Newport), 233

Greene, 176

Gregson, Thomas, 95, 110, 111, 131

Griffing, Jasper, 119, 120, 124

　　　Nathaniel, 124

Griswell, 274

Griswold, Matthew, 176

Guilford, *passim*

Hadley, 279

Haines, Joseph, 32

Halbidg, Halbidge, Arthur, 185, 246

Halleck, Fitz-Greene, 197

Hambleton Old Hall, 99

Hampton Court Palace, 195

Harrison, 132, 139

Hart, Isaac, 58, 60

Hartford, *passim*

Hayden, William, 175

Haynes, Governor, 16, 188

Hayward, James, 270

Hempstead, Robert, 125, 161, 162, 203, 210, 211, 219, 225, 241, 256

Herefordshire, 236, 237, 238

Hollister, 19, 53, 148, 211, 221, 231, 233, 234, 239

Hooker, Rev. Thomas, 7, 12, 16, 100, 105, 188, 241

　　　Thomas, 284

Hopkins, Governor Edward, 81, 184, 185, 275

Horton, Barnabas, 141

Hubbard, 111

Hurlbut, Thomas, 273

Inn, Elm Tree, 27, 28, 232, 239, 269

Ipswich, 149, 240

Jones, Mrs. Hannah, 107, 295

　　　Inigo, 231

　　　Governor William, 98, 106, 107, 295

Kent, 41, 236, 238, 239, 247, 252, 272

King Philip's War, 8, 49

Kinsman, 161, 169, 178, 211, 230, 249

Lamberton, 239

Lancashire, 236, 237

Lewis, Captain William, 28

　　　William, schoolmaster, 28

Lime Rock, 183

Lisbon, 161

Little Wenham Hall, 122

London, 41, 184, 255, 272

Long Island, 2, 140

Lord, Goodman, 174, 189

Lothrop, Samuel, 256

Ludlow, Mr., 260

Lyman, Richard, 270
Lyme, 176
Lynn, 159

Madison, 154, 197
Malvern Hill, 193
Manton, 125
Manton Shadrach, 125
Marsh, see Burnham
Massachusetts, 2, 49, 95, 183, 190,
            214, 240, 256, 260,
            275
        Bay, 2, 5, 94, 181, 225
Mather, Rev. Increase, 100, 102, 224,
    225, 230, 244, 260
Mattabesett River, 58
Merrill, Wilterton, 179
Middletown, 176
Miles, Richard, 97, 287, 295
Milford, 4, 52, 137, 144, 145, 155, 185,
    221, 241, 242, 266, 272
Montacute House, 99
Moore (Southold), 142
Moore, Deacon John, 37, 38
        John, Jr., 37, 38
        John, 3d, 37
Morrison, 133
Moshassuck, 196
Mowry, Roger, 125
Mowry, see Viall
Mullyner, Mr. 267
Munson, 270

Narragansett, 2, 5, 7, 74, 169
Nash, Joseph, 52

New Amsterdam, 141
New England, *passim*
New Hampshire, 231, 249
New Haven, *passim*
New London, *passim*
Newport, 5, 7, 74, 81, 113, 134, 184,
    233, 255
New York, 146
Norfolk, 140
Northampton, 230
Northamptonshire, 81
Norwich, 8, 9, 158, 159, 161, 169, 178,
    230, 231, 236, 249
Nowell, Thomas, 16
Noyes, Rev. Joseph, 109
Oldham, 245
Olmstead, James, 271
Olmsted, Captain Nicho, 183
Olney, Epenetus, 271
Oundle, 81, 275

Padley, 122
Painter, Thomas, 55, 132, 133, 185, 211,
    221, 231, 257
Pantry, William, 272
Payne, Mr., 273
Parkes, 274
Parmelee, Ebenezer, 147
Patterson, 19, 53, 54, 58, 148, 196, 215,
    224, 231, 233, 238, 239, 257, 263, 264,
    274, 276
Peck, Michael, 155
Pequot, 146
Perkins, 166
Pickering, 277

Plainfield, 243

Plymouth, 6, 169, 225, 245, 248, 249, 258

Porter, Erastus, 18, 19, 29

        Joseph, 31

Portsmouth (R. I.), 246

Potter, John, 273

Princess Anne County, 193

Providence, 5, 7, 11, 13, 15, 76, 79, 93,
   125, 145, 146, 159, 181, 183, 184, 193,
   223, 243, 249, 255, 258, 260

Pryce, Nathaniel, 159

Purkas, John, 271

Pulsifer, 55

Putnam, 161, 167

Pynchon, Joseph, 119

        Thomas, 119

Pyper, Richard, 272

Quaker Hill, 159, 178

Quinebaug, 161

Quinnipiac, 1, 2, 93, 94, 185, 239, 240,
   273

Rhode Island, *passim*

Richards, James, 52, 100

Rochambeau, 83

Rogers, Rev. Ezekiel, 239

Rouen, 246

Rowland, Rev. Joseph, 100

Rowley, 240

Ruggles, Rev. Thomas, 112, 119

Sandford, Zachary, 42, 280, 281

Salem, 6, 11, 101, 145, 148, 162, 166,
   198, 212, 251, 277

Saltonstall, 7, 149, 240

Saybrook, 1, 2, 4, 15, 134, 158, 169, 183,
   193, 236

Sayles, Israel, 77, 196

Saylesville, 77

Scott, Thomas, 178

Seamor, Richard, 179

Sewall, Judge Samuel, 224

Sheldon, Mr., 77; see Woodbridge,
   Sheldon

Sheldon (Deerfield), 38, 232, 242

Shelley, 197

Shipfield, Edward, 180

Shrewsbury, 239

Shropshire, 41, 236, 237, 238

Simsbury, 197, 254

Smith, William, 19

Sound, Long Island, 154, 158, 174, 186,
   236, 242

South County, 161, 178

Southold, 132, 140, 141, 181, 185, 248,
   249, 251

Stamford, 199

Standly, Timothy, 271

Stanley, Caleb, 183

Stanly, Engs Nathaniell, 183

Stanley, John, Sr., 31

Steel, Captain Ebenezer, 31

       George, 288

       James, 284, 285

       John, 18

Stell, John, 19

Stiles, Francis, 7, 16, 41, 272

       President Ezra, 98, 109, 110

Stoddard, John, 177

Stokesay Castle, 237
Stone, 12
Stoughton, 248
Stowe, 132, 137, 241, 242, 266
Suckiaug, 12
Suffolk, 122, 189, 247
Surrey, 225, 239, 247
Sussex, 236, 238, 239
Sutton Courtenay, 122

Talcott, John, 7, 13, 15
        Lieutenant-Colonel John, Jr.,
            13, 14, 159
        (Glastonbury), 193
        Major, 183
Thompson, Major Robert, 114, 120, 123
Thoroughgood, Adam, 2d, 193
Trowbridge, 193

United Colonies of New England, 5

Vere, Edward, 271
        Lady, 140
Versailles, 158, 161, 169, 211, 249
Viger, Thomas, 183, 197
Vigers, Thomas, 183, 184
Viall, 256
Virginia, 68, 120, 186, 193, 195

Wakeman, Jo, 97, 287, 295
Walker, 256
Ward, James, 267
        Nath, 280
Warner, 166
Warwick, 88, 166

Warwick Grant, 2
Washington, 83
Waterman, 193
Watertown, 12, 245
Webb, Joseph, 9, 83, 85, 87, 88, 89, 90,
        144, 177, 188, 211, 215, 225, 234, 267
Webster, Abagail, 283
        Ann, 283
        Daniel, 283
        Ebenezer, 283, 284, 285
        Jacob, 283, 285
        Governor John, 44, 282
        John, 282, 283, 284, 285
            Jr. (3d), 283
        Jonathan, 283, 284
        Matthew, 64, 284, 285
        Medad, 283, 284
        Robert, 44, 64, 282, 283, 286
        Samuel, 283, 284
        Sarah, 283
        Susannah Treat, 282, 283, 284
Welles, 83
Wells, Henry, 270
Wequetequock, 274
West Haven, 133, 185, 234
Wethersfield, passim
Whitfield, Rev. Henry, 96, 110, 112,
            113, 123, 177, 191, 273
        Nathaniel, 114
Whiting, Captain Joseph, 40, 41, 43,
            203, 228, 279, 280
            William, Sr., 41
Whitman, 31, and following
Wickham Court, 252
Wigglesworth, Michael, 95

Williams, Roger, 101, 143, 163, 166, 183, 184, 198, 212

Willson, Robberd, 19

Wilson, Robert, 18

Windham County, 243

Windsor, *passim*

        South, 195

Winsor, Sam., 271

Winthrop, Governor (Mass.), 2, 245, 260

        (Conn.), 4, 158, 159, 177, 183, 184, 207, 210, 214, 273

Wolcott, 85

Woodbridge, Sheldon, 10, 69, 76, 77, 86, 120, 143, 168, 181, 193, 197, 211, 215, 217, 258, 259, 261, 267, 269, 275, 276

        Rev. Dudley, 197, 254

Woodbury, 241

Wren, Sir Christopher, 9, 231

Wyllys, George, 16, 188, 253, 282

Wyman, Amos, 263

Yennicook, 140

York, 238

Yorkshire, 238, 239

Yorktown, 83